Matthias Michael Jöst

Personalized City Tours

Matthias Michael Jöst

Personalized City Tours

An Extension of the OGC® OpenLocation Specification

Südwestdeutscher Verlag für Hochschulschriften

Impressum / Imprint
Bibliografische Information der Deutschen Nationalbibliothek: Die Deutsche Nationalbibliothek verzeichnet diese Publikation in der Deutschen Nationalbibliografie; detaillierte bibliografische Daten sind im Internet über http://dnb.d-nb.de abrufbar.
Alle in diesem Buch genannten Marken und Produktnamen unterliegen warenzeichen-, marken- oder patentrechtlichem Schutz bzw. sind Warenzeichen oder eingetragene Warenzeichen der jeweiligen Inhaber. Die Wiedergabe von Marken, Produktnamen, Gebrauchsnamen, Handelsnamen, Warenbezeichnungen u.s.w. in diesem Werk berechtigt auch ohne besondere Kennzeichnung nicht zu der Annahme, dass solche Namen im Sinne der Warenzeichen- und Markenschutzgesetzgebung als frei zu betrachten wären und daher von jedermann benutzt werden dürften.

Bibliographic information published by the Deutsche Nationalbibliothek: The Deutsche Nationalbibliothek lists this publication in the Deutsche Nationalbibliografie; detailed bibliographic data are available in the Internet at http://dnb.d-nb.de.
Any brand names and product names mentioned in this book are subject to trademark, brand or patent protection and are trademarks or registered trademarks of their respective holders. The use of brand names, product names, common names, trade names, product descriptions etc. even without a particular marking in this work is in no way to be construed to mean that such names may be regarded as unrestricted in respect of trademark and brand protection legislation and could thus be used by anyone.

Verlag / Publisher:
Südwestdeutscher Verlag für Hochschulschriften
ist ein Imprint der / is a trademark of
OmniScriptum GmbH & Co. KG
Heinrich-Böcking-Str. 6-8, 66121 Saarbrücken, Deutschland / Germany
Email: info@svh-verlag.de

Herstellung: siehe letzte Seite /
Printed at: see last page
ISBN: 978-3-8381-1151-3

Zugl. / Approved by: Heidelberg, Universität, Diss., 2009

Copyright © 2009 OmniScriptum GmbH & Co. KG
Alle Rechte vorbehalten. / All rights reserved. Saarbrücken 2009

千里之行, 始於足下

(Eine Reise von tausend Meilen beginnt mit einem einzigen Schritt.)

Laozi (*Daodejing,* Kapitel 64; 6. Jahrhundert v.Chr.)

Danksagung

Zunächst und vor allem möchte ich Herrn Prof. Peter Meusburger für die Möglichkeit zur Promotion und seine Betreuung danken. Große inhaltliche Freiheit, jederzeit ein offenes Ohr und manch väterlicher Rat waren mir eine große Hilfe, das Projekt durchzustehen. Herrn Prof. Alexander Zipf möchte ich inbesondere für die vielen spannenden und fruchtbaren Diskussionen danken, die mich von der im Jahr 1998 begonnen Abschlussarbeit bis heute, zum Ende der Promotion begleitet haben und hoffentlich auch in der Zukunft Ansporn und Counterpart sein werden. Danken möchte ich auch Herrn Dr. Klaus Tschira und dem European Media Laboratory. Im dort durchgeführten Deep Map Projekt (1998 – 2001) durfte ich meine ersten wissenschaftlichen Schritte gehen, den Grundstein für diese Arbeit legen und die spannenden Aufbruchsjahre in einem neugegründeten Forschungsinstitut erleben.

In tiefer Schuld gilt mein Dank natürlich auch meiner geliebten Frau Annika, die mich an vielen Abenden, nach einem langen Bürotag noch mit der Promotion teilen musste. Ihre Fürsorge hat mir den Rücken freigehalten, unter anderem, um die knappe Freizeit mit unserem Sohn zu verbringen und dabei Kraft zu tanken. Danke möchte ich natürlich auf meinen Eltern, die mir alle Möglichkeiten eröffneten. *...ja ihr zwei, nun bin ich endlich fertig und es sind so viele Buchstaben...*

Zusammenfassung

Im vergangenen Monat eine Geschäftsreise nach London, nächsten Samstag für einen Tag nach Köln und im Herbst für ein romantisches Wochenende nach Paris – Dieses Beispiel verdeutlicht eine wesentliche Ausprägung des Tourismus in der heutigen Zeit: Bewohner der westlichen Hemisphäre bereisen oft und wiederholt Städte. Ein zentrales Problem, das all diesen Besuchen in fremden Städte gemein ist, ist die Frage – wohin gehe ich und was sehe ich mir in städtischen Mikrokosmos heutiger Großstädte und Metropolen an?

Dieser Fragestellung widmet sich diese Arbeit und präsentiert ein Konzept und eine Architektur für die Berechnung von nutzeradaptiven Stadtrundgängen. Tragende Säulen des Ansatzes sind Contextadaptivität und Personalisierung, wobei diese Arbeit einen integrativen Ansatz präsentiert. Die raum-zeitlichen Bedingtheiten eines Stadtbesuches werden auf Basis zeitgeographische Ansätze und deren algorithmische Umsetzungen berücksichtigt. Zur Lösung des mathematischen Grundproblems bei der Berechnung der Tour – dem Traveling Salesmen Problem – betrachtet die Arbeit Ansätze aus dem Bereich der kombinatorischen Optimierung und schlägt einen konkreten und heuristischer Ansatz vor.

Um den Anforderungen moderner Software-Architekturen hinsichtlich einer Komponentenorientierung und Diensteverteilung gerecht zu werden, wird der präsentierte Ansatz in eine service-orientiert Architektur auf Basis der OpenLocation Spezifikation des Open GeoSpatial Konsortiums eingebettet und erweitert dieses um eine Spezifikation für die personalisierten Touren.

Abstract

A business trip to London last month, a day visit in Cologne next saturday and romantic weekend in Paris in autumn – this example exhibits one of the central characteristics of today's tourism. People in the western hemisphere take much pleasure in frequent and repeated short term visits of cities. Every city visitor faces the general problems of where to go and what to see in the diverse microcosm of a metropolis.

This thesis presents a framework for the generation of personalized city tours - as extension of the Open Location Specification of the Open Geospatial Consortium. It is founded on context-awareness and personalization while at the same time proposing a combined approach to allow for adaption to the user. This framework considers TimeGeography and its algorithmic implementations to be able to cope with spatio-temporal constraints of a city tour. Traveling salesmen problems - for which a heuristic approach is proposed – are subjacent to the tour generation.

To meet the requirements of today's distributed and heterogeneous computing environments, the tour framework comprises individual services that expose standard-compliant interfaces and allow for integration in service oriented architectures.

Content

DANKSAGUNG 3

ZUSAMMENFASSUNG 5

ABSTRACT 7

CHAPTER 1. INTRODUCTION 17

CHAPTER 2. RESEARCH CHALLENGES 19

CHAPTER 3. APPLICATION DOMAIN – CITY TOURISM 21

    3.1. Classifications of City Tourism 23

    3.2. Economical Considerations and Statistics 24

    3.3. Motivations for City Trips 25

    3.4. Preferences and Interests 26

        3.4.1. General Trends 27

        3.4.2. Local Studies and Phenomena 27

    3.5. Information Sources 28

        3.5.1. Trip Preparation, Booking and Traveling 28

        3.5.2. Information Sources During the Journey 30

CHAPTER 4. ADAPTING TO THE USER 33

    4.1. Personalization and User Modeling 33

        4.1.1. Data Acquisition for Personalized Systems 34

        4.1.1.1. User Profile Data Acquisition 34

        4.1.1.2. System Usage Acquisition and Interaction Observation 35

            Selective actions 35

            Temporal viewing behavior 35

            Ratings 35

        4.1.1.3. Usage Patterns 36

            Usage frequency 36

            Information context – action correlations 36

            Task models and Action sequences 36

        4.1.1.4. User and System Context 36

        4.1.2. Inferences techniques for personalization 37

4.1.2.1.	Primary Inference	37
	Acquisition rules	37
	Plan recognition	37
	Stereotype reasoning	38
4.1.2.2.	Secondary Inference	38
	Logic-based inferences	38
	Representation and reasoning with uncertainty	39
	Inductive reasoning	41
4.2.	**Context and Context-Aware Applications**	**45**
4.2.1.1.	Context in Computing Science	45
4.2.1.2.	Context-Aware Applications	49
	Generic frameworks	51
	Context-aware indoor applications	64
	Outdoor applications	67
4.2.2.	Recent Developments in Context-Aware Applications	71
4.3.	**Focusing on the User – Combining Context-Awareness and User Modeling**	**72**
4.3.1.	User	73
4.3.2.	Context	73
4.3.3.	Knowledge	74

CHAPTER 5. SPATIAL INFORMATION - CONCEPTS, THEORY AND APPLICATIONS 75

5.1.	**Spatial Data Models**	**75**
5.2.	**Geographic Information Systems – GIS**	**78**
5.3.	**Interoperability for Spatial Data and Services**	**79**
5.3.1.	A Deeper Look into Ontologies	80
5.3.2.	Ontologies to Describe Spatial Data	81
5.3.3.	Ontologies for Spatial Service Integration	82
5.3.3.1.	Agent-Based Geographic Information Systems	82
5.3.3.2.	Web-enabled spatial services	84
	Open Geospatial consortium – Standardized spatial services	84
	Service oriented architecture - SOA	87
	GRID computing	88
5.4.	**Location-Based Services**	**89**
5.4.1.	Classification of Location-based services	93
5.4.2.	Example applications and services	94
5.4.2.1.	Global, Mobile and Location-Based Search	95
5.4.2.2.	Mobile Pedestrian Navigation	95
5.4.2.3.	Regional and Local Location-Based Services	96
5.4.2.4.	Further Location-Based Services	97

5.5.	Graph theory – Foundation for Navigation Services	97
5.5.1.	Shortest Paths – Algorithms and solutions	99
5.5.2.	Traveling Salesman Problem	101
5.5.2.1.	Combinatorial Optimization	102
5.5.2.2.	Heuristic Solutions for TSPs	103
5.5.2.3.	The Orienteering Problem and Enhanced Profitable Tours	104
5.5.2.4.	Problem Reduction for Geometric Optimizations	106
5.6.	**Time Geography**	**107**
5.6.1.	Accessibility Measure	107
5.6.2.	Space-Time Path and Prism	109
5.6.3.	Computational Approaches	111

CHAPTER 6. PERSONALIZED CITY TOURS 114

6.1.	The Geo Mobility Server – GMS	115
6.2.	**OpenLS Core Services**	**116**
6.2.1.	General Architecture and Data Types	116
6.2.2.	Implementations and Extensions	117
6.2.3.	The OpenLS Route Services Specification – a Closer Look	122
6.3.	**Tour Proposal Service Specification**	**125**
6.3.1.	Service Cascade for the Generation of Tour Proposals	125
6.3.2.	Services, Components and Interfaces	127
6.3.2.1.	Tour Proposal Service – *DetermineTourRequest*	127
6.3.2.2.	WPS Graph Builder	129
6.3.2.3.	WPS POI Weighter - WPS LS	135
	OpenLS Directory Service Request	135
	Context Server Service Request	136
	User Model Service Requests	137
	Processing user and context weight – an example	139
6.3.2.4.	WPS Feasibility Service	141
6.3.2.5.	WPS Graph Weighter	143
6.3.2.6.	WPS Tour Planner – WPS TP	145
6.3.2.7.	Tour Proposal Service – *DetermineTourResponse*	149

CHAPTER 7. CONCLUSION 152

REFERENCES 155

Figures

Figure 1: Visualizes the different research areas touched in this thesis	20
Figure 2: Development of spare time between 1840 and 2000 [according to Becker (2000)]	22
Figure 3: Ranking of holiday contents of Europeans in Germany 2006 as a percentage [GNTB (2006)]	23
Figure 4: Overnight stays in European cities in 2006 [TourMIS (2007)]	24
Figure 5: Sequence of activities in a typical historic city throughout the day [Data Hoffmann (2006)]	27
Figure 6: Information sources used by traveler to cities 2001 in Western Europe in 2001 [Atlas (2007)]	28
Figure 7: Booking methods for trips to Germany [GNTB (2005)]	29
Figure 8: Information sources for tourists in Heidelberg [Freytag (2003)]	30
Figure 9: Preferences for mobile location-based services [Data from Kölmel and Wirsing (2002)]	31
Figure 10: Graphical representation of a simple ontology	38
Figure 11: Fuzzy set A as part of a larger fuzzy set B	40
Figure 12: The Case-based reasoning cycle (modified after Aamondt (1994))	41
Figure 13: Clique-based filtering processes –(Kobsa, 2001)	42
Figure 14: Nearest neighbor – cloud of features and their selection	42
Figure 15: Decision tree	43
Figure 16: Neural network including in and output vectors	44
Figure 17: Context hierarchy [Pascoe (1996)]	48
Figure 18: Context feature space [Schmidt (1998)]	49
Figure 19: The StickeMap shows the user's current position (the '+' icon) relative to the stick-e notes [Pascoe (1996)]	51
Figure 20: Cool town architecture [Kindberg and Barton (2001)]	52
Figure 22: Context fabric architecture	55
Figure 23: Use-Case diagram showing the spatially related services that are demanded by location aware applications [Volz and Sester (2000)]	56
Figure 24: Architecture of the JFAX [Bardram (2005)]	57
Figure 25: An example operator graph with two sensors and two applications. The shaded squares are in-ports while unfilled squares are out-ports. The dashed lines are pull channels and the solid lines are push channels. [Chen, et al. (2004)]	58
Figure 26: Solar consists of a set of functionally equivalent nodes, named Planets (denoted P), which peer together to form a service overlay using a P2P routing protocol. Sources S and applications A may connect to any Planet. The filled circles are operators and the arrows represent data flow. [Chen, et al. (2004)]	59
Figure 27: Architecture of the Contextual Information Service [Judd and Steenkiste (2003)]	59
Figure 28: AURA - System architecture [Garlan and Sousa (2002)]	61
Figure 29: Ontology-framework for context-modeling	62
Figure 30 Components and their interactions [Schilit (1996) p.68]	65
Figure 31: Context model of SAiMotion [Eisenhauer and Kremke (2001)]	66
Figure 32: Architecture overview of the Conference Assistance system [Dey, et al. (1999)]	67
Figure 33: The CyberGuide Cartographer [Abowd, et al. (1997)]	68
Figure 34: The Guide object model [Cheverest, et al. (1999)]	69

Figures

Figure 36: comMotion architecture [Marmasse and Schmandt (2000)]	71
Figure 37: Combined user and context-model [Zipf and Jöst, (2005)]	74
Figure 38: Level-hierarchy to model space [Goodchild (1992)]	76
Figure 39: Spatial data model: raster representation	76
Figure 40: Spatial data model: vector representation	76
Figure 41: 9 - Intersection Model [Egenhofer and Herring (1991)]	77
Figure 42: Elements of the system ontology consisting of the agent communication and interaction and of the overall world knowledge of the system [Jöst and Merdes (2004)]	83
Figure 43: Adopted service-oriented architecture (SOA) for the discovery and retrieval of geospatial data.	88
Figure 44: LBS as an intersection of technologies [Brimicombe (2002)]	90
Figure 45: Mobile cellular subscribers and currently popular, network-enabled and mobile devices (e.g. mobile phones, video players and gaming console).	91
Figure 46: Primary location-based services	94
Figure 47: Secondary Location-based Services	94
Figure 48 - Location-based services provided by global internet search companies	95
Figure 49: Example LBS by navigation device manufactures and mobile phone manufacturers	96
Figure 50: Country-wide and local eamples	96
Figure 51: LBS examples focusing on specific functionalities	97
Figure 52 : Euler Tours - The seven brigdes of Königsberg	97
Figure 53: Simple pair graph	98
Figure 54: Direct graph - digraph D	99
Figure 55: Minimum spanning tree	99
Figure 56: Pseudo code of Dijkstra's shortest path algorithm [Connor (2001)]	100
Figure 57: Dodecahedron	101
Figure 58 – Classification of Traveling salesmen problems – [modified after (Feillet, et al (2005)]	103
Figure 59: Space-Time Path modified after Haegerstrand (1970)	109
Figure 60: Space-time path - after Lenntorp (1976)	110
Figure 61: Dynamic Potential Space considering feasible opportunity sets and possible activity durations [Kim and Kwan (2003)]	112
Figure 62: OGC Geo Mobility Server - modified after the OGC OpenLS 1.1	115
Figure 63: Abstract data types and the core services, modified after the OGC OpenLS Specification 1.1	117
Figure 64: Route maneuver type [Hansen, et al. (2006b)]	119
Figure 65: Orchestrated OpenLS services for the provision of focus maps [Neis and Zipf (2007)]	120
Figure 66: XML-encoded agent communication - map interaction request	120
Figure 67: Typical route planning procedure	122
Figure 68: The OGC OpenLS 1.01. Route service request suite	123
Figure 69: DetermineRouteResponse	124
Figure 70: Service cascade for personalized tour proposal. Orchestration of OGC OpenLS, Web Processing and Feature Service.	126
Figure 71: DetermineTourRequest	127

Figure 72: General UserType Element as Abstract Data Type.	128
Figure 73: TourPlan Request	129
Figure 74 OGC Web Processing Request – *ExecuteRequest*	130
Figure 75: OGC Web Processing Request – *ExecuteResponse*	131
Figure 76: WPS GraphBuilder - *GetGraph* request including an AccessibilityArea ADT	132
Figure 77: Graph ADT.	133
Figure 78: Edge and NodeDescriptor	134
Figure 79: DestinationType	134
Figure 80: OpenLS Directory Request and Response	135
Figure 81: *GetContextRequest*	137
Figure 82: Situational statements in GUMO	137
Figure 83: User Model service request exposed by the Deep Map application	138
Figure 84: *GetUserModelRequest*	139
Figure 85: Example for assigning Point of Interests with context and user weights	140
Figure 86: WPS Location service – *GetWeightedPOIs* request response pair requests	141
Figure 87: WPS Feasibility Service – *GetFeasibbleSet*	141
Figure 88: WPS Feasibility service– *DestinationType*	142
Figure 89: WPS Graph Reducer – *GetFeasibileSetResponse*	143
Figure 90: WPS Graph Weighter – *WeightGraphRequest*	146
Figure 91: Graph reduction [Stille (2001)]	147
Figure 92: Collapse and extension cycles [Stille (2001)]	148
Figure 93 WPS Tour Planner – *TourPlanRequest*	149
Figure 94: DetermineTourResponse	149
Figure 95: DetermineTourResponse – TourSummary and TourDuration	150
Figure 96: DetermineTourResponse – TourInstructionsList	151

Tables

Table 1: Different types of city visits – according to their duration and purpose. ... 24
Table 2: Direct and indirect effects of tourism [TSA (2007)] ... 25
Table 3 Main motivations for a city trips [Dettmer (2000)] ... 26
Table 4: Holiday content for Europeans on city breaks in Europe and Germany [GNTB (2006)] ... 26
Table 5: JCAF research scenarios ... 58
Table 6: Context, content sources and storage in SmartKom [Porzel, et al. (2005)] ... 62
Table 7: A comparison of Context Models and User Models [Byun and Cheverst (2001)] ... 73
Table 8: Knowledge representation languages [Bachman (1979), modified by Guardian (1994)] ... 81
Table 9: Five categorize of grid computing [Foster and Kesselman (1999)] ... 89
Table 10: OGC OpenLS 1.1 - Abstract Data Types ... 116
Table 11 Translation between the OpenLS address ADTs and the address specification of the ministry of interior / Taiwan [modified after Hui-Ting, et al. (2005)] ... 118
Table 12: Commercial OpenLS-compliant and registered products [OGC (2008)] ... 121

Equations

Equation 1: Specific Utility Function [Miller (1991)] 112
Equation 2: Calculation of the vertex prize – p(v) 144
Equation 3: Calculation of the normalized vertex prize 145
Equation 4: Calculation of the edge costs - c(e) 145
Equation 5: Calculation of the normalized edge costs 145

Chapter 1. Introduction

Almost every person in the western hemisphere is subject to a dramatic change in daily life in the past decade. Due to the continuing technological progress in physics, engineering and computer science the dawn of the age of Ubiquitous Computing as Mark Weiser proposed in (1991)[1] has begun. Computerized devices infiltrate our normal life in various forms, sometimes perceivable like mobile phones with integrated cameras and TV player, personal navigation assistance - PNAs or sometimes concealed as intelligent room heating or refrigerators with internet connection. This development is grounded on improvements various technical areas: like increasing computing power combined with a continued miniaturization; new sensors, advances in power supply be means of long-lasting batteries; ubiquitous communication with a proliferation of wireless networks; new materials allowing for new form factors of devices; new input devices like public displays, gesture based pointing devices and new interaction modalities such as gestures or speech

Aside from this more technical viewpoint a dramatic change has happened also with regard to computer applications and services, the information availability and the participation of individual users. During the mid nineties and the beginning of this century the World Wide Web has become one of the most, if not the most, important sources of information. More and more applications

---

[1] Mark Weiser describes Ubiquitous Computing: „as the third wave in computing, just now beginning. First were mainframes, each shared by lots of people. Now we are in the personal computing era, person and machine staring uneasily at each other across the desktop. Next comes ubiquitous computing, or the age of calm technology, when technology recedes into the background of our lives." http://www.ubiq.com/hypertext/weiser/weiser.html

relay on the distributed architecture of the Internet – even complete office solutions or customer relationship management – CRM applications are available online or become available when their users or on the move. All over the world humans interact and share their minds by means of so called Web 2.0 technologies like Mash-Ups, or escape the reality in virtual spaces such a Massive Multiplayer Online Games as WOW[2] or Second Live[3].

People in the so called *"developed world"* live and work in urban environments, which are characterized by high density of people, buildings, services, facilities and infrastructures. These urban areas are today fully covered with telecommunication facilities provided by mobile operators. Additionally in recent years many public authorities of cities – mainly in the United States - have started building up wireless networks to facilitate mobile broadband internet access. High speed networks and powerful handheld devices nowadays allow for mobile access to all these services provided by the internet.

Another social phenomenon of our times is the cities tourism boom. Cities have always been a center of attraction for people and but with the changing conditions in the professional life, the amount of short term visits has dramatically increased in the last years. A typical phenomenon in today's city tourism is the often quite short duration of the stay itself, sometimes limited to just a few hours. That counts especially for tourists from Asia and North America who visit Europe often in just a few days. Services that provide individual tailored city seeing tours through a city according to the various constrains like time budget etc. are expected to be very useful.

A tourist is a very challenging user of information services due to the fact that he spends his spare time and often money using such a service. For that reason he expects a very satisfactory information delivery. Moreover the range of potential personal preferences and indispositions is quite broad and also the variety of contexts of a mobile tourist can become very manifold.

This thesis will focus on digital and mobile services in today's city tourism, while exploiting the "new" technical possibilities. It aims in specifying a framework for adaptive, personalized and context-aware city tours. Those tours should bridge the gap between the mostly limited time budget and individual preference a tourist has. Additionally it extends the OpenLS specification of the Open Geospatial Consortium to allow for integration in open platforms and services.

---

[2] WOW – World of Warcraft. Largest online game community with about 8 million registered users and about 2000 simultaneous users.
[3] Second Life – Virtual world visible with personal avatars provided by Linden Labs

Chapter 2.   Research Challenges

This thesis aims to design, define and specify a framework for the provision of personalized city tours. Along the geographic tradition it follows an integrative approach at the intersection of various research areas. Approaches from fields like Human Computing Interaction, Ubiquitous Computing, Spatial Information Theory, Software Design and Time Geography are combined and fusioned.

Common ground and application scenario lies in the tourism domain, and more precisely in city tourism. The thesis will investigate core facets of today's city tourism and individual tourists, for example their preferences and information needs.

With increasing amount of information peoples are exposed to personalization and user modeling has gained a great momentum. Commonly the term personalization is used for user-driven adaptation of services – for example customization of an online shopping web site. But the origin of this term relies in the domain of information retrieval and recommender systems. With the dramatic increase of available digital information in the World Wide Web soon the need arose to find intelligent mechanisms to cluster, sort and search the huge information space in order deliver requested pieces of information. Personalization employs statistical methods from the domain of machine learning and demands a very broad data basis to provide reasonable results. Nowadays some approaches have succeeded to become commercial products such e.g. DynaPortal[4], FrontMind

---

[4] Found on 03.02.05 at: http://www.dynaportal.com/software/personalization.cfm

[Kobsa and Fink (2001)] or have been implemented within other services like at Amazon, the online store or O₂, a European telecommunication provider. Mostly personalization is targeted to textual information. So far there are only few and very initial approaches under discussion that try to provide also personalized access to spatial data. The thesis will review concepts and algorithms for personalization and user modeling known from the domain of data mining and knowledge discovery with regard to their applicability to geographic information systems.

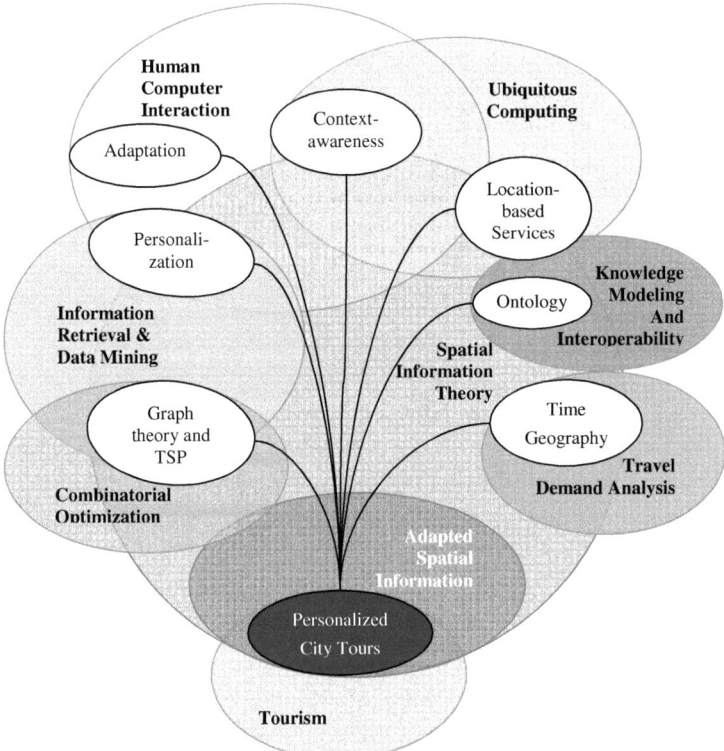

Figure 1: Visualizes the different research areas touched in this thesis

Covered by user interfaces today's information services are comprised of various, heterogeneous and often distributed components or services. Interoperability is a key item in current IT Landscapes. This thesis will investigate interoperability of spatial data and services. Subsequent it aims in extending the OpenLocation Specification of the Open Geospatial Consortium by means of proposing an OpenLS Tour Service and a subsequent set of Web Processing services.

Chapter 3. Application Domain – City Tourism

Tourism is a very prominent and influencing phenomenon in our times [Kasper (1998)]. This applies not only with regard to economical considerations but also to the great social effects. In western societies on average almost 15 percent of a humans life time is spend as a tourist – in case the complete spare time and an average amount of weekend trips is taken into account [Bieger (2005)]. But tourism itself is a broad term and subsumes multiple different areas, which changed along the changing working live and environment [Kaspar (1996)]. One can define tourism as:

Tourism summarizes all relations and phenomena that occur due to translocation and presences of humans, where the location is neither the domicile not the work place.

This definition emphasizes the diversity of touristy phenomena's with regard to economic social, environmental, technological and political implications.

Historically one can regard tourism as the mirror image of society. Already B.C. people traveled for example to big sport events like the Olympiad, during the Roman Empire the rich tried to escape the overpopulated Rome. During the medieval time the tourism succumb [Becker (2004)] except the pilgrimage to Christian places like the well-known Santiago di Compostela in Spain [Kaspar (1996)].

With the reconnaissance, the interest in natural phenomena and landscapes grew – triggered by the famous poets, painters and scientist – wealthy people started to travel, either to visit those landscapes or for recreational purpose by visiting spas resorts. By that time for a small proportion of the civil society, individual tourism based on personal interests was born [Benthien (1997)]. Only the upper class could afford to spend their time for travelling. On average, a worker had to work for at least 70 hours a week. Figure 2 describes how much the proportion of spare times has grown from 1840 to the year 2000 with respect to the weekly working time.

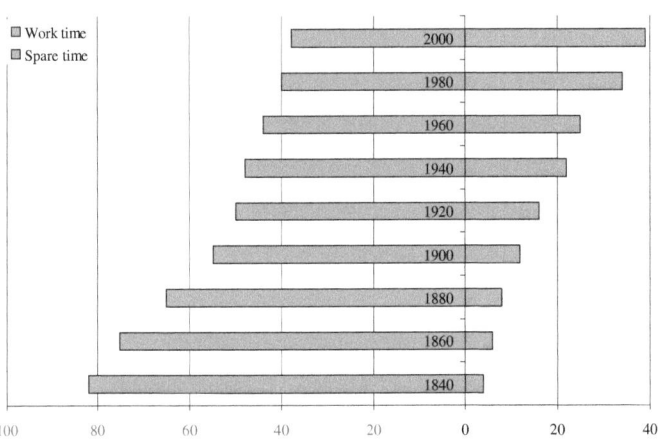

Figure 2: Development of spare time between 1840 and 2000 [according to Becker (2000)]

However the most influencing factor on the tourism was the improvement of the national and European transportation system. The construction of streets, steam shipping and especially the railway network brought tourism also to a broader class of population. In Germany another positive effect was caused by the collective labor law from 1918 that codifies for the first time on average 8 hours work per day and entitlement for an annual vacation [Benthien (1997)]. The economic crisis in the 30ties caused a sharp decrease of tourism [Kaspar (1996)]. Between the WW[5] I and WW II and especially after WW II the shape of tourism changed again due to the upcoming mobility based on individual motorization. Beginning with the 70ties the city tourism started to become popular [Quack (2006)].

Today the relation and necessary balance between work time, spare time and recreation is unchallenged. Tourism itself is a diverse phenomenon with various forms and types. Common classifications are: by destination, means of transportation or travel purpose. Reasons for traveling are very individual as they reflect needs, desires and expectation

---

[5] WW – World War

Chapter 3. Application Domain – City Tourism

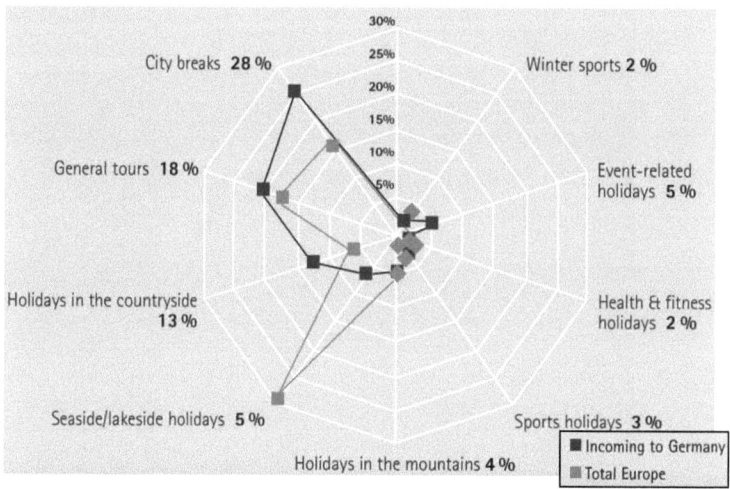

Figure 3: Ranking of holiday contents of Europeans in Germany 2006 as a percentage [GNTB (2006)]

City tourism is surely one of the prototypes of traveling [Lohman (1989)]. Cities – as the social, economical and culture centers of civilizations - posses always a great attractiveness for people in the proximity or in more distant regions. This applies even more since the first large traveling wave of the middle class in the nineteen's century. Figure 4 indicates that for Germany city breaks and general tours are the most important sectors of tourism. All other types, like seaside or sports holidays play a minor role.

In Figure 3 the different ranks of holiday content for Germany in relation to overall European trends are shown. One can identify that seaside and lake side holiday is less importance in contrast to other European countries. Also other types of holiday content like winter sports or event-related holiday are to disregard. For Germany especially general tours and city tourism is of great importance.

3.1. Classifications of City Tourism

The city tourism subsumes various different services and travel reasons. One can distinguish two main areas, first economically motivated tourism and second tourism due to private reasons. Economically motivated tourism subsumes all kinds of business trips to cities for example to visit a venue.

Another differentiator is the duration of city visits (see Table 1). The average duration for a city trip is between 1 and four days [Dettmer (2000)]. But here a high percentage of day visitors are unreflected. Figure 5 describes the overnights stays in some major European cities in 2006.

City tourism			
Overnight stay		One day tourism	
Economically motivated	Due to private reason	Economically motivated	Due to private reason
Multiple day business trip	City visit	One day business trip	Day trip/ Sightseeing tourism
Convention and congress visit	Visiting relatives	Convention and congress visit	Shopping tourism
Exhibition and Fair tourism		Exhibition and Fair visit	Evening visit
Incentive tourism			

Table 1: Different types of city visits – according to their duration and purpose.

In Germany more than 48% percent of the day trips have bigger cities as destination [DTV (2006)]. With 2.62 billion day trips in 2005 this is equivalent to around 1.26 billion trips to cities. Back in 1995 there were only 800 Mio day trips counted [Dettmer (2000)].

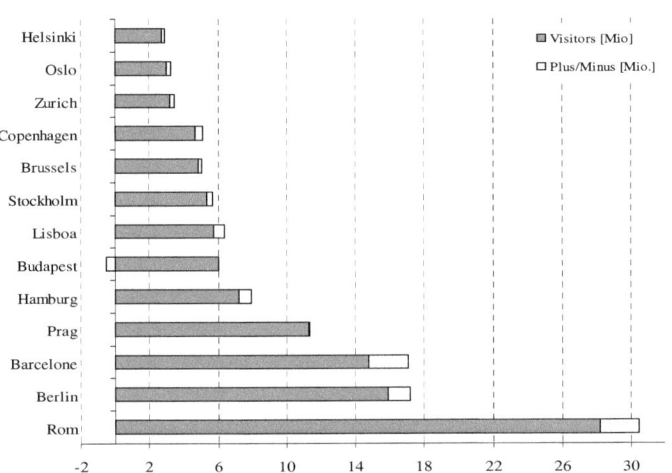

Figure 4: Overnight stays in European cities in 2006 [TourMIS (2007)]

3.2. Economical Considerations and Statistics

Today tourism is an important economic factor for the national and of course also for the local level. In 2006, the amount of dollars spends for tourism related demand in the United States was quantified by the Transportation and Security Administration – TSA with more than 1380 billion dollars [TSA (2007)]. A comparison of the direct and indirect effects of tourism in various countries can be seen in Table 2.

Tourism demands have a very broad impact as they flow through the national economies. They consist of goods and services produced for visitors and other more indirect activities such as retailing and construction.

For Germany, the direct effect in 2006 can be quantified with 78 billion dollars [TSA (2007)] and the overall with 267.7 billion dollars. Concerning city tourism a big proportion was due to business trips (71.5 million overnight stays with 38.5 billion US-$ spending and 540 million day trips with 14 billion US-$ spending) [GNTB (2006)].

Rank	Country	US-$ bn
1	USA	1.380,0
2	Japan	446,5
3	China	301,2
4	Germany	267,7
5	France	250,0
6	United Kingdom	212,8
7	Spain	212,3
8	Italy	192,5
9	Canada	131,8
10	Mexico	118,4

Table 2: Direct and indirect effects of tourism [TSA (2007)]

3.3. Motivations for City Trips

In contrast to the economically motivated city trips with a more or less clear business goal are private motivated trips often not planned but rather spontaneous [Dettmer (2000)]. They are based on the demand for consumption as recreational activity. The different motivations for city trips and the destination choices are manifold. According to the duration and motivation for a private cit trips Dettmer [Dettmer (2000)] differentiates three types:

1. Short city trips, which are motivated by cultural interest in order to do sightseeing and visit attractions, whereas the city itself is the main attraction.

2. Day visitors, here the interest is quite similar but the available time budget much more limited.

3. Event and Shopping visitors that visit cities to undertake a specific activity such as shopping or visiting friends. So the visited city itself is of minor interest.

But also economically motivated city trips cause demands for tourist services. Like for the event and shopping visitors, the broad offerings of a city itself is of minor interest, as the visitor needs to work but often some leisure activities are associated with the trip [Dettmer (2000)]. There is usually a short timeframe for sightseeing or at least a dinner and a short shopping tour.

Reason	
Visiting relatives or friends	27.8 %
Recreation	18.1 %
Shopping	11.8 %
Sight seeing	10.9 %
Visit of a specific event	10.5 %
Spontaneous trip	8.3 %
For a specific activity	4.0 %
Going out for dinner or lunch	3.0 %
Organized trips	2.0 %
Other reason	3.6 %

Table 3 Main motivations for a city trips [Dettmer (2000)]

3.4. Preferences and Interests

Visitors of cities find themselves in the great dilemma between the number of opportunities a city offers and the usually quite limited time budget.

Content of city breaks*	Total foreign city breaks 2006 by Europeans (frequency in %)	Rank 2006	City breaks to Germany by Europeans (frequency in %)	Rank 2006
Sightseeing	59	1	56	2
Enjoying atmosphere/ambience	49	2	61	1
Visiting museums	40	5	41	5
Enjoying food and drink	41	3	48	4
Shopping	41	4	53	3
Visiting exhibitions	23	8	30	6
Nightlife	26	6	28	8
Visiting parks/green areas	25	7	29	7

Table 4: Holiday content for Europeans on city breaks in Europe and Germany [GNTB (2006)]

Chapter 3. Application Domain – City Tourism

3.4.1. General Trends

A quite obvious trend for city tourism is the common interest to experience the local atmosphere, do sightseeing and enjoy the local food and drinks. Table 4 highlights this trend by visualizing the most common content of city breaks for Europeans, especially while visiting German cities.

Obviously, shopping is of high interest to city tourist. This counts especially for German cities, as the percentage is more than 10% higher as for other cities visited by Europeans. The data reveals also a high percentage of around 40% of visitors that intent to visit museums. This can be explained with the high recognition of local museums, especially in the capital Berlin and the other cities like Munich, Cologne or Hamburg.

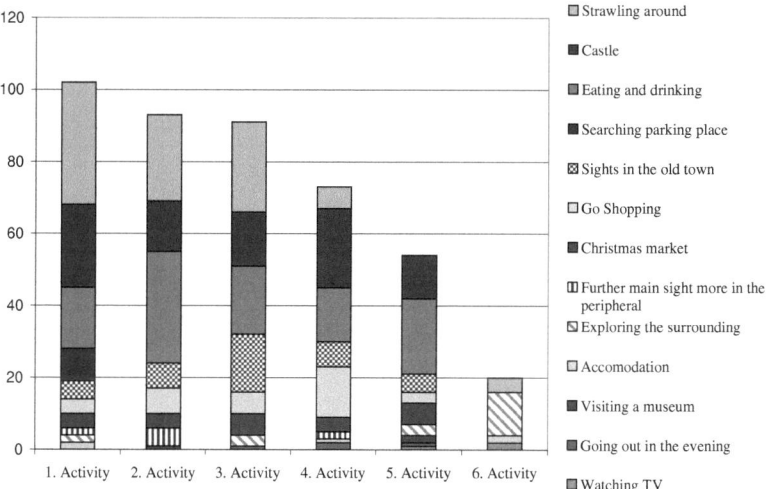

Figure 5: Sequence of activities in a typical historic city throughout the day [Data Hoffmann (2006)]

3.4.2. Local Studies and Phenomena

Local studies undertaken in different cities [Boedecker (2003), Freytag (2003), Hoffmann (2006), Kaul (1999), and Wiese (2007)] underline this general trend for sightseeing and experiencing the local atmosphere. They also indicate some common phenomena of city tourists [Cooper (1981), Dietvorst (1995), Thornton, et al. (1997)]:

1. Cities exhibit a limited amount of major sights that almost every first time visitors visit.

2. Commonly the flow of visitors follows specific tracks, often visiting the main sights in a certain order.

3. In European cities those tracks are usually within very limited areas be means of the inner cities and old-towns.

Also within the schedule of activities throughout the day one can identify specific patterns. An investigation by Hoffmann (2006) in a typical midsized historic city reveals that most city visitors start their visit either by just strolling around or going for the main sight.

Later in during the day, eating and drinking, further sights in the city centre as well as shopping are more frequently done. The number of activities is leveled around 3 – 5.

	Foreign tourists (including American tourists)	American tourists (n=277)	All respondents
Family, friends	29	26	31
Guide books	23	27	17
Internet	19	21	19
Previous visit	12	8	13
Tourist Board	9	9	10
Tour operator brochure	3	7	5
TV/radio	1	1	1
Newspaper, magazine	1	1	4

Figure 6: Information sources used by traveler to cities 2001 in Western Europe in 2001 [Atlas (2007)]

3.5. Information Sources

As of September 2007 an estimate of about 1250 million people all over the world are using the internet, which is equivalent to about 20 % of the world's population [InternetWorldStats (2007)]. In the last decade the internet and as part of it, the World Wide Web has revolutionized the way most people in the developed countries are gathering and working with information. This applies also for information related to traveling and trip preparation.

3.5.1. Trip Preparation, Booking and Traveling

According to a study undertaken by ATLAS[6] back in 2001 [Atlas (2007)] the main information source for the trip preparation used by travelers to cities have been relatives and friends, already

---

[6] ATLAS - Association for Tourism and Leisure Education

Chapter 3. Application Domain – City Tourism

directly followed by the internet [see Figure 6]. Recent findings by the IAB[7] [TravelMole (2006)] indicate that today search engines have become more used and trusted for information than friends and family. 88% of users rate information provided by search results higher than that of friends and family. In this study the friends and family category were at 78% while travel agents came in at 63%.

The proportion of young travelers who book online has increased from 10% to 50% in five years, according to the WY&SETC[8] global study of young independent travelers. And 80% use the internet to search for information before departing on their trip. A study by the GNTB[9]/WTM reveals that in 2005 trips to Germany have with 46 % already been book via Internet, whereas 24% still preferred the classical method via travel agencies.

But not only the destination selection and booking is nowadays dominated by the internet. Also the ways and methods travelers choose to prepare on how to get to the chosen city is heavily driven by services in the World Wide Web.

The recent eScape[10] Report 2007 highlights that 70% are using route planners when traveling by car

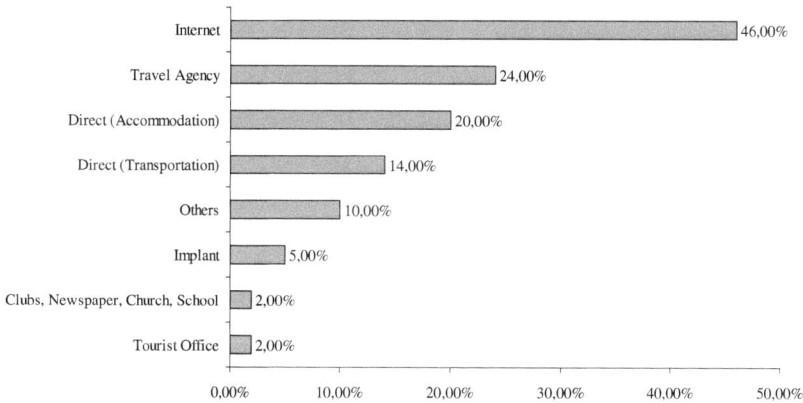

Figure 7: Booking methods for trips to Germany [GNTB (2005)]

(compared to 65% in 2006). Mapping applications in the internet in general are raising increasingly interest. Some of some are also offering time tables and route plans of public transportation of designated cities and areas [see Google Maps]. Almost every passenger transportation company has

---

[7] IAB - Internet Advertising Bureau - http://www.iab.net/
[8] WY&STEC – World Youth & Student Educational Travel Confederation's
[9] GNTB – German National Tourist Board
[10] eScape - http://www.escape-reports.com/

nowadays dedicated web presences including a broad range of services like airports announcing the start and landings, railway companies allowing for online booking and planning or local transportation companies offering even mobile web presence including schedules and time tables.

3.5.2. Information Sources During the Journey

While traveling that sources used for information on and about the current city are still rather classical by means of using personal recommendations, guidebooks or other print media. Freytag [Freytag (2004)] underlines this trend with local findings for Heidelberg/Germany [See Figure 8].

Another study by Hoffmann in 2006 [Hoffmann (2006)] supports this general observation. Amongst the main types of information sources of city tourists (guide books, personal tour guides, mobile information systems or guided audio tours), the classical approaches have been still the most preferred and less disliked ones [Hoffmann (2006)]. In this study mobile information systems have been the third preferred option but with a considerable discrepancy of participants that preferred those kind of services and those who dislike them.

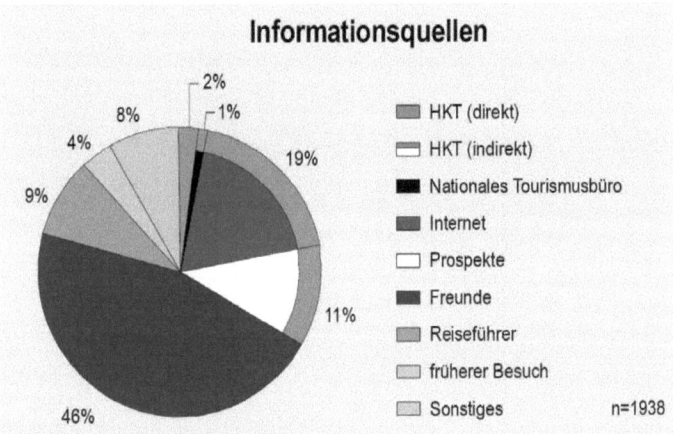

Figure 8: Information sources for tourists in Heidelberg [Freytag (2003)]

According to the ETC Report 2006 [ETC (2006)] new mobile services like PNAs[11] , guided audio tours and the mobile internet are getting significantly more influence in the near future on how travelers inform themselves during a city visit. Nowadays in the Internet there is an enormous amount and variety of interactive services available that touches city tourism in one way or the other. For example as city portals (e.g. www.meinestadt.de, www.stadtleben.de) event guides (e.g.

---

[11] PNA – Personal navigation assistance – Mobile device equipped with GPS Sensors and navigation software.

Chapter 3. Application Domain – City Tourism

www.godelta.de, www.prinz-online.de), navigation services (e.g. www.google.com/maps, www.maps.yahoo.com, www.local.live.com) and social networks (www.facebook.com, www.studivz.de) connecting people all over the world. As wireless technologies by means of network infrastructures (namely with UMTS, WIFI and WIMAX) and the availability of network enabled mobile devices (mobile phones, PDAs, gaming consoles and audio/video players) has gained a great momentum in the last years, people are able to connect to the internet almost wherever they are. According to a recent market research by Nielson Media [Nielson Media (2007)] among the 237 million wireless subscribers in the U.S more than 32 million accessed the Internet on their phones in September 2007.

Zipf and Jöst [Zipf and Jöst (2004)] investigated how young users of mobile city information systems judge and weight various types of digital content. The general observation was that especially maps, images as photos or panorama views, followed by textual information about sights were of higher interest whereas multimedia content like sounds or virtual characters were in sum of lower interest. With regard to mobile services, findings by Kölmel and Wirsing [Kölmel and Wirsing (2002)] show that potential users prefer assistance with regard to shopping, guidance and new forms of communication like buddy finder and location-based messaging.

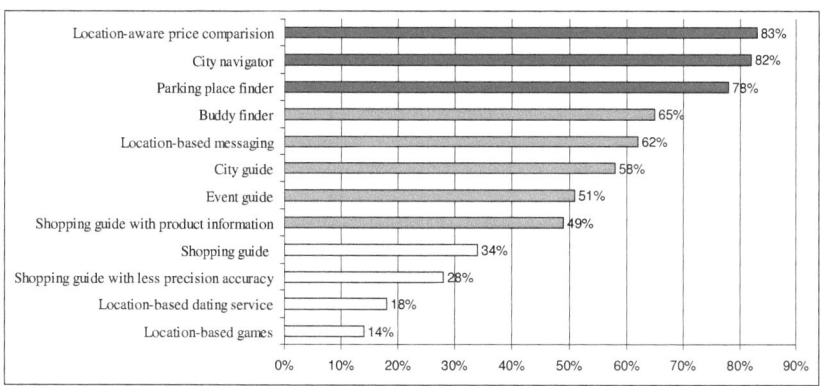

Figure 9: Preferences for mobile location-based services [Data from Kölmel and Wirsing (2002)]

In summary city tourism can be identify as a prominent and important phenomena of our times. It has significant effects economical and social impact on the cities. City tourism itself can be differentiated according to the main purpose of visit, whether it is business or privately motivated. Usually the duration is for a city visit is quite limited and the activities undertaken during the trip show often similar patterns. Especially strolling around to experience the local atmosphere, visiting the main sights, tasting local food and drinks and shopping is of high interest to city visitorsFor the trip selection and preparation the internet has already acquired the most important role whereas for information needs during the visit this is about to come with the increasing availability, accessibility and popularity of specific web sites, serving the needs of citizens for up to date content, even while on the go.

Chapter 4. Adapting to the User

To handle the complexity in today's computing environments adaptation is one of the key requirements. We are surrounded by a wide variety of electronic devices, at home, at work or en route. The following chapter focuses on the aspect of adaptation in computing with regard to the user. It presents key concepts of user modeling and personalization followed by an overview of context-awareness and context-aware applications.

4.1. Personalization and User Modeling

In the domain of information retrieval and information filtering, especially with the World Wide Web as application domain, there is a long tradition in employing statistical methods and approaches to tailor presented information to the users' needs. Many of those approaches use collaborative-filtering while others employ inferences based on user behavior. In recent years they even succeeded to become commercial available for example DynaPortal[12], FrontMind [Kobsa and Fink (2000)] or are implemented in other services like shopping web sites or community-driven travel web sites. To structure the diversity of personalization and user modeling approaches some definitions are given.

---

[12] Found on 03.02.05 at: http://www.dynaportal.com/software/personalization.cfm

Overall one can distinguish personalization approaches between *adaptable* and *adaptive* ones [Kobsa, et. al (2001)]. [Oppermann (1999)] defines a system as adaptable if the users are in control of the complete adaptation process. Systems are adaptive if these adaptations are done automatically without direct involvement of the user. Both approaches can coexist in one application with different weighting depending on the type of adaptation. A critical issue of adaptive and adaptable systems is their complexity by means of the directness of transformation between user inputs to system output. On can state [Kobsa, et. al (2001)] that the more explicit and direct this transformation is, the more appropriate results are gained.

4.1.1. Data Acquisition for Personalized Systems

To provide personalized and user tailored services an adaptable/adaptive system has to have a clear picture of the user, the interaction with him and the general context or situation both are in. The definition of this data is one of the fundamental steps during the design of a personalized system because these data represents the boundaries in which inference techniques can be applied. Often some aspects of the user, interaction and context information often cannot be gathered directly (either by user input or some sensors). It can only be inferred which has a great impact on the reliability of the personalization.

4.1.1.1. User Profile Data Acquisition

Profile data about a specific user is often provided explicitly by the user while asking him directly. This user profile data is the basement for every adaptation process. Obviously the most straight forward method to acquire user data like demographics or application specific background knowledge is asking the user directly. This is often done by means of an initial interview. J. M. Carrol [Carrol and Rosson (1986)] mentioned one of the most severe drawbacks of initial interview, as the "Paradox of the Active User". Users are eager to start using information systems or other adaptive applications. So they do not want to answer extensive questionnaires to allow the system to acquire a detailed profile. But on the other hand, such a profile might help them to find the needed information faster and more efficient. In the area of Web 2.0 this behavior has changed quite dramatically as active users of the world wide web leave quite detailed traces and profiles for example in today's social networking sites (e.g. Facebook, StudieVZ, LinkedIn, XING – formerly known as OpenBC – any others).

There are many example application mentioned in literature that employs initial questionnaires like Rich (1979), Boyle and Encarnacion (1994), and Fink et al. (1998).

4.1.1.2. System Usage Acquisition and Interaction Observation

Beside general user characteristics like origin, data gathered from the system usage and interaction observation are often used not directly on an individual level but rather as data to employ statistical inference techniques based on multiple users.

Selective actions

Selective action refers to the choice of the user to exploit a service in specific manner, e.g. request information via following a hyperlink or watching an online movie. They allow for direct inference on the potential interest of a user on the selected information item. A direct conclusion that a user is really interest in the content behind a chosen hyperlink can be dangerous due to the fact that the selection might be happened due to some random behavior. Additional to these direct selections more advanced selections of items are also possible e.g. when a user decides to buy a product or download, print or save a page locally on his desktop. With today ubiquitous computing environments and sensing technologies, selective actions outside a systems information space can also serve as evidence for a specific interest or intention.

Temporal viewing behavior

Temporal viewing behavior is also a very ambiguous in terms of inferring positive user interest on the selected information item. In nowadays desktop environments most systems can not distinguish whether a user is really focusing on the display information item or whether his attention is on something different [Joerding (1999)]. But temporal viewing behavior can be used as negative evidence for information items that are viewed only shortly. For none text based information items like videos streams, audio files, the fact that a user is listening from the beginning to the end can serve as a strong indicator for his interest.

Ratings

Ratings, if given by the users, are the most valuable source of information regarding the user interest, because here the users explicitly rate an information item according to their preferences and interest. The rating approach is the underlying concept of recommendation systems like user-driven Web 2.0 applications. These, mostly web based applications try to propose information according to recommendation given by users with similar profile. A major drawback of ratings is the fact that often users do not want to rate the information items.

4.1.1.3. Usage Patterns

The user's interaction with information systems is mostly embedded in complex tasks and software environments and follows a pattern. Therefore it is desirable to enhance inference results by employing additional information [Kobsa, et. al (2001)].

Usage frequency

Usage frequency is surely the most obvious additional information that can be used for inference, e.g. the fact that a user often returns to a specific web site might server as a strong indicator that he has interest on this site. The AVANTI system employs this approach by introducing shortcut links to frequently visited web pages in an additional navigation bar [Fink, et al. (1998)].

Information context – action correlations

The correlation of information demands with actions performed in parallel can provide useful information for the personalization process, e.g. a user is composing a business report and in order to do so he reads online news. This correlation of document type and news source can be exploited for further inferences [Dragunov, et al. (2005)].

Task models and Action sequences

Typical actions performed with computers often tend to follow an action sequence that can modeled during system desigg upfront or that be recorded, analyzed and predicted for the future (e.g. a user reads every morning the mails he received last night followed by a visit on some news portals) [Ahn, et al. (2008)].

4.1.1.4. User and System Context

With the migration of information systems from desktop oriented to mobile application the recognition of the user as well as the system context can be a very valuable source of information to tailor information and functionality to the users. For that reason one has to take a close look on context-aware application and derive a model of contextual information from them that can be used for personalization purposed. The description of context-aware application will follow in Chapter 4.2.

4.1.2. Inferences techniques for personalization

To facilitate adaptation and personalization applications and information systems need to infer, based on already existing knowledge about the user – either provided directly or gathered via system usage observation, potential goals, plans, information interests that are not yet given. One can distinguish between primary and secondary inference.

4.1.2.1. Primary Inference

Primary inference considers observations gathered directly from the user interaction. It tries to infer from these observation potential interests and preferences.

Acquisition rules

These rules are predefined actions that an adaptive system should apply, once new information about the user is available, e.g. due to another interaction with the system. Acquisition rules are usually straight forward interpretations of the user interaction e.g. *a user wants to perform a task x with the system so he is currently not interested in information y that relates to task y.* According to the type of acquisition rules and their implementation one can differentiate between application domain specific and domain independent rules. Most adaptive systems that apply acquisition rules use domain specific ones tailored to the requirements of the system and its users with the major drawback of less flexibility. An example of the employment of domain independent acquisition rules is KNOME application [Chin (1993)]. From a more linguistic point of view the interaction steps between user and system that lead to the applicability of acquisition rules can be named as dialog acts [Pohl, et al. (1995)]

Plan recognition

The aim of plan recognition is to identify the actual goal a user aims at by analyzing the necessary steps to achieve it based on his interaction history. Systems that employ plan or also called goal recognition need to have a task model of potential action that a user can perform, their combinations and sequences and the goals the system supports. Initial approaches focused on symbolic representation [Allen and Perrault (1980)] whereas newer approaches try to solve these problems by applying techniques from the domain on numerical optimization like graph based [Lesh and Etzioni (1995)] or numerical methods.

Stereotype reasoning

Another very prominent method to transform user data or interaction directly in a preference representation aims to match actual users in predefined stereotypes. These stereotypes comprise existing assumption about interests, preferences or even goals. Typical examples are groupings according to age categories or cultural background. A first system that facilitates stereotype reasoning back in 1979 was *GRUNDY* [Rich (1979)]. Nowadays this approach is more or less the common ground for all personalization and user model systems. The stereotype approach consists of three main elements: First the assumption about the users condensed into the stereotypes, second methods how to associate a new user to those stereotypes and finally methods on how to reassign already known users to stereotypes after a period of time.

4.1.2.2. Secondary Inference

Secondary inference aims to infer user preferences not from direct observations of only one single user but rather by transferring knowledge gained from other users. It is also called indirect inference, and one can differentiate between deductive and inductive approaches. Deduction means to reason from a specific case – that is thought to be valid – to a broader view, whereas induction is the reasoning process from a wide range of cases to the rationale behind them, in other words taking a bottom up or top-down approach. In both cases there is no direct link from assumptions to conclusions.

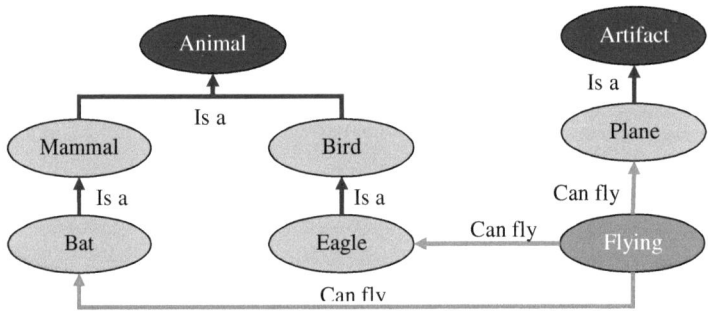

Figure 10: Graphical representation of a simple ontology

Logic-based inferences

The central concepts for logic-based reasoning in the context of personalization are assumptions / believes and their formal representation. One can differentiate between believes the user has about

Chapter 4. Adapting to the User

the real world (UB) and believes a system has about the real world and its user (SB). A basic logical formalism is the propositional calculus. Simple propositions like "*a Bat is an Animal*" are basic entities – also called atoms – of this formalism. These atoms can be combined by logical connectives like "like", "and" or "or to more complex statements. Most systems that use propositional calculus enhance this concept by graduated values like numeric or symbolic values [Pohl (1998)].

Other logic-based approaches are first-order predicate calculus (FOPC), and modal logic. A comprehensive overview of these approaches can be found in Pohl (1998). Another more recent approach to formalize logical concepts are ontologies. Ontology can be defined[13] as a branch of metaphysics concerned with nature and relations of being or a particular theory about nature of being or the kinds of existents. In more common sense - ontologies try to model concepts and entities in the real world and their relationships between each other. Figure 10 shows a graphical representation of a rather basic ontology that maps a simple hierarchy and a functional concept to each other.

In personalization systems information items are quite frequently associated with such formalized concepts and allow for inferences across them on the meta-level [Pretschner (1999), Gauch, et al. (2006)]. When there is an indication that a user has interest on an information item, the related concepts are also rated accordingly.

An eminent feature of human interests is the fact that they tend to change over time. Standard logic mechanisms have according to Kobsa (2001) difficulties to cope with these changes. Another drawback of logic approaches is their difficulties to deal with uncertainty.

Representation and reasoning with uncertainty

Uncertainty is a key attribute of most personalization techniques as they try to infer potential interest of their users via statistical methods based on existing knowledge about them. Various evidence-based approaches – methods from the domain of machine learning – have been adapted to the domain of personalization. Usually uncertainty is described as a linear parameter which is a numeric representation of probabilistic. They are commonly combined with feature value pairs that correspond to user characteristics and features [Sleeman (1985)].

- Bayesian Networks: The most prominent methods dealing with uncertainty are Bayesian Networks - BN or also called Belief Networks. These methods can be summarized as probabilistic graphical models. They span graph networks containing assumptions as nodes

---

[13] According to Merriam Webster Online Dictionary – Found on 01/05/2006

and their interdependencies as arcs between them. In case of Bayesian networks the graph network are directed and allow for upward and downward propagation of probabilistic. Other forms are Markov Random fields employing undirected graphs and Hidden Markov models employing dynamic networks. A short introduction can be found at Murphey (1998)[14]. Microsoft Office Assistance [Horvitz, et al. (1998)] as result of the Lumiere project is surely the most prominent examples that employ Bayesian networks and is available in an every day's product – the office product suite.

- Fuzzy logic: Fuzzy logic provides a framework to cover the coherence disambiguities of real world information and to reason under uncertainty. The term fuzzy sets and the derived term fuzzy logic were coined by Zadeh in 1965 [Zadeh (1965)]. He describes a fuzzy subset "A" of greater class "B" by assigning each "A" a value "b" that represents its degree of membership in B [see Figure 11]. So despite to standard logic with discrete finite set, in fuzzy logic the degree of truth can take continuous values from zero to one. There are two main arguments to employ fuzzy logic for user modeling mainly in the area of recommender systems. First, users reason about themselves also in vague concepts and second, the information that users might provide to such a system can be vague [Kobsa (2001)]. The process of conducting fuzzy logic follows a three step procedure [Frias-Martinez, et al. (2005)]: Fuzzifaction of the input data ➔ Conduction fuzzy reasoning based on the fuzzy information ➔ Defuzzification of the results into the final outcome. Personalization approaches that employ fuzzy logic can be found for example as shopping assistant [Popp and Lödel (1996)] or web recommendation system [Nasraoui, and Petenes (2003)].

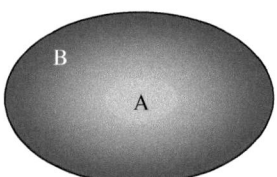

Figure 11: Fuzzy set A as part of a larger fuzzy set B

- Dempster-Shafer theory: The Dempster-Shafer theory[15] also known as the theory of belief networks goes back to thoughts of philosophers in the 17th century and was readopted by A. P. Dempster (1968) and Glenn Shafer (1976). It extends the classical Bayesian theory of subjective beliefs by allowing transfer beliefs from one proposition to a related one. Thus not all statements of interest have to have a directly related belief. A more detailed overview of

---

[14] found on 06/13/06 at http://www.cs.ubc.ca/~murphyk/Bayes/bnintro.html
[15] http://www.glennshafer.com/index.html found on: 01/17U/2006

Chapter 4. Adapting to the User

the previously mentioned three approaches to deal with uncertainty can be found at [Jameson (1996)]. Systems that employ the Dempster-Shafer theory are published for example by [Petrusin and Sinitsa (1993), Carberry (1990), Bauer (1996) or Tokuda & Fukuda (1993)].

Inductive reasoning

Induction is the reasoning process in which a conclusion is drawn from particular cases. In contrast to the previously described deductive reasoning there is no logical movement from beliefs to conclusions. The premises in inductive reasoning are based on observations. For personalization one can regard this process as "learning about the user" [Kobsa (2001)].

Induction can be applied along two dimensions: First by comparing features chosen by a single user. This approach is called case-based reasoning. And second by inferring interest among different users – the so called clique-based approaches. According to Aamondt and Plaza (1994), a general case-based reasoning cycle can be described by the following four processes:

1. **RETRIEVE** the most similar case or cases based on the distance metric of a feature vector.
2. **REUSE** the information and knowledge in that case to solve the problem.
3. **REVISE** the proposed solution.
4. **RETAIN** the parts of this experience likely to be useful for future problem solving.

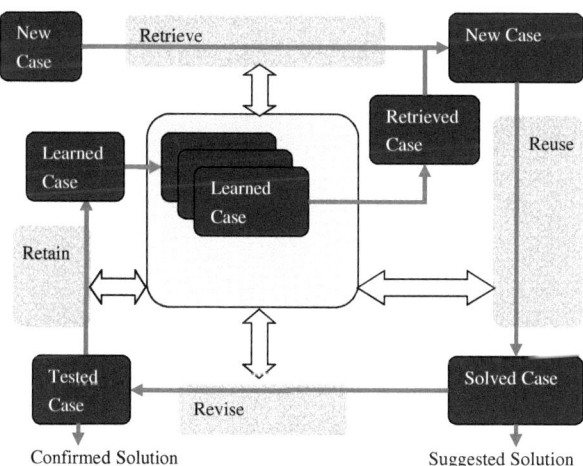

Figure 12: The Case-based reasoning cycle (modified after Aamondt (1994))

Alfred Kobsa [Kobsa, et al. (2001)] describes the process of generating recommendation as follows: Finding similar users – select the most relevant ones – generate recommendation based on their profiles (see Figure 13).

he term Clique-based approaches was coined by Alspector in 1997 [Alspector, et al. (1997)] and describes systems that aim at finding users who share similarities e.g. interests, preferences, information needs or goals. Depending on the system purpose, users with similarities are grouped into cliques. A major benefit of cliques is that they allow for prediction for new users that are assigned to one of the cliques. One can regard these systems as stereotype matching approaches in which the stereotypes are not predefined.

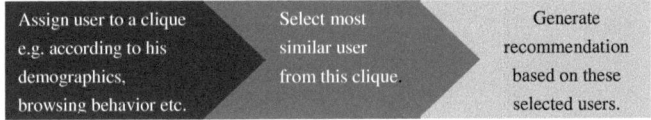

Figure 13: Clique-based filtering processes –(Kobsa, 2001)

A prominent example is the *GroupLens* system that computes correlations between readers of Usenet newsgroups by comparing their ratings of articles [Konstan; et al. (1997)]. Other examples regarding clique building based on web navigation patterns can be found in Yan et al. (1996) and Perkowitz and Etzioni (1998).

In the past years many algorithms and approaches from the domain of machine learning and artificial intelligence have been used to identify features that indicate user interest automatically.

- **Nearest-neighbor algorithm**: This approach as a prediction technique is among the oldest techniques used in area of data mining. Basically it ranks a set of known objects in terms of their distance from a new query object - q. The objects are represented as feature vectors and the measure of similarity is the computed distance in the n-dimensional vector space [Cost and Salzberg (1993)].

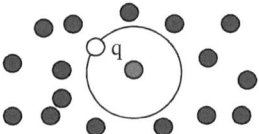

Figure 14: Nearest neighbor – cloud of features and their selection

Chapter 4. Adapting to the User

Although nearest-neighbor algorithms are quite effective for large training data sets that hold not too many noisy data, they have some disadvantages: The major problem is that computation costs are quite high because the vector distance will not necessarily be suitable for finding intuitively similar examples, especially if irrelevant attributes are present.

- **Decision trees**: "*A decision tree takes as input an object or situation described by a set of properties, and outputs a yes/no decision. Decision trees therefore represent Boolean functions. Functions with a larger range of outputs can also be represented....*" [Norvig and Russel (2003)]. Such a tree is composed of different types of nodes: intermediate nodes at which features or variables are tested during the decision process and leaf nodes that store and represent a final decision.

  Learning systems that employ decision trees are for example the rule-learning system RIPPER [Cohn (1996)], the agent-based approach presented by [Krulwich (1995)] or in combination with genetic algorithms shown in GA-ID3 [Bala, et al. (1995)]

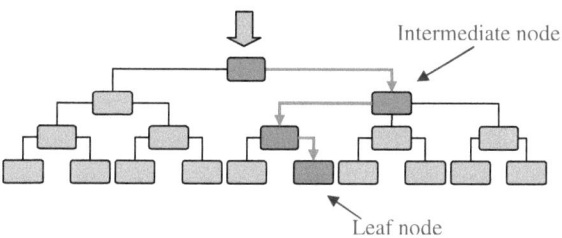

Figure 15: Decision tree

- **Genetic algorithms**: These algorithms – inspired by Darwin's[16] concept of survival of the fittest – try to mimic the natural selection process. They are typically employed in the area of optimization and search. The starting point in this approach is a set of potential solutions to a problem, called population. The population is combined and modified, resulting in a set of new solutions from which the ones closest to the optimum are selected. Another cycle starts. The fundamental element of this algorithm is the fitness function that characterizes the individual's utility via a numeric value. According to this score the individuals are selected for the next generation so that the best adapted one survives. Let's return to our example of the traveling businessman. Imagine him surfing the internet on his mobile — as the display size is quite limited, an optimization process should try to select the best combination of news items coming from different web sites to be displayed at once.

---

[16] http://www.amnh.org/exhibitions/darwin/ found on 01/18/2007

Genetic algorithms are often used for recommendation as a set of rules that can capture user goals or preferences [Min et al. (2001)] or for filtering [Fan et al. (2000)] and classification [Shin and Lee (2002)] due to their capability to deal with huge data sets. But this approach has limitations with regard to dynamic modeling [Frias-Martinez, et al. (2005)]

- **Neural networks**: Neural networks are also modeled on a corresponding concept in nature by means of imitating the construction of the human information processing unit, the brain. They are composed of single units – like neurons – that allow for multiple input streams that are then transformed into a single output stream. Usually a large amount of these units is employed in a highly-connected manner. Neural networks provide a unique benefit. They are able to discover patterns in unstructured data that are not observable by other means. One of the major drawbacks of neural networks is their need for training data and training time. So they are less capable of coping with dynamically changing information spaces. Furthermore, the outcome of the inference process is difficult to interpret due to the more or less hidden reasoning process within the network.

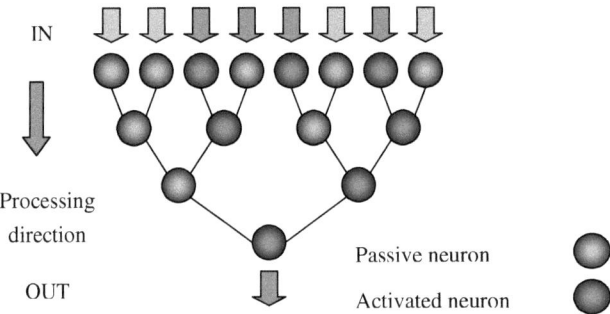

Figure 16: Neural network including in and output vectors

Neural networks are mainly used for classification [Bidel, et. al (2003), Hsieh (2004)] and recommendation [Roh, et al. (2003), Sas, et. al (2003)] but also for prediction tasks [Shepard et al. (2002)]. One of the major drawbacks of neural networks is their need for training data and training time. So they are less capable to cope with dynamically changing information spaces. Furthermore, the outcome of the inference process is difficult to interpret due to the more or less hidden reason process within the network.

The above mentioned feature-based approaches also show some drawbacks with regard to user-modeling and personalization. These drawbacks where summarized by Kobsa (2001) as:

- Content of objects like multimedia objects might be hard to be expressed as feature vectors. Furthermore it might be hard to analyze them.

- The content of object does not have to be the main aspect that causes the user interest.

- The interest might not even base on the features that should describe the content.

- A minimum set of rated features for each individual user are necessary to allow for some reasoning upon them.

Today the classical desktop paradigm describing one operator in front of an personal computer in office like environments is no longer valid, or at least no longer the only scenario where humans us computerized applications and services. Even so Mark Weisers [Weiser (1991)] proclamation of the age of ubiquitous computing might not yet be true in every aspect but it is already in broad variety of cases. Nowadays it is important to consider the usage situation – meaning the usage context – in order to provide the users with usable services. In the following aspects on context and context-aware applications are considered.

4.2. Context and Context-Aware Applications

Another important pillar to allow for adaptation is next personalization, knowledge about the context a user or system is in. Generally there is a great difficulty describing and defining context and context-aware applications. This is due to the lack of consensus concerning of the word itself. According to Merriam Webster Dictionary[17] Context is defined as the *"interrelated conditions in which something exists or occurs"*. Over the past years many researches in computing science and other areas gave various definitions: Ogden and Richards define context as entities (things or events) that are related in a certain way [Ogden and Richards (1946)]. Boy describes context as the paths of information retrieval [Boy (1991)]. Abu-Hakima regards context as a window on the screen [Abu-Hakima (1993)]. Cahour and Karsenty define context as a set of preferences or beliefs [Cahour and Karsenty (1993)] and Turner defines it as an infinite and partially known collection of assumptions [Turner (1993)].

4.2.1.1. Context in Computing Science

Each subject of computer science has a specific angle on context and for that reason it is hard to get an overview of the most significant publications and works with respect to context aware computing. Brezillion [Brezillion (2002)] tried to survey the different angles on context in artificial

---

[17] found on 01/29/2006 at: http://www.m-w.com/dictionary/context

intelligence research. His work provides the foundation for this section and the background definition for the context:

> *"Context is what constrains a problem solving without intervening in it explicitly".*

Databases:

The key role of context in the field of databases is to provide database users with a better control over the stored data. Context permits defining which knowledge/data should be considered and to what time, what are the activation conditions and what limits its validity [Brézillion (2002)]. To achieve interoperability among heterogeneous data sources Goh et al. [Goh (1995)] proposed a strategy based on the notion of context interchange in databases. In the framework, assumptions underlying the interpretations attributed to data are explicitly represented in the form of data contexts with regard to a shared ontology.

Natural language processing

The natural language discipline was the first which took context explicitly into account but still today context in NLP stays rather unexplored with the consequence that there is a theory ⇔ practice gap and work related to context aspects stays to vague and does not address the specific questions about context [Iwanska (1995)].

Frege, G. (1985): *On sense and meaning*. In: A.P:Martinich (ed.), *The Philosophy of Language*, Oxford University Press, pp. 212 – 220.

Arbab, B. (1992): *A formal language for representation of knowledge*, Proceedings of the AAAI'92 Workshop on propositional Knowledge Representation, Stanford, CA, pp. 1-8

Cuha, R. V. (1993): *Context dependence of representations in CYC*, Colloque ICO'93, Montreal

Moore, J.D. (1995): *Participating in Explanatory Dialogues. Interpreting and Responding to Questions in Context*. A Bradford Book, The MIT Press, Cambrigde, MA

Textbox 1: Literature on natural language processing and context

Communication

In communication, the context is considered as the history of everything that occurred over a certain period of time, the overall state of knowledge of the participants at a given moment, and the small set of things they are attending at the particular moment. Context appears as shared space of knowledge among the participants [Maskery and Meads (1992)]. Context can also be thought of as a kind of expert system that would be expert in 'predicting' what the user would likely want (need to do next) because of its knowledge of what had happened to either that specific user or other users with the same goals and needs [Maskery et. al. (1992)]. The key concept behind this definition of context is adapting the user interface according to the current task. In order to provide such functionality a system would need to know:

- The history of interaction between the user and the system
- The transaction history within the system
- The characteristics of the user
- The intention of the user
- The possible source of ambiguity
- The access rights of the user

Communication (and explanation of it) and context are dependent on each other. Context of the situation activates behaviors potential, which in turn modifies the context of the situation [Mittal and Paris [1995]]. Five types of components are essential to define the context of a dialogue after Cahour and Karsenty [Cahour and Karsenty (1993)]:

- Dialogue memory
- Task memory
- Environmental situation
- Psycho-social situation
- General knowledge about the world

For Grant [Grant (1992)] context is the conceptual entity which has some features in common with schemata developed in human cognition. The basic assumption in the contextual modular view is – that human knowledge structures are divided into small units. Regularities appropriate to certain contexts are stored together, and are accessible together. Grant [Grant (1994)] considers two different kinds of transitions between contextual modules:

- Learned (context-specific) transitions
- General (associative) transitions

Vision

In vision context can be an important factor in various areas, for example character or image recognition. Desvignees [Desvignes, et al. (1991)] defines context in the interpretation of a sequence of images as the set of properties that are associated with an entity according to the environment in which the entity is.

Mobile systems

The key-role of context in mobile systems is to adapt applications to the current situation a user and his device are in. This approach is a very challenging one because the user's environment is not static and can change very rapidly. Schilit [Schilit, et al. (1994)] considers that context in mobile systems consists of computing-context, user-context and environmental-context. There is a context-aware computing cycle with three phases:

- **Discovery** – learning about entities and their characteristics. This context information must have a representation, be capable of inspection, and be able to propagate to applications when changes occur.

- **Selection** – deciding which resources to use as the key concern of the context-awareness. The system should be capable to select entities based on the surrounding context.

- **Use** – employing the available resources.

Pascoe [Pascoe (1996)] modeled context in the Stick-e note project architecture also in a hierarchy whereas context becomes more specific as the hierarchy descends.

A generic context class is used to allow clients to use them as homogenous group. Devices, which capture context, are treated as separate objects with their own hierarchy. An environment class provides access to the general context categories, such as location. A pretend context can enrich the stick-e note model by allowing the user to pretend to be in a particular context.

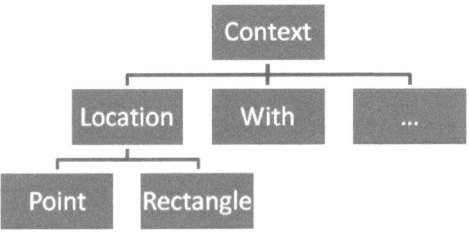

Figure 17: Context hierarchy [Pascoe (1996)]

Chapter 4. Adapting to the User

Schmidt [Schmidt (1998)] proposed a model to structure the concept of context: A context describes a situation and the environment a device or user is in. The context is identified by a unique name and there is a set of relevant features for each context. Each relevant feature has a range of values and is determined (implicitly or explicitly) by the context. This leads to the development of a hierarchical organized feature space for context. Between the context of human factors and context related to the physical environment is a distinction.

For Dey [Dey and Abowd (1999)] context is any information that can be used to characterize the situation of an entity. An entity is a person, place, or object that is considered relevant to the interaction between the user and an application, including the user and applications themselves.

Chen and Kotz [Chen and Kotz (2000)] defined Context as the set of environmental states and settings that either determines an application's behavior or in which an application event occurs and is interesting to the user. The authors distinguish between active and passive context:

- **Active context-awareness**: The application behavior is adapted automatically to the current context.

- **Passive context-awareness**: An application presents the current context to the user or stores the context for the user to be retrieved later [e.g. Stick-e note project].

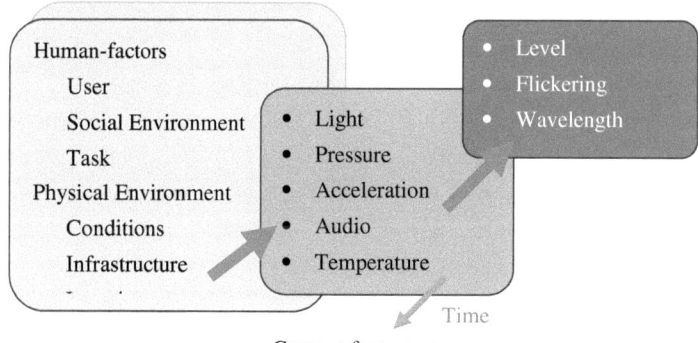

Figure 18: Context feature space [Schmidt (1998)]

4.2.1.2. Context-Aware Applications

Since the mid nineties many research group's attempts to create context-aware applications in different environments and with various user scenarios. According to the numerous definitions of context and the numerous approaches in this field there is a wide range of classification for them. Schilit [Schilit et. al (1994)] categorizes context-aware applications as follows:

1. **Proximate selection**: Objects located nearby are emphasized by the user interface.

2. **Automatic contextual reconfiguration**: This process modifies the current setting of available components; adds new ones, removes old ones or alters the connection between the components due to the change of the context.

3. **Contextual information and commands**: According to the context in which they are issued, they can lead to different results.

4. **Context-triggered actions**: These are simple IF-THEN rules used to specify how the system should behave according to the context.

Hong [Hong (2001)] suggests categorizing context-awareness and its associated adaptation process as:

1. **Triggers**: Notification if a context change occurs.

2. **Metadata tagging**: Context logging at various tasks.

3. **Reconfiguration and Streamlining**: Modification of the environment depending on the actual context.

4. **Input specification**: Especially important in the field of speech recognition.

5. **Presentation**: Adoption to the current context.

The following list presents some of the most accepted approaches for context aware applications. The approaches are classified into generic frameworks, indoor and outdoor applications. These generic framework usually propose a rather general context-definition that can be used in multiple application scenarios whereas indoor our outdoor approaches usually come up with specific context definitions tailored to their needs.

Each presented approach will be classified according to Chen and Kotz [Chen and Kotz (2000)] definition of context. Furthermore brief document descriptions will be given at the beginning in tabular form.

Chapter 4. Adapting to the User

Generic frameworks

This chapter focuses on approaches which introduce new ways how to handle and/or implement a certain aspect of context and its awareness. Some of these approaches remain on the design level whereas others are implemented in prototyped systems.

Mobisaic

The Mobisaic system, developed in 1994 at the University of Washington, is an information system in the World Wide Web, designed to serve users in a mobile environment. The system extends Web documents by allowing them to refer and react to changing contextual information [Voelker and Bershad (1995)]. It incorporates two new concepts, Dynamic URLs and Active Documents. The dynamic URL depends on the current user context at the time it is resolved (e.g. http://www/places/$(Location).html). Active documents automatically update their context in response to a change in the user context. Within the system context information is represented as variable / value pairs.

In this approach the user location serves as active context, whereas no passive context is considered.

Stick-e note

The Stick-e note application developed at the University of Kent proposes a redefinition of the human-computer interface, extending its boundaries to encompass interaction with the user's physical environment.

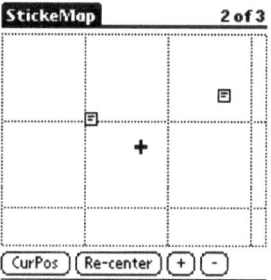

Figure 19: The StickeMap shows the user's current position (the '+' icon) relative to the stick-e notes [Pascoe (1996)]

The system architecture offers a universal means of providing context-awareness through an easily understood metaphor based on the Post-It note [Pascoe (1996)].

Within the general architecture contexts are modeled in a hierarchy [See Figure 17]. A stick-e note object is defined in terms of the context it is attached to. The context indicates the conditions for which a note is invoked (trigger-condition) [Pascoe (1996)].

The concept of situated information spaces proposes the idea of attaching information to objects within the user's physical environment. This has much in common with the ubiquitous computing philosophy where the prime concern is in providing computer interfaces transparently throughout the user's environment so that computer services can be provided wherever and whenever a user requires them [Weiser (1991)]. A driving principle of situated information spaces is to embed computer interfaces throughout the user's environment while retaining the conventional physical interfaces that are beneficial to the user.

There is no active context considered in this approach. As passive contexts the user location, time, additional values (temperature etc.) are taken into account.

Cool Town

The Cool Town project ties web resources to physical objects and offers a web model to support nomadic users. It should enable the automatic discovery of URLs from the physical surroundings by using localized web servers.

Within the application real world objects are for example tagged with bar code that represents URLs. A mobile devices equipped with a bar code scanner is able to read them and load dynamically localized web pages. There are further approaches to not only read localized web content but to upload dynamic content to a web presences [Kindberg and Barton (2001)].

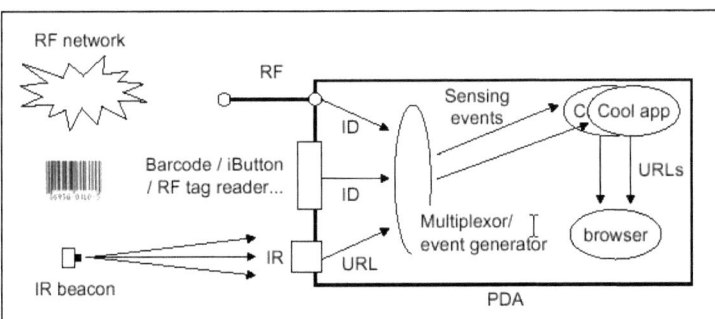

Figure 20: Cool town architecture [Kindberg and Barton (2001)]

Analog to the Mobisaic system in Cool Town the user location serves as active context, whereas no passive context is considered.

Cyberdesk

The CyberDesk project aimed to provide a flexible framework and the necessary infrastructure for self-integrating software in which the integration is driven by the user's actions. Dey [Dey, et al.

Chapter 4. Adapting to the User

(1998)] refers to this as context-aware integration. It was based on the CAMEO infrastructure a component-based framework in which individual components can observe the activity of others and manipulate their interfaces [Wood (1998)]. CAMEO had a centralized service that allows the dynamic registration of components and run-time support for querying the interfaces of registered components.

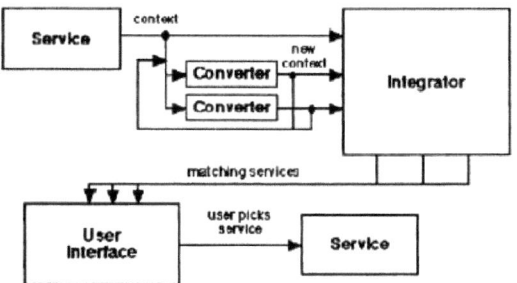

Figure 21: Run-time Architecture of the CyberDesk System [Abowd et al. (1998)], The arrows indicate the information flow in the system

Cyberdesk consists of five main components:

1. **Registry**: The Registry maintains a directory of all the other components of the system, their interfaces and the data types they provide. The Registry provides a white and a yellow page service.

2. **Information Services:** These services are end-user functions that perform actions on the supplied data. They can be stand-alone or part of a larger application and do not necessarily provide functionality to the user but they can also provide data to the system. Wrappers are used to integrate these services into CyberDesk.

3. **Type converters**: The converters try to transform received data types in other data types which can be used by other services. They provide a separable context-inference engine. Further conversion abilities improve the systems ability to make relevant service suggestions. Type converters are services which monitor other services via the Registry in order to get necessary and appropriate data.

4. **Integrators**: The integrators also observe other system components that can provide data. It uses this information to find services which can act on the provided data.

5. **User interface**: The UI represent the adapted and converted service results.

All sorts of active and passive contexts can be processed in this general processing pipeline.

Context toolkit

The Context Toolkit introduces the concept of context widgets that mediate between the environment and the application [Salber et al. (1999)]. A context widget is a software component that provides applications with access to context information from their operating system. It hides the sensor complexity from the application level, abstracts the context information and provides reusable and customizable elements

A context widget has a certain state and behavior. The state is a set of attributes which are gathered via sensors from the environment and can be queried by the application. The behaviors are call backs to the environment if a context change happens. This toolkit was used to implement three different applications:

1. **In / out board**: This board is used to indicate which employees are currently in a building. It uses an *"IdentityPresence"* widget which is associated to each employee and senses his current location (build upon the Active Badge Architecture).

2. **Information Display**: It shows the users who are currently around the display and their research group and the information which is relevant for the research group. This application uses a *"GroupURLPresence"* widget that is installed near to the display and looks for present users.

3. **DUMMBO Meeting Board**: The Dynamic Ubiquitous Mobile Meeting Board is an instrumented digitized whiteboard that supports the capture and access of informal und spontaneous meetings.

Due to the widget and the abstract from sensor level to application level, the context toolkit can also facilitate various passive and active contexts.

Context fabric

The Context Fabric provides another basic infrastructure for context-aware applications. Key abstraction within this architecture is a XML-based Context Specification Language.

Within the Context Fabric there are four basic services which should serve the applications with the necessary context information.

1. **Context Event Service**: This service is intended to be a universal event system for context-aware applications. It takes subscriptions requests, stores them and asynchronously notifies interested subscribers whenever a specific context event occurs.

2. **Context Query Service**: Provides a generic mechanism for querying the current context state. This interface processes the queries synchronously.

Chapter 4. Adapting to the User

3. **Automatic Path Creation Service**: If a context need is specified by an application this services manages different sensors in order to serve the need. It provides a generic abstraction layer for any kind of sensors and manages the data flow from them in order to extract the appropriate context.

4. **Sensor Management Service**: This service handles the automatic registration of sensors to the system.

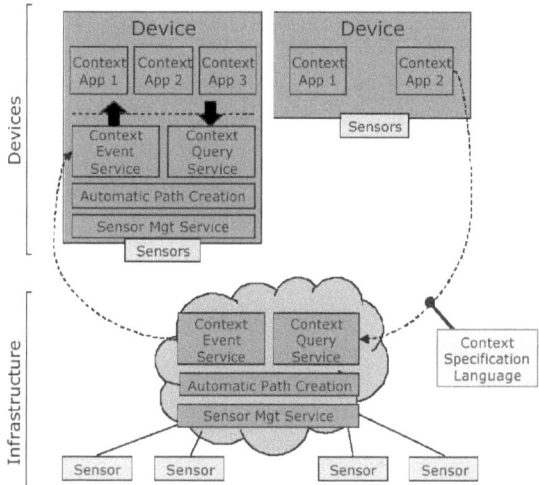

Figure 22: Context fabric architecture

Nexus

The aim of the research project nexus at the University of Stuttgart is the development of a generic platform that supports location aware applications with mobile users. The main task of the nexus platform concerns the management of dynamic spatial models that represent the real world as well as virtual object [Fritsch, et al. (2000), Blessing, et al. (2006)].

The Use-case diagram shows the spatial related requirements of location aware clients:

- Present Area, e.g. show a map.

- Navigate, e.g. calculate shortest path.

- Analyze Model, e.g. perform queries on spatial properties

- Generate Zone, e.g. create a 2D/3D buffer around spatial objects.
- Calculate Values, e.g. spatial measurements
- Subscribe Event, e.g. get notification on changes of an spatial object
- Change object, e.g. modify the properties of an spatial object
- Load Model, e.g. for thick clients which can perform spatial operations on their own.

Within the system there are three different applications dealing with location awareness. More global approaches like city- or traffic information systems stand opposite to rather local applications like exhibition guides [Volz and Sester (2000)].

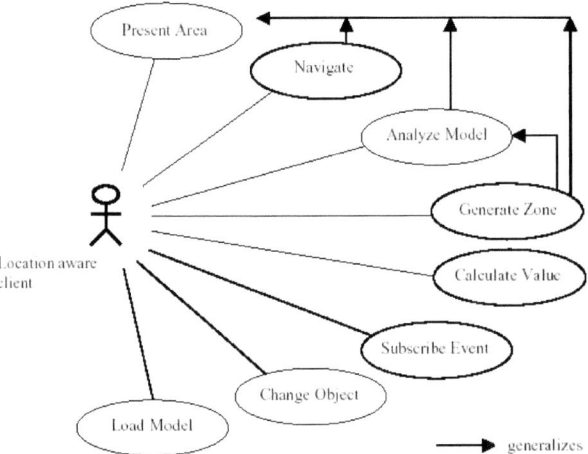

Figure 23: Use-Case diagram showing the spatially related services that are demanded by location aware applications [Volz and Sester (2000)]

Java Context Aware Framework (JCAF)

The goal of JCAF was to create a general-purpose, robust, event-based, and service-oriented Infrastructure and a generic programming framework in Java for the development and of deployment context-aware applications [Bardram (2005)]. The runtime infrastructure was developed following several core design principles:

- Distributed and Cooperating Services – Services are distributed and loosely coupled, while maintaining ways of cooperating in a peer-to-peer or hierarchical fashion.

- Event-based Infrastructure – To support the subscription to relevant context events

- Security and Privacy – Via authentication and secure communication

- Extensible – At runtime with further services and context transformers.

The general application programming interface – API followed supported also various requirements:

- Semantic-free modeling abstractions – Context information can be modeled independent of a specific application domain.

- Context Quality – Quality measures of context information are maintained through all transformation processes.

- Support for Activities - Reasoning on the level user-activities rather than in the application logic alone.

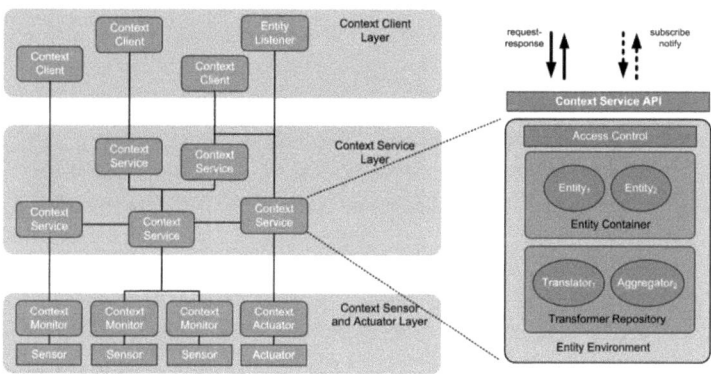

Figure 24: Architecture of the JFAX [Bardram (2005)]

The overall architecture consists of the central *Context Services Tier* and the peripheral *Context Client Tier*. *Context Monitors* and *Context Actuators* at the client tier are listening and performing actions depending on contextual changes. At the service layer, programmers can add Context Transformers to a central Context Transformer Repository. Those transformers can be queried at runtime.

The JCAF was deployed in various research scenarios.

Application	Description
Proximity-Based User Authentication	Enables a user to log in to a computer by physically approaching it.
Context-Aware Hospital Bed	A hospital bed that adjust itself and react according to entities in its physical environment, like patient, medicine, and medical equipment.
Bang & Olufsen AV Home	Using context-awareness to make B&O AV appliances adjust themselves according to the location of people and things.
AWARE Framework	A system that distributes context information about users, thereby facilitating a social, peripheral Awareness, which helps users coordinate their cooperation.
Wearable Computers for Emergency Personnel	A wearable system for emergency workers, like ambulance personnel. Helps them react to changes in the work context.

Table 5: JCAF research scenarios

Context Fusion Network – Solar

Solar builds an infrastructure model that allows context aware applications to select distributed data sources and compose them with customized data-fusion operators into a directed acyclic information fusion graph [Chen, et al. (2004)]. It employs a context fusion network – CFN – that provides four characteristics: First, flexibility to allow for integration of further sensors and implementation of arbitrary context fusion algorithms; second, scalability to allow for large sets on sensor nodes; third, mobility to allow mobile devices to access context data and fourth self-management. The authors envision two application areas for CFNs: *smart spaces* and *emergency response*.

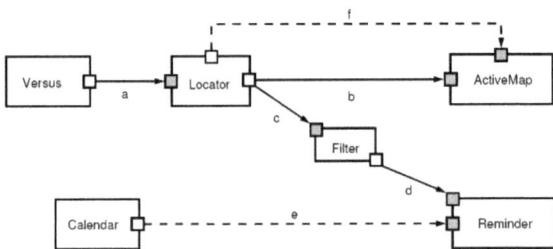

Figure 25: An example operator graph with two sensors and two applications. The shaded squares are in-ports while unfilled squares are out-ports. The dashed lines are pull channels and the solid lines are push channels. [Chen, et al. (2004)]

Given logical operator-graph specifications, a CFN provides a platform to connect the distributed sensors and applications and to execute the operators. To handle the complexity of CFN's, Solar as service platform overlays a set of functionally equivalent hosts, named Planets, which group together the different sensor nodes and allow for self-organization and self-repairing in a peer-to-peer like fashion.

Solar is following the filter-pipe approach, in which filters are named as operators and pipes are named as channels. A channel connects to a *source* at one end, and to a *sink* at the other end. A *sensor* provides (raw) data to Solar while an *application* consumes (contextual) data from Solar. A sensor is also a source and an application is also a sink. An operator is both a source and a sink. An operator is a self-contained data-processing component, which takes one or more data sources as input and acts as another data source. Each operator has a set of *input ports* and a set of *output ports*. Ports can either be pull or push-based.

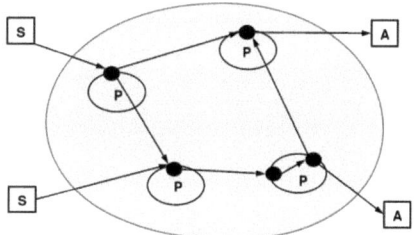

Figure 26: Solar consists of a set of functionally equivalent nodes, named Planets (denoted P), which peer together to form a service overlay using a P2P routing protocol. Sources S and applications A may connect to any Planet. The filled circles are operators and the arrows represent data flow. [Chen, et al. (2004)]

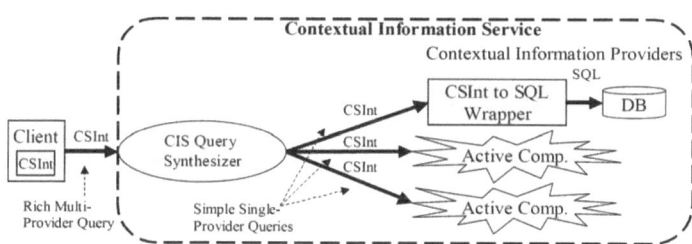

Figure 27: Architecture of the Contextual Information Service [Judd and Steenkiste (2003)]

Contextual Information Service- CIS

The CIS [Judd and Steenkiste (2003)] provides applications with a SQL-like query interface and is organized like a virtual context database [see Figure 27]. The requested information is stored, or collected on demand, by a distributed infrastructure of contextual information providers.

It allows clients to easily synthesize required contextual information. It facilitates the implementation of efficient information providers. Furthermore the CIS supports dynamic attributes enhanced by metadata like accuracy, confidence, update-time and sample interval.

AURA – Architectural framework for ubiquitous computing applications

The Architectural framework for ubiquitous computing applications – AURA - enables mobile users to make the most of ubiquitous computing environments, while shielding these users from managing heterogeneity and dynamic variability of capabilities and resources [Garlan and Sousa (2002)]. AURA act as a proxy for mobile users. When a user enters a new environment, the system marshals the appropriate resources to support the user's tasks. Additionally AURA captures the current physical context which may be of influence. There are two competing goals within this scenario: The first one is to maximize the use of available resources and the second one is to minimize user distraction and the drains of users' attention.

The system provides three key features:

- User tasks become first class entities that are represented explicitly and autonomously from a specific environment.

- User tasks are represented as coalitions of abstract services.

- Environments are equipped to self-monitor and renegotiate task support in the presence of run time variation of capabilities and resources.

Furthermore the *Prism* reacts on context changes through the adoption of the different tasks. A *context observer* provides information about the physical context of the users. Within different environment the observer may have different degree of sophistication depending on the sensors deployed in the environment. The *environment manager* is aware of the different services that are available to support a specific task in a certain environment. He also hides low level management functionalities from the user (e.g. manages distributed file access). *Connectors* facilitate the exchange between the different core components on the various locations autonomously.

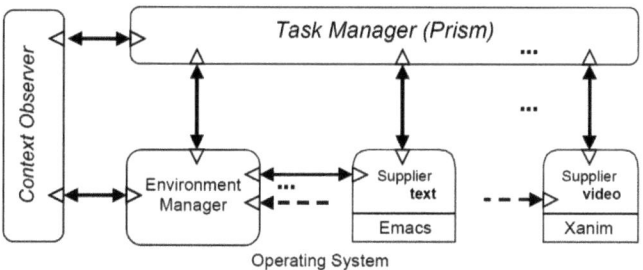

Figure 28: AURA - System architecture [Garlan and Sousa (2002)]

Ontology-driven context framework

Thomas Springer [Springer, et al. (2006)] presented an ontology-driven context modeling approach that facilitates different layers of context descriptions. At first a Meta model defines elements for representing contextual information that are not associated with any semantics. For different domains individual models are comprised of semantic and structural information. The semantic layer defines the semantics of terms for the structure definition based on ontologies. A structural layer defines the representation and interrelation of contextual information relevant for a certain domain. The different context models are specified in OWL – the web ontology language.[18]

To access the context information a context service provides mechanisms for seamless integration of heterogeneous data sources and efficient and scalable distribution handling. The overall architecture consists of independent components including a context broker that facilitates the access to remote context sources and allows for peer to peer distribution of contextual information. The architecture feature:

- Local handling of context sources and local access to context services.

- Multiple views on information dependent on the application domain.

- Domain independence due to the layered context modelling

- Abstract view on context sources.

---

[18] OWL – Web Ontology Language – http://www.w3.org/OWL

Personalized City Tours - An Extension of the OGC® OpenLS Specification

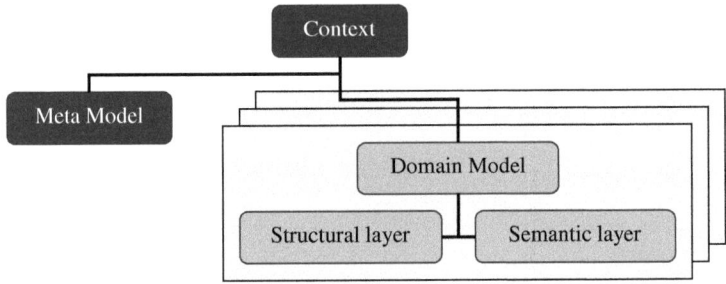

Figure 29: Ontology-framework for context-modeling

This ontology-driven approach is used in adaptive mobile messengers, providing video-communication in a 4G environment.

Multiplatform - Verbmobil, SmartKom, SmartWeb

Multiplatform is a general framework for building integrated natural-language and multimodal dialog systems. It was incipiently developed during the VerbMobil project that aimed in developing a speaker-independent, bidirectional speech to- speech translation system [Wahlster, eds. (2000)]. For that purpose speaker context was also considered to improve the translation result.

Type of context	Content	Knowledge store
Dialogical context	What has been said by whom	Dialog Model
Ontological context	World/Conceptual Model	Domain Model
Situational context	Time, place, etc.	Situation Model
Interlocutionary context	Properties of the interlocutors	User Model

Table 6: Context, content sources and storage in SmartKom [Porzel, et al. (2005)]

The core Multiplatform relied on a distributed component model employing a communication framework featuring XML-based interfaces. It has no central-control mechanism and relies purely on an event-trigger approach.

Its successor project SmartKom aimed in developing mixed-initiative dialog systems in various deployment scenarios like at home, in the office, in the car and as a pedestrian in a city [Wahlster, eds. (2006)]. With regard to dialog system the context-model was enhanced to cope with the different aspects of the human-computing interaction

The follower project SmartWeb aimed in building an intelligent speech-driven answering application that extracts information from the World Wide Web and provides it multimodal to users in different usage scenarios, with a strong focus on mobile access [Sonntag, et al. (2007)].

Summary

The early frameworks facilitating context-awareness incorporated their context storage and reasoning capabilities implicitly in the application logic and provided only quite limited external interfaces via a Uniform Resource Locator – URL approach [see Mobisaic, Stick-e note, Cool Town and Cyberdesk)]. In the following years more advanced approaches focused on the integration of further context sources and the externalization of context information via detailed application programming interfaces – APIs or a the structural query language – SQL [See JCAF, Solar or CIS]. Recent approaches attempt to model context and context-reasoning quite generally and allow for the extension of these modeling attempts. Context knowledge is stored in Ontology's and accessible via XML interfaces like web services.

Since the early beginnings of context-aware applications back in the 1990ies a broad range of applications and frameworks have been built by research groups all over the world. A specific emphasis in many of these is the automatic association and combination of services with regard to changing conditions of a mobile system usage. For that reason agent-based and component-based applications are in the research focus. Some examples are:

- **QoSDREAM** framework was focusing on the development support for context-aware multimedia applications. It provided an event messaging component, data storage and distributed multimedia service [Naguib, et al. (2001).

- **Crumpet**: The crumpet system was comprised of different software agents on top of an agent infrastructure to provide tourism services in European cities. It considered the location-context and employed statistical algorithm to support personalization [Poslad, et al (2001), Zipf and Aras (2002)].

- **CAPNET** - Component-based framework for context-aware multimedia applications. The middleware offered functionality for service discovery, asynchronous messaging, publish/subscribe event management, storing and management of context information. It provided a common interface for external context sources. The context information was forwarded to a central repository to allow other services to use them [Davidyuk, et al. (2004)]

- **SCaLaDE**: This middleware facilitates a mobile agent infrastructure for mobile internet services. It is comprised of high-level services (like QoS or Transaction services) and low lever services (like presentation planning or event handling). The framework provides location-awareness and context-awareness with regard to available resources. It has been deployed as a mobile museum guide. [Bellavista, et al. (2006)]

Context-aware indoor applications

Active Badge

The Active Badge application developed at the Olivetti Research Lab was the first indoor location system employing infrared beacons. Within a building a user of the systems wears small badges which send out a small IR signal every 15 seconds to receivers [Harter and Hopper (1993)]. The Active Badge was primarily developed to support the telephone forwarding in a large building complex [Hopper et. al (1994)], but later further approaches have been developed which uses this localization technique. For example the teleporting application that allows for an automatic display transfer to any workstation within the building.

Both applications considered only the location as active context and have no passive context information.

ParcTab

The ParcTab application was developed at Xerox PARC with the purpose to assist mobile employees in an office environment. Within the system the handled information is categorized in: *Devices*, *People* and their *Context*. The architecture was composed of several *device agents*, *active map service* and *user agents* [Schilit (1995)]. Devices were the tools that could be used to get the task at hand done. The term devise was used in a very generic sense for printers, display mobile hosts, thermostats, phones etc. The active map service was providing the functionality to obtain contextual information because context is defined as user's relationship to other objects in space within the system. The user agent was handling personal preferences and customizations.

The active map dynamic environment handled located objects and allowed to spatial queries (containment and travel distance). The network architecture was built on infrared communication

Each of the components of the ParcTab system was associated with a so-called, *dynamic environment*, which provides an abstraction layer to obtain a uniform way to see environment changes. The communication about environment changes is driven by a data-oriented model and uses a publish/subscribe mechanism to decrease the network traffic [Schilit (1996)]. Clients of the interface update information about objects and/or submit queries to obtain information about other published objects.

The approach had various disadvantages. Locations where associated with user interactions. For that reason only one application at a time was informed about a location change. Nearby searches of other users were not easily be done. Also the information about locations was quite limited.

Chapter 4. Adapting to the User

The ParcTab application employs location information as passive context, whereas no active context was considered.

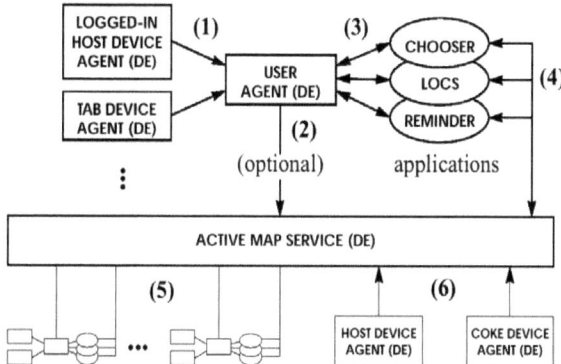

Figure 30 Components and their interactions [Schilit (1996) p.68]

Hippie

Hippie, developed at the German GMD was an internet-based guide supporting several of activities during the preparation, the execution and the evaluation of a museum/fair visit [Oppermann, et al. (1999)]. The system facilitates a user-model and incorporates a rule-based mechanism which contains thresholds on interest and associates information items with common attributes (e.g. author, style, and genre). The Hippie system has several adaptive methods [Oppermann and Specht (2000)]:

- Adaptive navigation support (e.g. tour module)

- Adaptive maps contain the current user position and annotated exhibits.

- Adaptive recommendation (e.g. alerts the user if a exhibit of interest is in his/her closer physical area)

- Adaptive interface (according to the user and the context)

In this approach only the location was considered as passive context.

SaiMotion

Situation Awareness in Motion' (SAiMotion) was concentrating on context modeling and Human-Computer Interaction. The project aimed to provide an exhaustive situation model identifying and

Personalized City Tours - An Extension of the OGC® OpenLS Specification

using all relevant situative parameters for proactive information supply and user interaction for the mobile use on exhibitions and fairs [Eisenhauer and Kremke (2001)].

In SaiMotion not only the location but also the current task, time and environmental parameters were considered as active context.

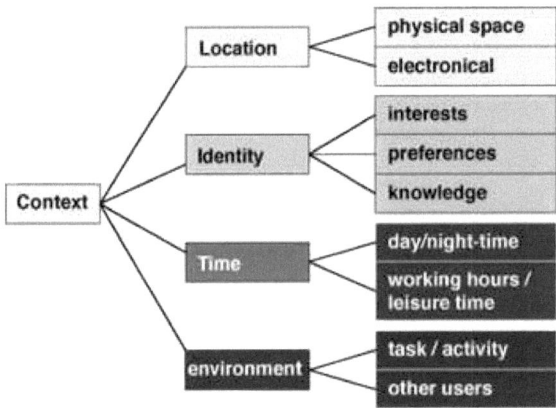

Figure 31: Context model of SAiMotion [Eisenhauer and Kremke (2001)]

The process of information contextualization requires filtering, annotating and aggregation of information contents. Context adapted services are dependent on the reception of the situation of the user, implying the physical environment (location, objects in the vicinity, light intensity, volume) actual tasks and targets of the user. Furthermore the current state of affairs in the processing of the task, the characteristics of the device – concerning in- and output of information, as well as the user's profile of interests and preferences [Eisenhauer and Kremke (2001)].

Conference Assistant

The Conference Assistant developed at Georgia Institute of Technology was a prototype of a mobile and context-aware application that assists conference attendees during a conference and afterwards [Dey, et al. (1999)]. It was build upon the context toolkit architecture [Salber, et al. (1999)] and incorporated four aspects of context: time, identity, location and activity of a user.

The general architecture consists of three types of components:

1. Widgets, that encapsulate a certain type of context information and the corresponding sensors

2. Servers, that merge the context information of different widgets

Chapter 4. Adapting to the User

3. Interpreters, which are used to abstract and interpret the current context.

The different context components are instantiated and executed independently of each other in separated threads and possibly on different devices. Within the Conference Assistant system the user server which handles all user preferences and acts as an interface for the other system components is the central component

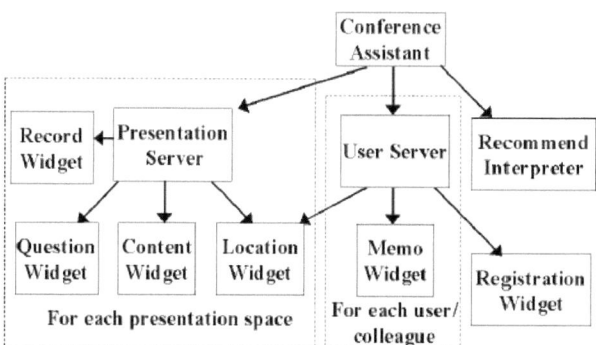

Figure 32: Architecture overview of the Conference Assistance system [Dey, et al. (1999)]

The conference assistant took time, location, identity and activity passively as well as actively into account.

Driven by the initial context-aware applications and frameworks, end of 1999 the area of ubiquitous computing – proposed by Mark Weise in his famous article on *the computer of the 21th century* [Weiser (1991)] – gained more momentum. Since than a wide range of new approaches focusing on intelligent indoor environments like meeting rooms, living rooms or office spaces have been developed.

Some examples are: Aware Home [Kidd, et al. (1999)], KidsRoom [Bobick, et al. (1999)], Classroom 2000 [Abowd (2000)], Smart Office [Gal, et al. (2000)], iRoom [Fox, et al. (2000)], Smart Kindergarten [Srivastava, et al. (2001)], Gator Tech House [Hellal, et al. (2005)], Embassi [Ludwig, et al. (2006)], Dynamite [Heider, T. and Kirste, T. (2002)]. An overview of mobile location-aware museum guides can be found at [Raptis, et al. (2005)]

Outdoor applications

Almost parallel to the research of context-aware indoor applications, outdoor approaches have been developed in the last years. Initially those approaches considered only time and location as context parameters but nowadays many applications take also a wider range of further context values into account like weather, social context and the like.

CyberGuide

On of the first approaches providing a first foretaste of context-awareness in outdoor scenarios was the CyberGuide system, developed at the Georgia Institute of Technology. The mobile information system, which was primarily intended for an indoor use, was extended to allow an outdoor use later on.

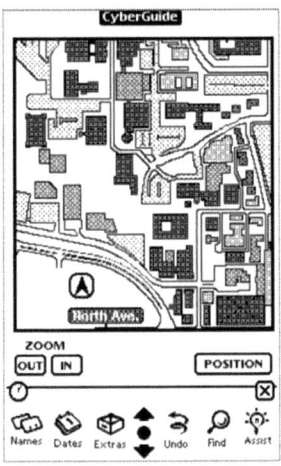

Figure 33: The CyberGuide Cartographer [Abowd, et al. (1997)]

Within the CyberGuide system context-awareness is considered to [Abowd, et al. (1997)]:

1. Collect information about the user's physical environment, informational and emotional state.

2. Analyze the date either independently or by combining different information collected recently or in the past.

3. Perform some actions based on the information.

4. Repeat the cycle.

Chapter 4. Adapting to the User

Guide

The Guide project developed at the University of Lancaster was explicitly tailored to the needs of tourists who endeavor a city with a mobile device at their hand. The general requirements of the system were [Cheverest, et al. (1998 and 2000]:

- Flexibility: Tourists should use the system as much or as little as they like.

- Context-Sensitive Information: The presented information should be context-sensitive. There are two kinds of context, the context of the visitor (his interests, current location, etc.) and the physical environment (time of day, weather, season, state of the cities transportation system etc.).

- Support for dynamic information which should be available when the context seems to be appropriate.

- Support for interactive service e.g. communication with the tourist information for actual information.

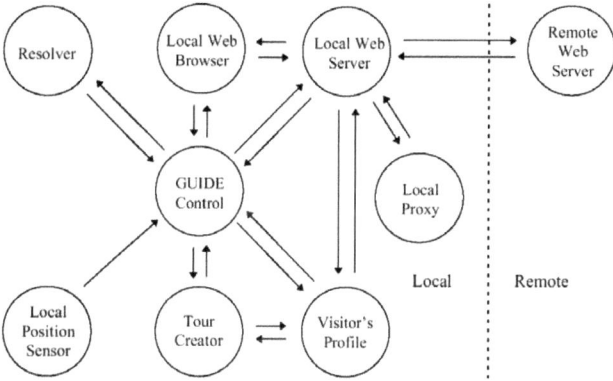

Figure 34: The Guide object model [Cheverest, et al. (1999)]

In general the Guide system was based on a distributed cellular architecture, comprising a number of strategically located base stations that also provide the positioning service. The complete system uses Web technologies including HTML pages to provide and present the information. In order to offer context-aware information these HTML pages are splitted into small information blocks that are combined according to the current situation of the user.

Within the Guide approach, location and time were considered as passive context information, whereas no active context was taken into account.

DeepMap

The Deep Map application developed at the European Media Laboratory, a private research institute located in Heidelberg/Germany, focused also on mobile tourist [Zipf (1998), Malaka and Zipf (2000)]. It aimed at providing mobile multimedia service featuring multimodal user interaction.

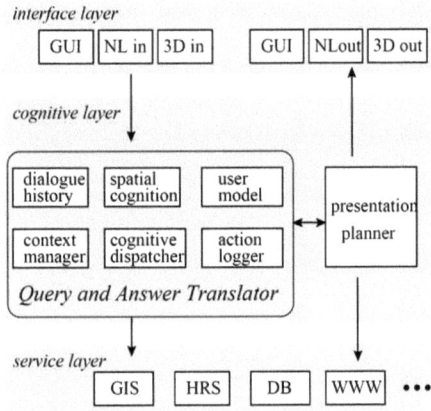

Figure 35: Agents in Deep Map where located in three layers: interface, cognitive, and service layer. The main direction of interaction went from upper left (user input) through middle left (QUATRA components) to the service layer and back up on the right side to output to the user [Malaka, et al. (2001)]

There was a strong emphasis on the integration of spatial information and reasoning. Yet another focus was on intelligent, self-organizing application infrastructures, employing autonomous software agents [Malaka, et al. (2000)].

The Deep Map system considered user location and time as passive context-parameters. Furthermore, it integrated a personalization component facilitating machine learning algorithms to tailor information to user preferences. [Fink and Kobsa (2002), Jöst and Stille (2002), Zipf (2002)]

comMotion

The comMotion application was a multi-modal, location-aware computing environment that linked personal information to locations [Marmasse, Schmandt (2000)]. The system noticed frequently visited locations and asked the user to specify these locations. Additionally it associated a to-do list in which the user or authorized others could add some tasks.

Chapter 4. Adapting to the User

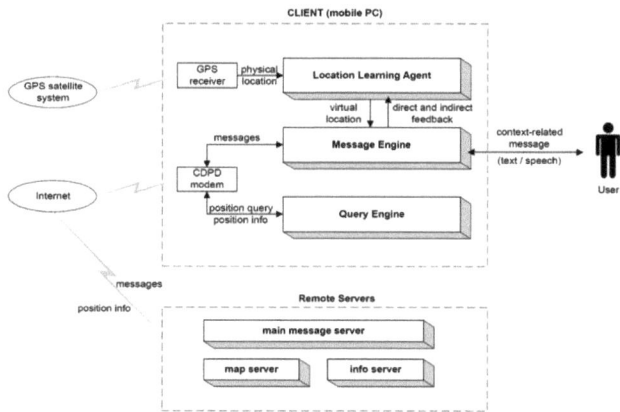

Figure 36: comMotion architecture [Marmasse and Schmandt (2000)]

4.2.2. Recent Developments in Context-Aware Applications

Today the array of context-aware approaches is diverse and manifold. The most relevant approaches to model context in those approaches include Key-Value, Markup Scheme, and Graphical, Object-oriented, Logic-based and Ontology-based models [Strang and Linnhoff-Popien (2004)]. Their conclusion shows that ontologies are the most expressive models and fulfil most of their requirements.

Korpipää and Mäntyjärvi present some requirements and goals for context ontologies: First, *simplicity* with regard to the used expressions and relations; Second, *flexibility and extensibility* to support an addition of new context elements; Third, *generic* to support a wide range of types of context and fourth, *expressiveness* to describe as much context states as possible in arbitrary detail(s)? [Korpipää and Mäntyjärvi (2003)].

Bolchini, et al. survey context-aware approaches with regard to the context data that is modelled as such [Bolchini, et al. (2007)]. The authors analyze recent context-aware frameworks with regard to modeled context parameters (like location, time, subject, etc.), to the representation features (like level of formality, flexibility or granularity) and to context management and usage (e.g. context construction, reasoning, ambiguity resolving or automatic learning).

Yet another survey by Baldauf et al. put emphasis on context-aware middleware with regard to context information acquisition and exchange [Baldauf, et al. (2007)].

Today one can observe two major trends for context-aware mobile applications. The first one is that the initial approaches and concepts focusing on the context of individual users have reached a mature state and can be found in various mobile commercial applications. So far those approaches consider only some aspects of context, but nevertheless mobile context-aware computing can be found widely distributed. The most prominent examples are location-based services. The second observation is that the research on mobile-context aware applications focuses nowadays on aspects of context-distribution middleware that facilitate a peer to peer interaction. Examples can be found at [Leureiro, et al (2006), Le Sommer, et al. (2006), Shriram and Sugumaran (2007), Springer, et al. (2006)].

4.3. Focusing on the User – Combining Context-Awareness and User Modeling

Knowledge about the context in which a services, or application is used is a crucial requirement to users and it is a key requirement for personalized adaptation. But as humans, their interests and their behavior are complex and manifold, it is fundamental for the success of an adaptation process to incorporate some formal model of the users. The user model should structure the information that will be collected about its users by the service. Furthermore it should be open to incorporate new knowledge that is for example not gathered directly from the user but that is inferred from other users that have shown a similar behavior.

But to focus on the users solely is not enough, especially since this would not account for adaptation in ubiquitous computing scenarios. Here the classical desktop computing schema with a user sitting in front of a PC does not fit anymore.

In fact the user is situated somewhere and experiences all sorts of i nfluences from his current surrounding. For example, changing light conditions, noise levels, he might be in a hurry or surrounded by his family. Contextual and personal factors involve each other [Jameson (2001)]. Personal characteristics determine a humans behavior and the behavior determines the context (and vice versa). [Zipf and Jöst (2005)] propose a combined user and context model order to integrate these effects. This model consists of three main components namely, the representation of the *user*, the *knowledge* and the *context* which are explained in turn.

Chapter 4. Adapting to the User

Issues	Context Models	User Models
Data Acquisition	Largely from sensors	Largely from interaction with the users
Coupling to Applications	Can be insulated from applications	To be part of an application could be more efficient.
Representation	A data model	A data model, a behavior model, or a combination of the two.
Period required for Data Acquisition	There is no time gap to capture a user's context	Sufficient time and interaction needed for a behavior model to learn a user's behavior.

Table 7: A comparison of Context Models and User Models [Byun and Cheverst (2001)]

4.3.1. User

The system's representation of the user incorporates a user model. It describes the user by assumptions about his knowledge and preferences, interaction history and a description of his current situation.

A distinction between interests and behavioral preferences is proposed for dealing with preferences. Interest preferences depict the user's interest in certain topics, for example buildings of a specific architectural style or an historical event. One can distinguish such interests between only a short duration or as a general long-term interest in order to reflect the concept of interest shift during the use of the system.

Behavioral preferences should represent some aspects of the user's general demeanor. An example might be if the user usually does not like to wait in line at an entrance to a sight or if he likes to have a tea break in the afternoon.

The interaction history comprises the different interactions between the user and the system either via natural language or a graphical user interface.

4.3.2. Context

The overall context is comprised of the user context and the general context. The user context attempts to describe the user's current situation with its various characteristics in the real world. Some of these occurrences can be gathered more or less directly through the use of external sensors like the user's current position. Others can only be inferred through indirect indicators derived from the context model. An example for the latter might be the emotional or social state or the physiological condition of the user.

The general context distinguishes three different user independent aspects: First, the overall status of the system (e.g. whether some services are temporarily unavailable), second the device context (e.g. battery or memory status of the device) and third the environmental context (e.g. whether it is raining or some museums are closed).

4.3.3. Knowledge

The third main component is a representation of the user's and the system's knowledge. The user knowledge provides references to information, which was already given by the system in order to allow an adequate interaction and to refine the user preferences. The system knowledge should represent the system's overall knowledge about the world.

This combined consideration of the user and the usage context can serve as a solid basis for adaptation processes. Obviously most applications can not gather information for all aspects of the described schema, and actually if they do so, such an Orwell like information collection would harm all privacy consideration [Langheinrich (2007)], but on the other hand, for effective adaptation to the user some aspects need to be gathered.

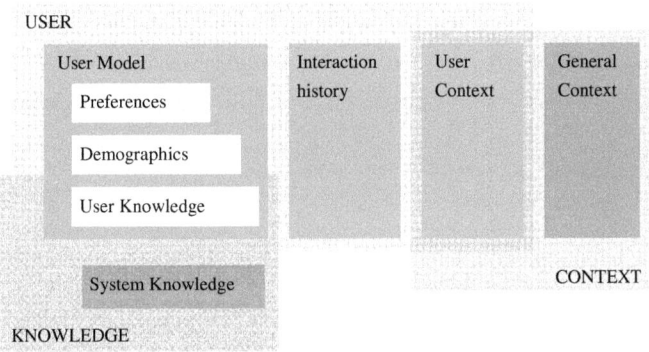

Figure 37: Combined user and context-model [Zipf and Jöst, (2005)]

Chapter 5. Spatial Information - Concepts, Theory and Applications

When speaking about adapting to the user in today's mobile computing scenarios at home, work or on the move, basic and important information that requires for adaptation is the spatial information by means of maps, routes and the like. This chapter will present basic concepts for spatial data handling by means of spatial data models and geographic information systems. Due to the complexity and diversity of present distributed computing environments in the age of the internet, aspects for the provision of interoperability for spatial services will be presented. Location-based services – as one of those services requiring for interoperability – will be introduced. Prototypical location-based service is mobile navigation, namely routing, way finding and guidance, especially for city tourists on sightseeing tours. Graph theory, heuristic algorithms and time geography will be presented in order to decrease the complexity of the challenging computational problem for calculation of individual and personalized city tours.

5.1. Spatial Data Models

One can identify a general three level-hierarchy to model space in information systems [Goodchild (1992)]: Firstly general *spatial concepts* that subsume the perception and understanding of space and spatial phenomena. Secondly *spatial and geometric models*, that are implementable and follow formal definitions and finally, *spatial data structures* that allow to store, retrieve and manipulate spatial data on computers.

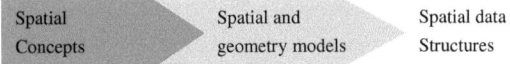

Figure 38: Level-hierarchy to model space [Goodchild (1992)]

Entities in space have geometric properties that can be modeled by measurements, properties, and relationships of points, lines, angles, and surfaces. There are two types of spatial data models prevalent in information systems: *Vector* data and *Raster* data [Peuquet (1984)].

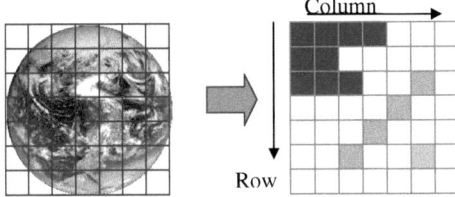

Figure 39: Spatial data model: raster representation

The raster data model is build upon a cellular organization in a discrete space [Baumann (1994)]. The two-dimensional space is divided into a series of units were each unit is generally similar in size to another. Most common raster representations are the grid cells. Spatial features of a specific type, for example a forest area or a complex of buildings are divided into cellular arrays. Each cell has an assigned coordinate (x, y) and a feature value. This association allows for registration in a geographic reference system. Common data formats are standard image formats like JPG, GIG, BMP or TIF.

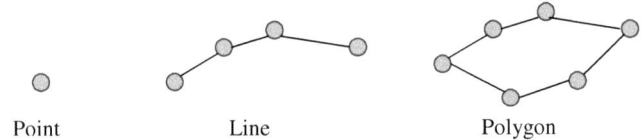

Figure 40: Spatial data model: vector representation

The vector data model assumes that space is continuous rather than discrete. It has – in theory – an infinite set of coordinates [Frank (1992)]. The vector data model is composed of one basic element – a point. In traditional mathematical theory of space, points are considered as primary spatial primitives and all other objects space, either in 2 dimension or 3 dimensions are sets of points. A

Chapter 5. Spatial Information – Concepts, Theory and Applications

point has a single set of coordinates (X, Y and in 3D also Z) in a coordinate space. It has no dimension but can be attached with attribute values. Lines are composed of connected points (nodes) and have no width. A polygon is a closed area that is built of a circuit of line segments.

There are two main data models: field-based and object-based data models. Field-based models consider the world as a continuous surface with different layers, over which features (e.g., land usage, elevation or soil) vary [Shekhar, et al (1997)]. Different layers can be manipulated via set of layer algebra operations (as intersection) to produce new layers. The object-based model treats the world as a surface with almost unlimited recognizable objects (e.g., houses, trees, streets or mountains), which exist independent of their locations [Nunes (1991), Couclelis (1992)].

There are relationships and especially topological relationships between different objects in space. These relations can be described as a particular subset of geometric relations with the characteristic that they are preserved under topological transformations like translation, rotation, and scaling. It is based on algebraic topology [Alexandroff (1961)] a branch of geometry which deals with the algebraic manipulation of symbols that represent geometric configurations and their relationships to one another.

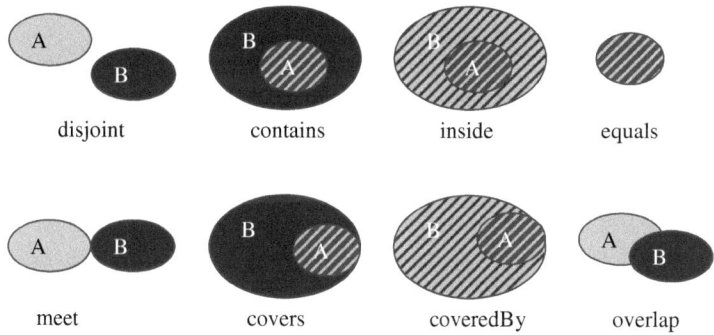

Figure 41: 9 - Intersection Model [Egenhofer and Herring (1991)]

For example, two individual countries that are tangent to each other in a planar map will be tangent to each other on a spherical globe, too [Egenhofer and Herring (1991)]. Topological information is a purely qualitative property and excludes any consideration of quantitative measures.

The algebraic-topology spatial data model is based on primitive geometric objects, called cells. These cells are defined for different spatial dimensions:

- 0-cell is a node (the minimal 0-dimensional object)

- 1-cell is the link between two distinct 0-cells
- 2-cell is the area described by closed sequences of three non-intersecting 1-cells.
- A face of a 0-cell is any A (0 ...n)-cell that is contained in A.

Cells may have arbitrarily shaped interiors. There are four topological primitives: closure, interior, boundary, and exterior of a cell [Egenhofer and Herring (1991)]. For all possible topological relations one can identify eight models that subsume most cases.

There is one main difference with regard to the two geometrical data models. In contrast to vector boundary raster boundary has a spatial dimension [Winter (1998)].

5.2. Geographic Information Systems – GIS

Geographic information systems – GIS are systems that manage information about cities, rural areas, and the environment for many different purposes [Antenucci (1991)]. Basic computerized implementations have already been built in the 1960s in the analog method of overlaying different maps to show varying combinations of features [Schmidt and Zafft (1975)].

Initial geographic information systems have been used mainly for all sorts of planning processes like urban planning, regional planning and the like. But nowadays GIS are almost ubiquitously used – in small personal navigational assistance, as web mapping application or integrated in corporate business intelligence solutions.

In the early days of geographic information systems they have been rather isolated solutions for different application areas, mostly in the domain of urban planning. The data models of these systems have been internal data structures following classical database structures employing table structures according to entity-relationship models. As a consequence the modeling process did not offer possibilities to match the representation of the reality, the user's mental model of it and the internal data structures. The consequences of these limitations have been manifold, as spatial models often need to deal with for example location or time constraints, accuracy or topological relations.

At the beginning of the 1990ies GIS Software started to gain more and more momentum, conquering almost every domain and business area: from public to military, from enterprise to private user services. Nowadays GIS solutions have widely penetrated our private lives for example by means of internet mapping services (like Google Maps, Yahoo Maps, and Microsoft Live search), in-car navigation devices or mobile PNAs'[19]. Today's GIS environments are highly heterogeneous and distributed regarding spatial data sources, spatial data repositories, application types, services and usage situations.

5.3. Interoperability for Spatial Data and Services

As the collection and maintenance of spatial data is a resource intensive process regarding human and financial resources there was a lot of emphasis on spatial data integration and exchange already in the early days of GIS. Almost every integration approach known from other fields in information technologies has been adopted by GIS in the past [Fonseca, et al (2003)] like federated database with schema integration [Sheth and Larson (1990)], object orientation [Papakonstantinou, et al. (1995)] or ontologies [Fonseca, et al (2000), Hakimpour and Timpf (2002)].

Generally speaking, the usage of metadata standards is regarded as the key to information sharing, integration and analysis for geographic information systems. Today there are several public bodies that aim at standardizing the definition and usage of metadata. These include:

- Federal Geographic Data Committee (FGDC)

- International Standards Organization (ISO) for geospatial metadata.

- Spatial Data Infrastructures. In recent years spatial data infrastructure – SDI [Groot and McLaughlin (2000)] have been set up or are about to be setup to facilitate an exchange of spatial data across political entities like regions, countries or nations [e.g Brox, et al. (2002)]. The European Initiative Inspire[20] aims at establishing a SDI across Europe. The same applies for the NSDI in the United States. In this context, spatial ontology's can facilitate a semantic enhanced exchange of spatial data [Lutz (2005)].

All these bodies try to overcome data inconsistencies and incompatibilities called semantic heterogeneity and caused by of different conceptualizations and database representations of a real world fact [Bishr (1998)] via standard forms of documentation of spatial data and clearly defined processes for data conversion.

One can define ontology as a branch of metaphysics concerned with the properties of objects, with their model of existence and with questions like how they can be divided into parts and fill space [Smith (1982)]. Frank and Mark state, that a GIS is built to present a model of some aspect of

---

[19] PNA – Personal Navigational Assistant = Small digital device including GPS receiver and navigation software. For example: TomTom, Navigon, Garmin.
[20] Inspire WebSite: http://geoportal.jrc.it/geoportal/ found on 17.10.2007

reality [Frank and Mark (1991)]. This model must reflect observable properties of this reality. It is useless if there are any substantial systematic deficiencies in the correspondence between observed reality and the model [Frank (1997)].

5.3.1. A Deeper Look into Ontologies

Back in the 1980s, ontologies started their triumphal procession to conquer today's information systems. Back then such kinds of philosophical interests have been almost confined to very specific topics in the field of "theoretical" knowledge representation in AI[21] research. Questions on granularity [Hobbs (1985a)] or existential assumptions [Hobbs (1985b), Hirst (1991)] have been considered with regard to ontologies. In general, knowledge was defined in a strictly functional way [Newell (1982)]. Knowledge modelling methodologies tended to focus on individual subsystems only, viewing domain knowledge as strongly dependent on the particular task at hand [Guarino (1995)].

With the beginning of the 1990ies, a new school of thought which aims to a logical formalization of commonsense reality based on a rigorous characterization of fundamental ontological categories like those regarding space, time, and structure of physical objects, was slowly emerging in the AI community.

Ontology was considered as the study of the organization and the nature of the *world* independently from the form of our knowledge about it. The term *formal ontology* has been defined as "the systematic, formal, axiomatic development of the logic of all forms and modes of being" [Cocchiarella (1991)].

Back in 1979 Brachman classified different knowledge representation languages according to the various primitives offered to the user [Bachman (1979)]. The two main poles of consideration are on the one hand the logical level with clear functional properties and on the other hand the linguistic levels in which primitives directly refer to verbs and nouns. At the *conceptual* level, primitives have a definite cognitive interpretation, corresponding to language-independent concepts like elementary actions or thematic roles. The epistemological level describes the nature and sources of knowledge" [Nutter 1987]. A usual logical interpretation is that knowledge consists of *propositions*, whose *formal structure* is the source of new knowledge. One can differentiate between structuring and non-structuring relations of primitives. Unary structuring relations are usually called *concepts*, *kinds* or *types*, and binary structuring relations are called *roles*, *attributes* or *slots*. Non-structuring unary relations are called *(assert ional) properties* or sometimes *qualities*, while non-structuring binary relations are usually called *constraints*

---

[21] AI – artificial intelligence

Level	Primitives	Interpretation	Main feature
Linguistic	Linguistic terms	Subjective	Language dependency
Conceptual	Conceptual relations	Subjective	Conceptualization
Ontological	Ontological relations	Constrained	Meaning
Epistemological	Structuring relations	Arbitrary	Structure
Logical	Predicates, functions	Arbitrary	Formalization

Table 8: Knowledge representation languages [Bachman (1979), modified by Guardian (1994)]

Guerin proposed the introduction of a further level – the *ontological level* – intermediate between the epistemological and the conceptual one [Guerin (1994)]. At the ontological level, a central issue is the distinction between the logical relations which contribute to the taxonomic structure of the domain and those which do not, providing instead additional information on already identified objects.

Gruber [Gruber (1995)] defines a basic set of requirements for the formularization of concepts in ontology: It should describe concepts clear and coherently, allow for extensibility, reduce encoding biases and have as minimal ontological commitment as possible.

One can classify ontology according to their specific task or point of view [Guerin (1997)]:

- *Top-level ontology* describes very general concepts.

- *Domain ontology* describes the vocabulary related to a generic domain.

- *Task ontology* describes a task or activity.

- *Application ontology* describes concepts depending on both a particular domain and a task, and is usually a specialization of them. This ontology is created from the combination of high-level ontology. They represent the user needs regarding a specific application.

5.3.2. Ontologies to Describe Spatial Data

There are multiple ways to describe and categorize objects and "things" in the real world. Taxonomies or kind-of hierarchies familiar to us from the Linnaean classification of plants and animals is only one way to organize knowledge. Another way to organize knowledge is in terms of a cognitive partonomy [e.g., Miller and Johnson-Laird (1976); Tversky (1990)]. Like taxonomy, a partonomy is a hierarchy, but based on a part-of relation rather than on a kind-of relation.

Initial work on spatial categorization focused on dictionaries of geographic terms [e.g. Moor (1978); Mayhew (1997)] on spatial data standards [Fegas, et al. (1992)] and human studies on spatial categorization [e.g. Battig and Montagues (1968); Tversky and Hemenway (1983); Rugg and Schmidth (1986); Lloyd, et al. (1996)].

Smith and Mark [Smith and Mark (1998, 1999)] argue that there is a certain difference between objects in the *"geographic realm"* and *"objects at surveyable scales"*:

- Spatial objects are on or near the earth surface with a minimal scale. Usually they are complex. For this reason ontology for spatial objects must have a concept of part/whole or a mereology.

- Spatial objects have boundaries (open or closed). The concepts of boundary, contiguity and closure are topological notions. Thus an adequate ontology of spatial objects must contain a *qualitative topology*, a theory of boundaries and interiors, of connectedness and separation, which is integrated with a mereological theory of parts and wholes to form a *mereotopology* [Smith (1996)]. [...] *Boundaries give rise to important and complex issues—for example pertaining to the oppositions: fiat vs. bona fide, crisp vs. graded—which do not arise, or have not been studied, in relation to the artifacts and living things on which most work on object-categorization has been focused hitherto.* [...] [Smith and Mark (1999)].

Spatial objects are often conceptualized not in terms of their usage, function or behavior, but rather in terms of topology, geometry, location, and orientation.

5.3.3. Ontologies for Spatial Service Integration

Software systems – especially in the business world – have become increasingly complex along with the widespread of geographic information systems in the 1990ies. Driven by research on software design and architectures, object orientation as programming paradigm and component-based software architectures have become widely accepted [Buehler and Farley (1994)].

5.3.3.1. Agent-Based Geographic Information Systems

Agent-based applications were yet another approach to master the increasing complexity of software next to the pure component-based composition was.

The agent-based software design is more flexible than other distributed architectures because of the ad-hoc integration of agents [Jennings and Wooldridge (1999), Jennings (2001)]. Agents are realized as independent entities that communicate with others in order to solve a problem. A number of agent platforms has been developed and proposed for mobile and distributed information systems like. FIPA[22]. In general, agents communicate via a shared communication language. The most popular ones are the Knowledge Query and Messaging Language - KQML [Finin, et al. (1994)] resulting from the Knowledge Sharing Effort - KSE and the FIPA Agent Communication Language (ACL) [15].

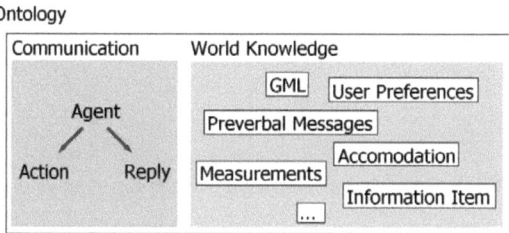

Figure 42: Elements of the system ontology consisting of the agent communication and interaction and of the overall world knowledge of the system [Jöst and Merdes (2004)]

[Malaka et al. (2000); Zipf and Aras (2002); Schmidt-Belz, et al. (2003); Jöst and Merdes (2004)] present Multi-Agent Systems – MAS like the Deep Map I + II or the CRUMPET system that provide location-based services for mobile users. In these approaches software agents facilitate various spatial services (like mapping, spatial search or routing) via autonomous communication between each other.

These MAS employs FIPA – ACL that consist of several attributes like sender, receiver, communication type, and a content slot as the generic container for the message itself. The message content is expressed in terms of a system-wide ontology corresponding to the structural part of the world knowledge of the tourist and city history domains. It therefore comprises all real world objects and topics that are possible discourse topics of the agent community and the user. Moreover, not only world objects are modeled, but also the operations on them and their resulting objects can be expressed. Thus the ontology covers all of the agents' capabilities.

One can classify these approaches according to Wache [Wache, et al. (2001)] as a Single Ontology Approach with the benefit of a straightforward implementation of agents supporting the ontology. Additionally they provide less/no semantic heterogeneity during the communication between agents. Their major drawback is the need for adaptation of the agents if the global ontology changes.

---

[22] FIPA - Foundation for Intelligent Physical Agents – http://www.fipa.org

Timpf [Timpf (2002)] describes the usage of a central ontology for the purpose of way finding in urban environments. Zipf and Jöst [Zipf and Jöst (2005)] employ ontologies to describe various spatial services like search or mapping in a software agent application.

5.3.3.2. Web-enabled spatial services

By the mid-1980s, geographic information system software was heavily used in natural resources and defense domains, especially within government agencies [OGC History (2007)]. Other market sectors, like state and local government, civil engineering, transportation and business marketing were seriously exploring this *"new"* technology but also discovered severe limitations. Additional to the already mentioned inability to share spatial data, the expensive GIS software was very limited in matters of functional extensibility and flexibility. This caused significant costs as inefficient, time consuming and error-prone data transfer methods had to be used or individual solutions had to be developed. Back then initial attempts were undertaken to overcome this narrow, software vendor centric view but even today, in the age of service centric software internet architecture, the GIS community is still struggling. In 2002 Max Egenhofer described his vision of a geospatial web that allows for reasoning and interpretation of spatial terms in web searches [Egenhofer (2002)]. This vision is still yet to come, but today there are technical approaches and public entities available helping to reach for it.

Open Geospatial consortium – Standardized spatial services

One of the very popular raster GIS applications at that time – and even now - was the Unix-based *Geographic Resources Analysis Support System* –GRASS. It was developed in the early 1980s at the U. S. Army Corps of Engineers' Construction Engineering Research Laboratory (CERL) and became one of the first global open source software projects [OGC History (2007)]. In 1992, the GRASS user community formed a non-profit organization -- the Open GRASS Foundation (OGF) which transformed into the *Open Geospatial Consortium* – OGC in 1994. Initially the OGC was founded by eight institutions and grew up to now to 348 members from universities, non profit organization, political entities and commercial companies. The OGC aims at

- Making more commercial as well as non-commercial geo-processing choices available.

- Acting as a sounding board for the user community.

- Aligning user demands with product development plans.

Until now the OGC has specified industry-wide accepted collection of standards on spatial data formats and services. A basic set of abstract specification defines the common ground for all further

Chapter 5. Spatial Information – Concepts, Theory and Applications

higher services specifications. These abstract specifications can be considered as the basic OGC ontology's.

Important OGC specifications are:

- Geographic Markup Language – GML: The Geography Markup Language is an XML grammar written in XML Schema for the description of application schemas as well as the transport and storage of geographic information [OGC GML (2007)]. According to the ISO 19101 a feature is an abstraction of real world phenomena, it is a geographic feature if it is associated with a location relative to the Earth. So a digital representation of the real world may be thought of as a set of features. The state of a feature is defined by a set of properties, in which each property may be thought of as a {name, type, value} triple [OGC GML (2007)].

- Catalogue services: This service defines common interfaces to discover, browse, and query metadata about data, services, and other potential resources [OGC CAT (2007)] on external resources available in the internet.

- Coordinate transformation service: The specification provides means to identify coordinate systems and to access coordinate transformation services which support accuracy calculation [Specht (2002)]. As there is a broad variety of projections and coordinate systems used all over the world for different purposes (like nautical navigation or property identification). This service eases the data exchange. If an application cannot import data in a given coordinate system, a compliant server will transform the coordinates to the supported coordinate system.

- Filter encoding: [...] *defines an XML encoding for filter expressions. A filter expression constrains property values to create a subset of a group of objects* [...] [OGC FIL (2007)]. This encoding is used to filter spatial features based on their property values, for example for visualization purposes on a web map server.

- Styled Layer descriptor – SLD: Such styled layer descriptors are used to define the appearance of spatial features on mapping services such as WMS [OGC SLD (2007)].

- Web Map Server – WMS: The web mapping specification is an URL encoding schema that defines three main operations [OGC WMS (2007)].
    - *GetCapabilities* – to request the basic capabilities of a WMS by means of available features, SLDs etc
    - *GetMap* – to request a map with specific properties like extent, projection, layers and styling.

- o *GetFeatureInfo* – to request attribute information for a spatial feature at a specific coordinates.

- Open Location Service – OpenLS: This collection of standards is aimed at describing and standardizing various types of location-based services [OGC OpenLS (2004)] by means of:

  - o *Directory service*: provides access to an online directory (e.g. Yellow Pages) to find the location of a *specific* or *nearest* place, product or service.

  - o *Gateway service*: This service fetches the position of mobile terminal from a give network and is modeled after the Mobile Location Protocol (MLP)[23],

  - o *Location Utility* service: Subsumes geo-coding or reverse geo-coding to resolve a given address to a coordinate and vice versa.

  - o *Routing service*: specifies the calculation of a route from start to an endpoint, including visit locations and means of transportation. The result might be given as a summary information, geometry, map or turn instructions.

  - o *Presentation service*: The service allows to summarize results of other OpenLS services in map presentations.

- Web Processing Service – WPS [...] *provides client access across a network to pre-programmed calculations and/or computation models that operate on spatially referenced data. The calculation can be extremely simple or highly complex, with any number of data inputs and outputs* [...] [OGC WPS (2005)]. A WPS Interface defines three basic services

  - o GetCapabilities – This operation allows a client to request and receive back service metadata about the specific server implementation documents that describe the abilities of the specific server implementation. The GetCapabilities operation provides the names and general descriptions of each of the processes offered by a WPS instance. This operation also supports negotiation of the specification versions being used for client-server interactions [OGC WPS (2005)].

  - o DescribeProcess allows a client to obtain detailed information about the processes that can be executed, including the input parameters and formats as well as the outputs [OGC WPS (2005)].

---

[23] The OMA Mobile Location Protocol (MLP) is an application-level protocol for obtaining the position of mobile stations (mobile phones, wireless personal digital assistants, etc.) independent of underlying network technology. See http://www.openmobilealliance.org

Chapter 5. Spatial Information – Concepts, Theory and Applications

o Execute – This operation allows a client to run a specified process implemented by the WPS using provided input parameter values and returning the outputs produced [OGC WPS (2005)].

Yet there are only few approaches available that demonstrate the potential of web processing services. Essid, at al [Essid, et al (2003)] proposed a mediation system, called VirGIS [Boucelma, et al. (2003)] that complies with the OGC GML and WFS standard. It provides a uniform interface to different data sources via a common model. Queries are posed against a virtual and global schema which transforms this query into various sub-queries send to local resources. Other approaches have been presented by [Comert (2004), Stollberg and Zipf (2007)].

In recent years many approaches have been proposed and discussed to build complex application and service for spatial data analysis [Kemp, et al. (2007)]. In heterogeneous and distributed environments two main approaches have gained momentum in recent years: *service oriented architectures* and grid computing.

Service oriented architecture - SOA

Service oriented architecture - SOA can be described as a flexible and standardized architecture which is able to unify business processes by structuring large distributed applications in a set of smaller individual modules, called services. Usually a SOA consists of three main component types.: 1.) a service provider that offers specific services for example access to data repositories or computing resources, 2.) a services requestor that is in need of specific services and finally 3.) a service broker that collects all service descriptions including their capabilities as well as constraints and facilitates their exchange. Figure 43 visualizes the handshakes between the three main components by means of service registration, definition of a shared vocabulary and definition of the service ontology.

In order to facilitate this brokerage, services have to be described either with free text, some metadata or via a central ontology. Free text obviously has limitation regarding search ability. The metadata-based approach for catalogue definitions can lead to problems when querying and interpreting search results of different distributed catalogues. These Problems caused by semantic heterogeneous descriptions play a crucial role during the task of finding relevant information within a GI web service environment [Wache, et al (2001)]. Bishr [Bishr (1998)] defines semantic heterogeneity as the consequence of different conceptualizations and database representations of a real world fact.

A service oriented architecture including an ontology based service broker for enterprise wide GIS application was described by Paul and Gosh. Their approach facilitates service querying via an XML based query language XQuery [Paul and Gosh (2006)].

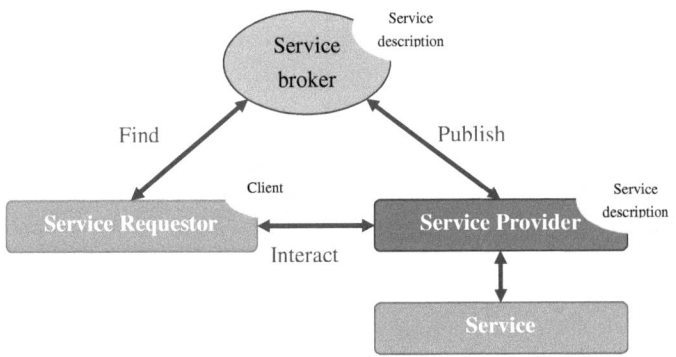

Figure 43: Adopted service-oriented architecture (SOA) for the discovery and retrieval of geospatial data.

GRID computing

In the last decade another web-based approach named Grid computing has gained momentum. Driven by an increasing demand of access to computational power - mainly in the research and university world – a new paradigm was found that tries to utilize idle capacity. A computational grid can be described as an infrastructure that provides dependable, consistent and cheap access to a large pool of resources – by means of computer cycles, data, sensors or even people [Foster and Kesselman (1999)]. Five main grid computing categories can be described: distributed super computing, high throughput computing, on demand computing, data intensive computing and collaborative computing.

As geo-processing and spatial analysis is also resource intensive application areas also grid-based computing approaches have been employed. Traffic prediction based on real time data, fluid dynamics in slope processes, floods or earthquakes are only some examples. But currently no coherent framework for developing and deploying geo processing applications on the grid exists.

An example build on top of OGC-compliant web processing services is the MOSE application [Folino, et al. (2007)]. This grid-based approach aims to spatial-temporal modeling of environmental evolutionary processes. A central workflow executor acts as application core that distributes individual processing task to various web services.

Category	Characteristics	Examples
Distributed supercomputing	Very large problems needing lots of CPU, memory, etc.	Distributed interactive simulation, stellar dynamics, *ab initio* chemistry
High throughput	Harness many otherwise idle resources to increase aggregate throughput	Chip design
On demand	Remote resources integrate with local computation, often for bounded amount of time	Medical instrumentation, network-enabled solvers, cloud detection
Data intensive	Synthesis of new information from many large data sources	Sky survey, physics data, data assimilation
Collaborative	Support communicative or collaborative work between multiple participants.	Collaborative design, data exploration, education

Table 9: Five categorize of grid computing [Foster and Kesselman (1999)]

5.4. Location-Based Services

The origin of location-based service can be found back in 1995. The Federal Communications Commission – FCC[24] was issuing a mandate requiring that wireless carriers should be able to locate 911 callers within 50 meters of their location [VanDeMeer (2002)]. The dot.com area was just taking off as many new start-up companies heading to build services in order to capitalize this new mandate. Soon there was a hype about location-based services as the new killer application and mass market but it took more than a decade until these services are about to reach the mass market.

In the last couple of months the worlds biggest software companies (such as Google or Microsoft), the biggest telecom operators (for example Vodafone) and the biggest manufacturer of mobile phone have started to battle for this mass market.

But what are location-based services? There is a plethora of definitions around and also the geospatial community is still struggling for a common definition [Francica and Schutzberg (2007)]. With a user-centric view one can define location-based services as [Zipf and Malaka (2001)]:

Services for mobile users
that take the current position of the user into account
when performing their task.

---

[24] Federate Communication Commission - http://www.fcc.gov/

With a more system oriented-view in mind, one can identify location-based services as an *"intersecting field of various technologies"* [Brimcombe (2002)], namely: GIS, Internet and Mobile Networks/Devices (see Figure 44).

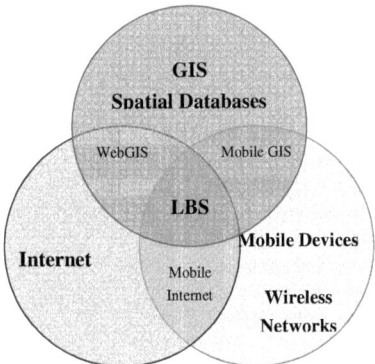

Figure 44: LBS as an intersection of technologies [Brimcombe (2002)]

Along these two viewpoints various service areas can be found that consider location:

- Localization – *Where am I? Where is the product X?*

- Orientation – *How do I get to? Where do I need to drive?*

- Navigation/Mapping – *How does the area nearby look like?*

- Search – *Where do I find X?*

There are several main components required – namely mobile devices, communication networks, localization techniques, service and content providers for the provision of location-based service.

- Mobile devices: In order to request mobile location-based services a user has to be equipped with a mobile device. In previous years the amount and variety of mobile devices has skyrocketed. For example:

    o According to actual statistics by the ITC more than 40% of the world population are mobile telephone subscribers.

    o The amount of personal navigational assistant devices – PNAs will grow to more than 100 million units annually by 2011 [ABI Research (2008)].

Chapter 5. Spatial Information – Concepts, Theory and Applications

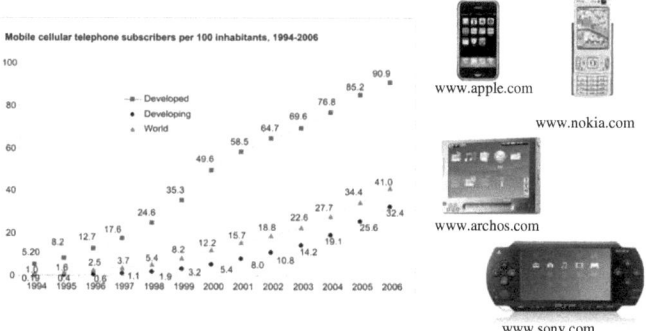

Figure 45: Mobile cellular subscribers[25] and currently popular, network-enabled and mobile devices (e.g. mobile phones, video players and gaming console).

But today not only mobile phones are getting internet enabled. Also other appliances like mp3 players, video players or even gaming consoles support network connectivity in one way or the other.

- Communication networks: In contrast to popular PNA's are location-based services are in most cases not stand-alone applications but rather services that require some sort of network connectivity. This is due to complexity of the service and the need for actual data gathered for example from the internet. Today there are two main network approaches competing for the provision of LBS.

    o Cellular networks: Owned by telecommunication companies these networks were the most classical and standard ones and in the past – primarily targeted for voice communication. In recent years they have been rebuilt also for data communication featuring higher bandwidths. Commonly cellular networks are today described as 3G networks, referring to the third generation of underlying network technology. Several data standards exists, like GSM[26] or UMTS[27] and various extensions like GPRS[28], EGDE[29] or HSCSD [30].

---

[25] ITU - International Telecommunication Union (2007), found on 2007/12/11 at: http://www.itu.int/ITU-D/ict/statistics/ict/index.html

[26] GSM – Global Standard for Mobile communication
[27] UMTS – Universal Mobil Telecommunication System
[28] GPRS – General Packet Radio Service
[29] EDGE – Enhanced Data rates for GSM Evalution
[30] HSCSD - High Speed Circuit Switched Data

o Wireless local area networks: Initially these networks were used to wireless connect different stationary desktop computers in indoor, home and office scenarios. This local wireless technology evolved to broad outdoor installation like city-wide, municipal WLAN. Today Wi-Fi[31] is the de facto standard for WLAN's. It was initiated and is driven by the Wi-Fi alliance[32]. Wimax[33] is yet an extension of the network standard to cover wide areas.

o Personal area networks: There are several other technologies available to cover close areas like infrared transmission or short range radio transmission named Bluetooth but due to their spatial limitation for the provision of location-based services they play only a minor role.

Positioning component or service: Positioning is the third technical pillar for the provision of location-based services. One can differentiate two main approaches to determine a mobile devices current location: Self and remote positioning [Zeimpekis, et al, (2002)].

Self-positioning labels a devices capability to determine its current location by itself. In most cases the mobile terminal uses signals transmitted by the gateways/antennas to calculate its own position. A widely distributed approach – currently even been integrated into mobile phones – computes satellite signals from the orbit, named Global Positioning System – GPS (or competing approaches like GLONAS or yet to come the GALILEO system). Other self-positioning techniques using "spatial labels" for localization identifying landmarks via image recognition [Davies, at al. (2005)], Bar-codes [Knights and Lanza (2001)] or URLs [Kindberg, et al. (2002)] attached to objects in space.

Exactly the opposite of self positioning is remote positioning. Here mobile devices can be located by measuring signals traveling to and from a set of receivers. In most cases the signals are electromagnetic waves used for the network connectivity, but in some cases also ultrasound or infrared are used. In order to define a mobile terminals position from a remote location, several physical and mathematical methods can be used, all founding in the principle of triangulation or trilateration. Those approaches are for example measuring the direction or angel of arrival, time delays or strength of the signals. Another quite simple approach

---

[31] Wi-Fi: This acronym has no corresponding long description as it was invented for marketing purposes.
[32] Wi-Fi Alliance: http://www.wi-fi.org/
[33] Wimax - Worldwide Interoperability for Microwave Access

employed in GSM networks is using Cell Identification. As mobile phones are connected to one base station, this information can be used to allow for a quite precise localization.

- Service and application provider: Given mobile users and their devices, wireless networks and localization techniques, provider combine these three aspects for the provision of location-based application and services. Nowadays there is a huge variety of location-based services around. Almost all major telecommunication providers (T-Mobile, Verizon, Orange, Vodafone etc.), internet companies (like Google, Microsoft, Yahoo) and mobile device manufactures (TomTom, Garmin, Navigon, Mio, Nokia etc.) are offering location-based services. But there are also many smaller companies aiming for niche or regional markets

- Data and content provider: Especially for location-based services precise and actual – spatial- and non-spatial – content is very important. This content is maintained and provided by public bodies (like municipal departments and ordnance surveys) or private companies (e.g. NAVTEQ[34], TeleAtlas[35]) focusing for example on spatial vector data or remote sensing data (like satellite images and aerial photos). Other location-specific content providers are local news agencies, local yellow pages or classifies. For the provision of location-based services – either as professional services or tailored for private users – all five components need to be combined and interweaved.

5.4.1. Classification of Location-based services

Generally one can classify location-based services in primary and secondary, services. Primary services – as the basic building blocks for LBS – can be divided into visualization, navigation, search, tracking, communication and billing services. These basic elements are the foundation for secondary services by means of more complex applications and services.

---

[34] www.navteq.com
[35] www.teleatlas.com

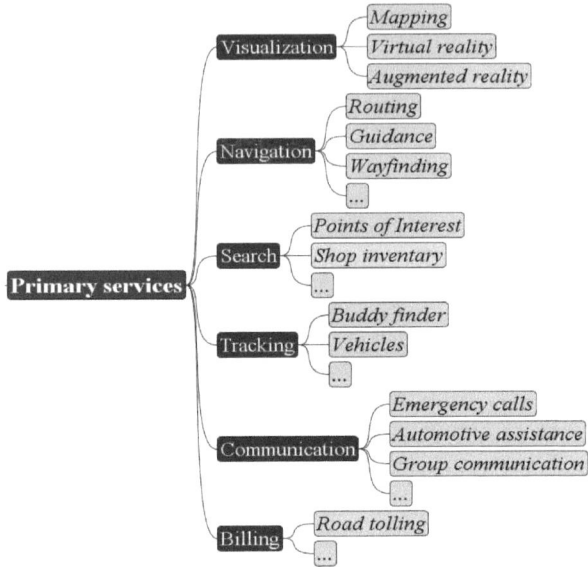

Figure 46: Primary location-based services

Figure 47: Secondary Location-based Services

5.4.2. Example applications and services

The array of examples for LBS is manifold and diverse. In the past years a huge proliferation of different location-based approaches aiming at various application areas and target markets has happened. In 2007 the speed of innovation and market penetration has even increased dramatically, which was facilitated by the convergence of mobile communication, mobile internet, Web 2.0 technologies and new mobile devices.

Google Maps Mobile   Yahoo! Go Local   M.Live Search

Figure 48 - Location-based services provided by global internet search companies

5.4.2.1. Global, Mobile and Location-Based Search

Location-based service offerings provided by the big global internet search engine companies like Google, Yahoo, Microsoft Network – MSN and others are very prominent examples are the. In the past years these services have moved on from pure web search to mobile search and later also to more sophisticated location-based service offerings like routing, buddy finders, or mobile access to public transportation schedules. But nevertheless these services still focus strongly on location-based search as their business model is built based on selling advertisement. So far these services are the only ones aiming at global data coverage.

5.4.2.2. Mobile Pedestrian Navigation

Another service category – namely mobile navigation - has gained increasing popularity in the past years. These devices, which were initiated by in-car navigation systems and movable devices like after-market equipment, have also entered the mobile handheld market to provide navigation services for pedestrians. According to a study by ABI Research[36] more than 27 million PNA units were sold in 2007 and until 2012 this amount is expected to increase by 20.5 % p.a. Individual manufacturers and models often offer further mobile services like Point-of- Interest search or multimedia services.

But not only specialized navigation device manufacturers are aiming at pedestrian navigation services. Mobile phone manufactures are also entering the market by extending the mobile phones with GPS Chips and navigation software. A prominent example is the cellular manufacturer Nokia,

---

[36] ABI Research - http://www.abiresearch.com/ found at 08.01.08

with a market share of about 40 %, which acquired the spatial data provider NAVTEQ[37] in 2007 for about 6 billion dollar.

               Garmin Navü   TomTom One   Nokia Maps on N95
        [Source www.garmin.com]   [Source: www.tomtom.com]   [Source: www.nokia.com]

Figure 49: Example LBS by navigation device manufactures and mobile phone manufacturers

5.4.2.3. Regional and Local Location-Based Services

On the regional or local level one can find a big variety of approaches frequently based on internet technologies. Figure 50 presents a small subset for Germany.

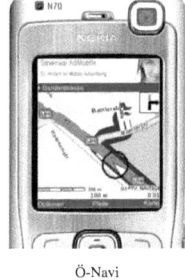  

              Ö-Navi   mobil.stuttgart   Heidelberg Mobil
       [Source: www.oe-navi.de]   [Source: mobil.stuttgart.de]   [Source: www.heidelberg-mobil.de]

Figure 50: Country-wide and local eamples

The "*Ö-Navi*" application is the mobile derivate of the official phone book and yellow page service – "*Das Örtliche*". "*Mobil.Stuttgart*" was initiated for the Soccer World Championships 2006 to serve visitors with basic information about Stuttgart (which was one of the venues).

Heidelberg can be traced back to a research project on location-based services called Deep Map in Heidelberg/Germany [Zipf (1998)] and has evolved recently to complete product suite.

---

[37] Source:http://investor.navteq.com/phoenix.zhtml?c=179528&p=irol-newsArticle
&ID=1086681 found on 08.01.08

Chapter 5. Spatial Information – Concepts, Theory and Applications

5.4.2.4. Further Location-Based Services

Mobile and location-based services are available for many different application domains, embracing content sharing, recommendation services, messaging and games. Figure 51 shows some representatives for these service categories.

| Mobile Content Sharing | Geo tagging | Mobile buddy finder | Mobile games |
| [Source: www.gypsii.com] | [Source: www.plazes.com] | [Source: www.qiro.de] | [Source: pacmanhattan.com] |

Figure 51: LBS examples focusing on specific functionalities

5.5. Graph theory – Foundation for Navigation Services.

The graph theory – as foundation of any navigaundtion services – is a *[...] branch of mathematics concerned with networks of points connected by lines [...]* [Encyclopedia Britannica (2007)].

It has its origin in recreational math problems, namely the Königsberg Bridge problem. This problem was a puzzle concerned with specific arrangement of bridges in an Old Prussian city. There were seven bridges over a forked river building an island. The task was to find a path over every one of the seven bridges without crossing a bridge twice. Leonhard Euler, a Swiss mathematician [Burckhardt, et al. (1983)], argued that no such path exists due to the physical arrangement of bridges and thereby proved the first theorem in graph theory.

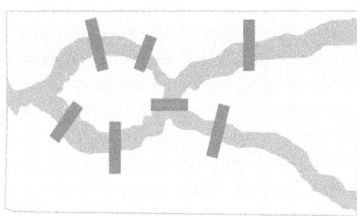 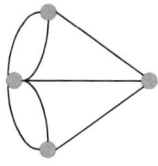

Figure 52 : Euler Tours - The seven brigdes of Königsberg

A graph is an ordered triple (V(G), E(G), Ψ_G) consisting of a nonempty set of vertices V(G), a set of edges E(G) that is disjoint from V(G) and an incidence function G that associates an unordered pair of vertices to each edge of G. If a is an edge, A and B are vertices such that $\Psi_G(a)$ = AB, then A and B are called the ends of the edge a. See Figure 53. Graphs are named because they can be represented graphically by indicating vertices as points and an edge as line connecting the vertices.

This graphical representation helps understanding many of the graph properties [Bondy and Murty (1976)].

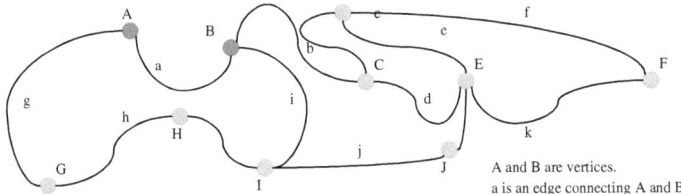

Figure 53: Simple pair graph

Today the graph theory has diffused into many areas of mathematical research including applications in chemistry (for example on chemical pathways), operations research (e.g. data warehousing and business intelligence), social sciences (e.g. population models) and computer science (e.g. computer networks, navigation).

Generally one can distinguish two main concepts and problem-solving types in graph theory: structure-based and edge-based approaches. Structure based approaches consider and operate on the structural components of a graph meaning its formation and composition of different sub graphs. Edge-based approaches emphasize edge and associated cost functions for example defined by the edge length [Musser and Osman (2003)]. There are three main categories for edge-based algorithms:

- Spanning tree algorithm: This category subsumes algorithms that calculate the least weight spanning tree of some graph. A spanning tree is an acyclic, connected sub graph of a given graph that includes all of its vertices. In fact a graph has many spanning trees but the problem is to find the one with the minimum weight, where the weight is defined by some edge property.

- Flow algorithm: Calculates the quantity of flow in graph from a source vertex to a sink vertex. This is one aspect of a larger field that studies flow networks.

- Shortest path algorithm: These algorithms compute the shortest paths from a given start vertices to one or multiple end vertices.

Focus in this sub chapter is on the navigational aspects of the graph theory and the subsequent application areas. Here the plain definition of graphs is not sufficient enough as traffic networks contain one way tracks so that traffic is prohibited in one direction and allowed in the other. An extension of graphs are directed graphs or digraphs D. Formally D is an ordered Triple (V(D), a(D), Ψ (D)) consisting of a nonempty set V(D) of vertices, a set a(D), disjoint from V(D), of arcs and a

Chapter 5. Spatial Information – Concepts, Theory and Applications

incidence function Ψ (D) that associated with each arc of D an order pair of vertices D. If *a* is an arc and A and B are vertices such that $\Psi_D(a) = (A, B)$. Then *a* is said to join A and B, A is the tail of *a* and B is the head [Bondy and Murty (1976)].

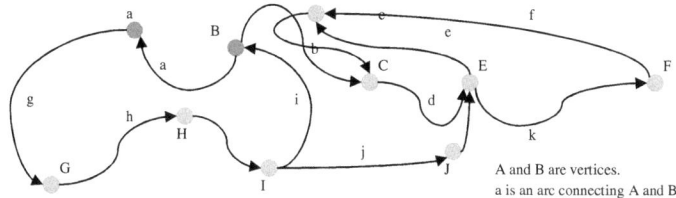

Figure 54: Direct graph - digraph D

5.5.1. Shortest Paths – Algorithms and solutions

Shortest path problems – which mean finding the shortest way to a given destination – are one of the most prominent navigation and especially location-based services. Shortest path algorithms have been studied extensively since the 1950ies and many different approaches have been proposed so far. The problem is easy in the sense that a shortest path in a graph of *n* vertices and *m* edges can be found in O (n^2) time.

The meaning of a shortest path is not restricted to the distance but rather refers to a path connecting the start and destination vertices with the least costs. The bases for this are weighted graphs. G is called a weighted graph if for each edge *e* (G) there are real number weights *w* (e).

There are two types of shortest path algorithms: Single source and all pair's shortest path algorithms. The first calculates the shortest path from a source vertex to all other vertices in a given graph, the latter compute the shortest path between all pairs of vertices in a given graph. All known algorithms for solving the all pairs problem must solve all or part of the single source problem. The all-pairs problem can be viewed as *n* single source problems and solved accordingly. Therefore the single source problem, i.e. find the shortest paths from r to all other nodes is the fundamental problem [Connor (2001)].

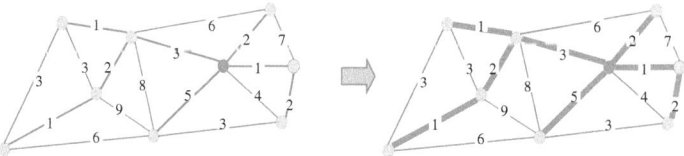

Figure 55: Minimum spanning tree

The optimum solution to the single-source shortest path problem is a set of n−1 shortest paths and their lengths. Such a solution can be succinctly described by a spanning tree T(r) whose root is r. The unique path from r to any u in T(r) is the shortest path from r to u in G. The length of any path from r to u in T(r) is the shortest distance from r to u in G and is denoted by D_u [Connor (2001)].

Figure 55 presents a minimum spanning tree of shortest paths from a source vertex A. The most prominent shortest path algorithm spanning such a tree is Dijkstras algorithm developed in 1959 [Diijkstra (1959)]. While building the tree this algorithm follows the theorem:

If graph G has positive arc distances then when any vertex u is selected from a list S its distance D[u] is optimal and it is never added to S again.

A pseudo code example of this algorithm is depicted in Figure X.

```
{S is represented as an unordered list}
Initialize (r, G, p, D)
S := N;  D[r] := 0;  p[r] := null
while S is not empty do
    u := DeleteMin (S)
    for each v ∈ Adj(u) do
        if D[v] > D[u] + d_uv then
            D[v] := D[u] + d_uv
            p[v] := u
        endif
    endfor
endwhile
endalg  {Dijkstra-SPathTree}
```

N - Nodes
S – Selection set
D – Distance
G – Graph
r – root vertex
u – current vertex
v – target vertex
p – path

Figure 56: Pseudo code of Dijkstra's shortest path algorithm [Connor (2001)]

The shortest paths problem (and its extension – the all-pair's shortest path problem) is one of the most well known problems in algorithm design; yet its complexity has remained open until today. Since the 1950s several hundreds of approaches tried to decrease its computational complexity on order to speed up processing time by introducing additional constraints like geometric constraints [Aleksandrov, et al. (2000)], planar graphs [Frederickson (1987), Chen (1995)] or randomly chosen edge weights [Spira (1973)]. Another common assumption for shortest path problem is that graphs are integer-weighted, which means in principle structurally unrestricted. A wide range of approaches focuses on pre-processing of edge weights to enter Dijkstra-like algorithms with pre-sorted lists. Examples are algorithms on scaling [Gabow (1985), Goldenberg (1993)], fast matrix multiplication [Dobosiewics (1990), Seidel (1992)] or hierarchy-based approaches [Thorup (1999)]

Since 1959 the computational time has been degreased from O (n³) to $O(n^3 \log^3 \log n / \log^2 n)$ in 2007 [Chen (2007)].

5.5.2. Traveling Salesman Problem

A further extension of the rather "simple" problem finding a shortest route from a starting point to an endpoint considers visiting additional – if not all – possible stops on a graph. A path considering all vertices of a graph is named as Hamilton cycle, after Hamilton [Hamilton (1856)], who described a mathematic game on the dodecahedron in which one person sticks five pins in any five consecutive vertices and the other is required to complete the path so formed to a spanning cycle. A graph is a Hamiltonian if it contains a Hamilton cycle.

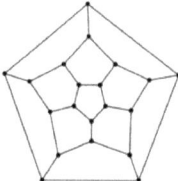

Figure 57: Dodecahedron

In contrast to the Euler graph, no nontrivial necessary and sufficient conditions for a graph to be Hamiltonian are known. The problem of finding such a condition is one of the main unsolved problems in graph theory. A further extension is the traveling salesman problem:

A traveling salesman wished to visit a number of cities and return to his starting point. He intends to visit all cities in as shortest time as possible, given that the travel between cities is associated with travel times.

In graphical terms, the aim is to find a minimum weight Hamilton cycle on a weighted complete graph. The Traveling Salesman problem has an interesting history [Appelgate, et al. (1998)]. In the 1929s the mathematician and economist Karl Menger publicized the Traveling Salesman problem among his colleagues in Vienna. Ten years later it reappeared in the mathematical circles of Princeton and vanished afterwards for almost a decade. In the 1949s it was studied by statisticians in connection with an agricultural application [Mahalanobis (1940)]. In the following year it became the prototype of hard problems in combinatorial optimization.

5.5.2.1. Combinatorial Optimization

The roots of combinatorial optimization in general lie in economics research by means of efficient resource and operations planning [Graham, et al. (1995)]. In classical optimization theory the number of possibilities is infinite whereas in case of combinatorial optimization this number is finite. Nevertheless due to various additional constraints or requirements often an optimal solution often cannot be computed in polynomial time. For that reason heuristic approaches try to find a solution that can be considered as optimal for example by relaxing one of the given constraints.

Yet another typical challenge appearing in today's problem areas and requiring for optimization is the circumstance that heuristic solutions can not be pre-computed because input constraints can be very dynamic. One just needs to consider a potential portfolio selection and a volatile stock exchange.

The application areas that can be mapped to combinatorial optimization problems are manifold and not only limited to the already mentioned Traveling Salesman problem like gene sequencing, job assignment, VLSI[38] for chip manufacturing, computer network optimization and many more. In the past decades many attempts to find optimal solutions have been presented. According to their general fundamental principles they can grouped into:

- Local search or greedy algorithms: These approaches rely on the assumption that a local optimum might also reflect a global optimum. A well-known approach is the Kruskal minimal spanning sub tree that aims at finding a tree in a connected, weighted graph that contains all vertices where the weight of the edges in minimized [Kruskal (1956), Weiner, et al. (1973)].

- Local improvement algorithms: They follow the idea that once a good solution is found, with small changes an even better solution might appear. This methodology is analog to genetic algorithm. In graph theory these approaches are also called local search algorithms as they often start at an initial start vertex). In case the improvement is done along an already computed path, these algorithms are called augmenting path algorithms [Grötschel and Lòvasz (1993)].

- Relaxation algorithms: A general problem with heuristic algorithms is that an optimum solution is hard to prove. Relaxation algorithms try to relax one or more constraints in order to achieve an optimum in the other ones. Typical examples are branch and bound algorithms where constraints are associated with a valuation that expresses the impact of violating the constraint or the quality of the solution [Schiex, et al. (1995)].

---

[38] VLSI – very large-scale integration

Chapter 5. Spatial Information – Concepts, Theory and Applications

- Dynamic programming describes the process of solving combinatorial optimization problems as multistage [Bellman (2003)] or discrete-time sequential decision processes. Given an initial starting state, a number of potential following states are possible. In order to approach an optimal solution the best one need to be chosen. The general goal is to maximize the value of the terminating state. An example from the Traveling Salesmen problems would be finding the optimal tour given the constraints [Fonlupt and Nachef (1993)]

- Linear programming[39], in general, is concerned with finding the best outcome for a given list of constraints [Gass (1984)]. The constraints are specified in a real-valued affine function. A best-candidate solution can be described as a point in a polytope space (e.g. a polygon or polyhedron). A wide range of heuristic approaches try to translate their specific problem into a linear programming one [Yannakakis (1988)].

- Changing the objective function – the basic idea for these approaches is that in case an optimization problem is associated with some weights; change the weights without harming the overall optimal solution. One of the most prominent approaches is called scaling. It aims at transforming weights into more easily computable forms by multiplication with a positive scalar value and rounding to the next integer [Edmonds and Karp (1972)].

5.5.2.2. Heuristic Solutions for TSPs

Optimization problems like TSPs offer verifiable solution unfortunately not in polynomial-time. They are NP-Hard and solvable only by heuristics as suboptimal solutions.

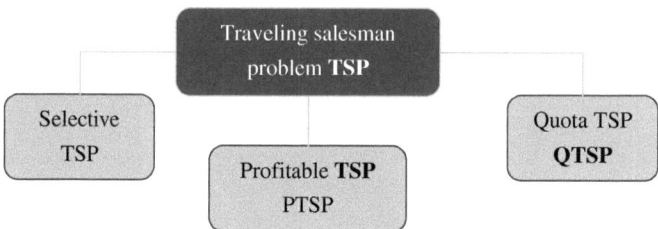

Figure 58 – Classification of Traveling salesmen problems – [modified after (Feillet, et al (2005)]

On can differentiate Traveling Salesman problems in classical ones – aiming at finding a tour visiting all cities, and TSP's with additional constraints where a visit of all cities is not compulsory. Selective Traveling Salesman problems (STSP) aim at finding a circuit on the graph that maximizes collected profit so that travel costs do not exceed a preset value c_{max}. This was for example

---

[39] The term programming in this context refers to its mathematical meaning

described as an inventory routing problem [Golden, et al. 1984] or in an orienteering competition context [Tsiligirides (1984)]. Quota Traveling Salesman Problems - Quota TSP where introduced by Awerbuch and his colleagues [Awerbuch et al. (1998)]. Here heuristics try to identify circuits on a graph whose collected profits are not smaller than a preset value p_{min}. Some more insights on heuristic approaches for geometric optimization problems can be found at Arora [Arora (2003)]. Problems that combine both these objectives in the objective function are named as Profitable Tour Problems [Dell'Amico et al. (1995)].

A given graph contains edges with non-negative costs $c(e)$ for each edge $e \in (E)$ and vertices with non-negative vertices prizes $p(v)$ for each vertex $v \in (V)$.

These two extreme types of routes are respectively optimal for the travel cost objective or the profit objective. But at the same time, each one of the constraints can possibly yield a very bad value for the other one. Thus, the purpose of heuristic procedures is to balance the quality of both objectives. In case there is a given root node $v_0 \in (V)$ this problem is described as price-collecting Steiner Tree Problem [Johnson, et al. (2000)].

In order to balance both objectives in profitable tour problems, four main operations may be used to transform a route [Feillet, et al. (2005)]:

- Adding a vertex to the route

- Deleting a vertex from the route

- Re-Sequencing the route

- Replacing a vertex of the route with a vertex outside the route

The application areas for these Traveling Salesmen problems with profits are manifold, ranging e.g. from salesmen scheduling [Gensch (1978)], inventory routing [Golden, et al. (1984)], job scheduling [Pekny and Miller (1990)], carrier transportation problems [Diaby and Ramesh (1995)] or touristic bus tours [Deitch and Ladny (2000)]. More examples can be found at [Feillet, et al. (2005)].

5.5.2.3. The Orienteering Problem and Enhanced Profitable Tours

In the context of this thesis profitable Traveling Salesman problems are considered with regard to sightseeing tours. Sightseeing in cities shown some special characteristics. Quite often tourists start from a given starting location – for example a bus stop or hotel and usually they also need to return to this location. Other constraints are potential distance or time limits when visitors need to pick up the coach or return to the hotel for the night.

In this context one can distinguish three main classes of problems. First the Orienteering problem [Arkin, et al. (1998)] that aims at designing a network on a graph that visits a maximum number of nodes, subject to an upper bound on the total length of the network. Second, the Vehicle Routing problem, taken from the real world problem of delivering goods with predefined time slots [Toth and Vigo (2002)] and third Enhanced Profitable Tour that considers additional overall time limits for a tour.

For the Orienteering problem exact and heuristic approaches have been proposed. Exact enumerative methods were introduced by Ramesh, Laporte and Martello or Leifer and Rosenwein [Ramesh, et al. (1992), Laporte and Martello (1990), Leifer and Rosenwein (1994)].

Tsiligirides [Tsiligirides (1994)] proposed an approach for the Orienteering problem based on the Monte Carlo method[40] a large number of solutions are generated to select the best one among them as a final solution. Each route is constructed in such a way that every point not included in the route is assigned a desirability measure. Among a set of points with normalized desirability measures one is selected and insert. This procedure is repeated until no more point can be added without violating the maximum distance constraint.

Golden [Golden, et al. (1987)] presented a heuristic algorithm to solve the OP in three steps:

1. Route construction: An initial route is constructed based on a weighted ranking including a score rank S_j, a distance to center-of-gravity rank C_j, and a sum of the distances to the two foci of an ellipse rank E_j. Each node which is not a part of the route is assigned a weighted measure to determine the next node to be inserted.

2. Route improvement by applying a 2-opt heuristic, which is followed by a cheapest insertion procedure in which the maximum possible numbers of nodes are inserted onto the route without violating the maximum distance constraint.

3. Computation of the center of gravity based on the route obtained in the second step.

These three steps are repeated until the two successive routes are identical to each other.

An efficient four-phase heuristic consisting of vertex insertion, cost improvement, vertex deletion and maximal insertions was developed by Ramesh and Brown [Ramesh and Karwan (1992)]. In the first phase insertion rules are employed to construct an initial solution. This solution is then improved local search routines. The third phase attempts to achieve a decrease in the length of the path in a way that one point is removed and another is inserted. The final phase deals with a

---

[40] A Monte Carlo method relies on repeated random sampling as input vector.

systematic attempt to include each unvisited node in the path. The last three phases are repeated to find a very good solution.

The approach developed by Chao [Chao, et al. (1996)] is considered as one of the fastest and most efficient for the orienteering problem. It consists of an iterative two step process. First, via a greedy method a set of solution is generated and the best one is picked. This solution is the optimized via a two-point exchange method, repeated until the solution becomes infeasible and the total score does not increase anymore.

Tasgetiren [Tasgetiren (1984)] propose a genetic algorithm that includes an adaptive penalty function. After the crossing of the individuals in the population, a mutation schema is used. This mutation schema aims at enriching and diversifying the populations by using add, omit, replace and swap operations on the newly created offspring's. The penalty function is used to penalize infeasible solutions [Goemans and Williamson (1992)].

In contrast to the well-investigated problem domain of minimizing the tour length given some additional constraints, the behavior of optimization problems that seek to maximize some function on the nodes visited, subject to constraints on the length of the path used or the time spans the nodes are being visited, is not as well understood [Chen and Har-Peled (2006)]. Generally this problem can be described as the Enhanced Profitable Tour Problem – EPTP. It is defined as the following.

A given graph contains edges with non-negative costs c(e) and times t(e) for each edge e ϵ (E) and vertices with non-negative vertices prizes p(v) and times t(v) for each vertex v ϵ (V).

The EPTP consists of finding a particular cycle $\chi = (V_\chi, E_\chi)$, $V_\chi \subseteq V$ and $E_\chi \subseteq E$ that maximizes the sum of prizes of edges and vertices it is composed of, whereas each node is visited at most once. The total amount of time required for this cycle must not exceed a given t_{max}.

5.5.2.4. Problem Reduction for Geometric Optimizations

Problem simplification is a very important step for optimization problems and their solutions is. Especially in NP-complete problems computation times scales exponentially, for example with $O(n^a)$. For geometric optimization is graph reduction a widely used approach. It considers removing unnecessary edges and vertices. Classical examples of graph reduction concern spanning trees, series-parallel graphs and flowcharts [Arnborg, et al. (1993)].

Functional programming languages and their compilation to computational byte code are other examples. Here a program is represented as a graph, where multiple program pointers might reference the same node. These nodes represented a computation result and multiple pointers to this result avoid additional computations [Pfaltz, et al. (2003)]. A further application domain for graph reduction is symbolic circuit analysis during chip design.

With regard to sightseeing city tours not only graph reduction and simplification can aid with reducing the problem size. As pedestrians are bound to spatial-temporal constraints, a restriction of the graph span to reachable areas results in significant improvements in processing time. Time geography focuses on the spatial and temporal constraints of human interaction and participation in spatial actions.

5.6. Time Geography

Until the late sixties of the 20th century there was no broadly accepted model in social sciences and geography was capable to link the behavior of humans with spatial and temporal capabilities and restrictions. Studies of human beings and behavior mainly considered only groups and aggregated population in the first place. At that time Haegerstrand, professor at the Department of Social and Economic Geography at Lund University, Sweden, who had studied human migration, published a paper in which he argued that the study of human beings which is restricted to groups and aggregate populations hides the true movement patterns of individuals [Haegerstrand (1970)].

While focusing on individuals as the unit of studies Haegerstrand also argues that time as of special importance in the human activity.

"Time has a critical importance when it comes to fitting people and things together for functioning in socio-economic systems".

A primary concern in time geography is assessing an individual's accessibility or ability to participate in events at limited locations and durations in space and time. Some notions and definitions in the scope of time geography are:

- *Time budget* – that is available for travel and activity participation

- *Activity time* – minimum required time to participate in an activity.

- *Stations* – location in space, where path can bundle or cluster in space and time.

5.6.1. Accessibility Measure

Accessibility is a multi-faceted concept that ultimately centers on an individual ability to conduct activities within a given environment [Weibull 1980]. It assesses an individual's freedom to participate in activities in a given travel environment rather than explaining or predicting actual travel choices. Conventional accessibility measures focus on the tradeoffs between the attractiveness of opportunities and the travel costs required to obtain these opportunities - see, e.g. [Geertman and Van Eck (1995)].

Accessibility measures summarize usually different types of measures [Miller (2005)]:

- Distance measures between different opportunities. Cumulative opportunity measures are an extension of distance measures that count the number of relevant destinations or opportunities within a fixed distance of an origin.

- Topological measures examine the degree and pattern of connectivity of nodes within a network.

- Attraction-accessibility measures postulate a trade-off between the utility of a destination and its required travel cost relative to a given origin.

- Benefit measures draw from the random utility framework and the microeconomic theory of consumer surplus. These measures equate accessibility with the benefits provided to an individual from a spatial choice situation

Accessibility measures often neglect the fact that the temporal dimension also affects individual accessibility. Time policy research suggests that space-time accessibility affects individual travel behavior both in space and time [Tacken (1997)]. Adding temporal constraints that affect the size of the individual's choice set can improve prediction accuracy of behavioral choice models [Landeau, et al. (1981), Landeau, et al. 1982)]. Landau coined those spatial constraints as feasible opportunity sets.

An analysis by Kwan [Kwan (1998)] suggests that space-time measures are more sensitive in capturing interpersonal differences in individual accessibility. The space-time constraints framework provides the fundamental physical constraints to define individual's potential action space [Dijst and Vidakovice (1997)].

Space time accessibility measures evaluate individual accessibility by delimiting the space-time prism, which is determined by the *locations of activities*, the *distances between relevant locations*, and the amount of time available for travel and activity participation, as well as travel speed [Burns (1979)].

Chapter 5. Spatial Information – Concepts, Theory and Applications

5.6.2. Space-Time Path and Prism

The space-time path model demonstrates that individual spatial behavior is often predefined by spatial limitations. Haegerstrand invented to model the individual movement pattern in the spatial and temporal environment [Haegerstrand (1970)].

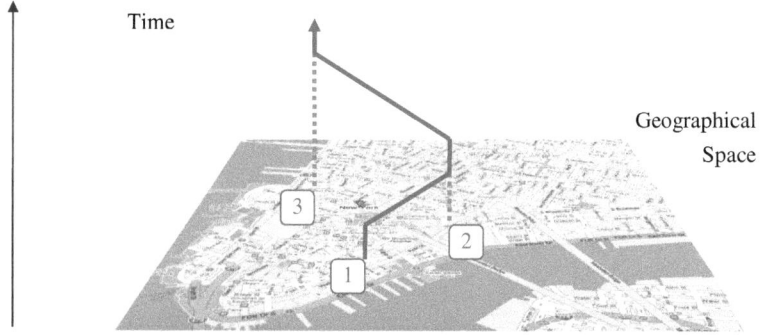

Figure 59: Space-Time Path modified after Haegerstrand (1970)

The model itself reduces the physical area around a given individual into a two-dimensional plan, on which his or her location and destination are represented as zero dimensional point. Time is represented by the vertical axis, creating a three dimensional cube that represents a specific partition of space and time.

Haegerstrand identified three different categories of limitations: *capability*, *coupling* and *restrictions*.

- Capability defines the time for spatial movement solely, e.g. an individual's restriction by the driving schedules of the public transportation or the opening hours of a museum.

- Coupling identifies limitations with regard to other individuals or spatial entities, for example a scheduled meeting in the office.

- Restrictions, by means of an individual's limitation to access certain areas, e.g. military areas.

An extension of the *space-time path* is the *space-time prism*. It incorporates additional durations of fixed activities [Lenntorp (1976)]. One can distinguish two different activity types, mandatory and discretionary ones. The limits of the space time path create an accessibility regime that is connected and a continuous set of positions in space-time (see Figure 60).

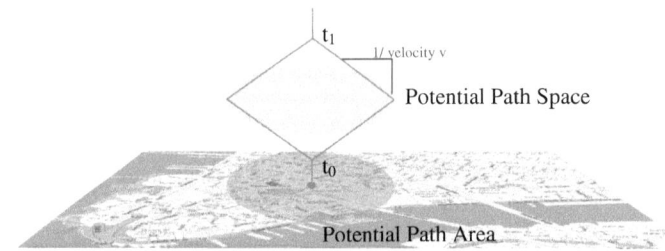

Figure 60: Space-time path - after Lenntorp (1976)

The Potential Path Space – PPS is determined by the time budget, spatial constraints and the travel velocity. The three dimensional prism is projected to 2D resulting in a PPA – potential path area.

Accessibility measures based on the space-time prism usually include the following elements [Wu and Miller (2002)]:

- A fixed activity event in space and time as reference from where and when the accessibility of an individual to other locations is measured.

- A set of destinations (activity locations) and their attributes representing the discretionary opportunities available to an individual.

- A transportation system that enables an individual to overcome the spatial temporal separation of activity sites.

Lenntorp's initial model of the space time prism does not incorporate all space-time properties of opportunities and the urban space realistically. It ignores the uneven spatial distribution of opportunities, the restricted mobility due to the geometry of the transport network, variable travel speeds throughout the urban environment and the temporal availability of opportunities associated with limited opening hours. These spatial disparities have been investigated by Kramer with regard to individual temporal expenses on mobility [Kramer (2005)].

So far the amount of approaches providing complete and consistent analytical statements of basic time geographic concepts is quite limited. "Analytical" in this context refers to the ability to construct continuous mathematical functions and computable procedures that are defined for any neighborhood on a surface like the plane. The most complete time geographic systems are informal descriptions of constructible objects that support the geometric calculations [Burns (1979) and Lenntorp (1976)].

5.6.3. Computational Approaches

The limited amount of computational approaches for space-time paths and prisms focus mostly on network graphs as spatial representation and simplification. The Network Time Prism – NTP can be described as a transportation network graph consisting of edges and nodes. It can be considered as more realistic representation of the real world as it incorporates inconstant travel velocities across space. A Potential Path Tree – PPT is a sub tree with this network graph consisting of nodes and arcs reachable given fixed activity locations and a time budget. The root of this tree might be travel origin or travel destination.

An approach by Kwan and Hong take cognitive constraints like individual spatial knowledge into account to identify feasible opportunities within the PPT [Kwan and Hong (1998)]. More specifically it delimits the set of feasible opportunities travel and activity participation in a bounded region [Kwan (1998), Weber and Kwan (2002), Dijst and Vidakovic (2002)]. Miller developed an operational method employing GIS procedures to implement a network-based space time prism incorporating link-based travel speed (instead of uniform travel conditions) [Miller (1991)]. The network-based prisms offer some analytical restriction, but only for a particular time geographic product (the prism) and a specific case (within a transportation network). Miller also developed the *space-time accessibility measures* (STAMs) of user benefits based on the PPT in 1999 [Miller (1999)]. It incorporates concepts of behavioral choice theory as well as the Weibull framework of spatial interaction-based accessibility measures [Weibull (1976)]. Its basic element is a specific utility function, which considers the activity at a location a, the time for participation T and the travel time t.

$$u_{ij}(a_k, T_k, t_k) = a_k^\alpha T_k^\beta \exp(-\lambda t_k)$$

Where

$$t_k = (d(x_i, x_k) + d(x_k, x_j))v^{-1}$$

x_i = location vector for i

$d(x_i, x_k)$ = distance from location i to location k.

v = constant velocity of travel

$$T_k = \begin{cases} t_j - t_i - t_k \rangle 0 \\ 0 \quad else \end{cases}$$

Personalized City Tours - An Extension of the OGC® OpenLS Specification

Equation 1: Specific Utility Function [Miller (1991)]

1. Focusing more on temporal aspects, Kim and Kwan introduce the concept of static and dynamic delay times during a journey to a location and combine them with the minimum activity time at the location to the extended minimum delay time [Kim and Kwan (2003)].

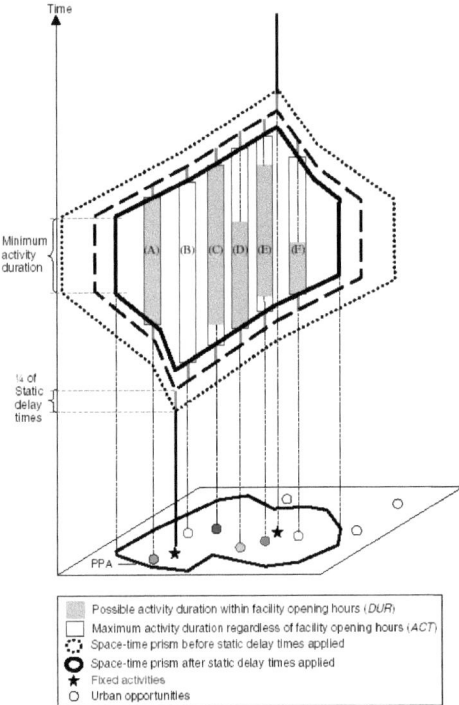

Figure 61: Dynamic Potential Space considering feasible opportunity sets and possible activity durations [Kim and Kwan (2003)]

The authors propose an algorithm to identify all feasible opportunities within a space-time prism while limiting the spatial search boundary. Its basic steps are:

1. Verify if the space-time prism can be be constructed by calculating the extended minimum activity time and the available time.

2. Delimit the initial search areas for feasible opportunity sets - using Service Area functions - and find the opportunity candidates within the search area.

3. Identify opportunities within the potential path area and calculate the maximum activity duration possible at each opportunity.

Chapter 5. Spatial Information – Concepts, Theory and Applications

4. Identify the final FOS (given the effect of facility opening hours) and calculate accessibility of an individual. Figure 61 visualizes a dynamic potential space including activity duration and delay times.

Hornsby and Egenhofer [Hornsby and Egenhofer (2002)] developed a framework for multi-granularity representations of space- time paths, prisms and composite paths/prisms to support space-time queries – but they invent a non-standard terminology for these entities. Their framework uses simultaneous inequalities to describe these entities. These are inconvenient for analytical statements about measurement and uncertainty propagation since they describe the entities only implicitly.

Raubal, et al. [Raubal, et al. (2004)] enhances the space-time prism and the spatial opportunities by the extended theory of affordances [41]. Physical, social-institutional and mental affordances, especially with regard to means of transportation, are transferred into additional space-time stations that are intersected with existing space-time stations and incorporated into an adjusted space-time prism.

Buliung and Kanaroglou [Buliung and Kanaroglou (2006)] present an overview on the quite limited amounts of approaches of spatial and spatiotemporal models describing individual and household activities.

---

[41] The term affordance was coined by James J. Gibson who investigated how people visually perceive their environment [Gibson (1977)]. An affordance is described as the quality of an environment or an object that allows an individual to perform an action.

Chapter 6. Personalized City Tours

In the previous chapters various different research areas have been mentioned - ranging from human computer interaction to spatial information theory, from context-awareness to combinatorial optimization – in order to introduce important concepts which are needed to propose a framework for the provision of adaptive spatial information. The following chapter aims at combining those concepts to extent the current OGC OpenLS for a new tour proposal services specification.

As already introduced in chapter 5.3.3.2 the OGC OpenLS describes interfaces for different types of location-based services, like directory, gateway, and routing and presentation services. Its primary objective is to define access to core services and Abstract Data Types (ADT) to build an open location services platform. The current official version 1.1, dated from May 2005, was produced following the OpenLS 1/1.1 test bed initiatives that took place from October 2001 to October 2002.

Submitting companies that define the current specification have are mostly based in North America like Autodesk, deCarta, ESRI, Intergraph, NAVTEQ, Oracle and SUN Microsystems. Only Webraska/French and Tele Atlas/Belgium have been contributors from Europe. Surprisingly one of the dominating companies concerning public attention for mobile location-aware services – Google Inc. – did not take part in the contribution process as Google was not an official member of OGC then.

6.1. The Geo Mobility Server – GMS

The OpenLS core services are embedded in a service layer which brokers between physical network and service providers facing the user - the Geo Mobility Server GMS. The OpenLS core services represent the central, binding element between spatial data, location-aware applications and position information. Its embedding into the GMS's architecture is depicted in Figure 62.

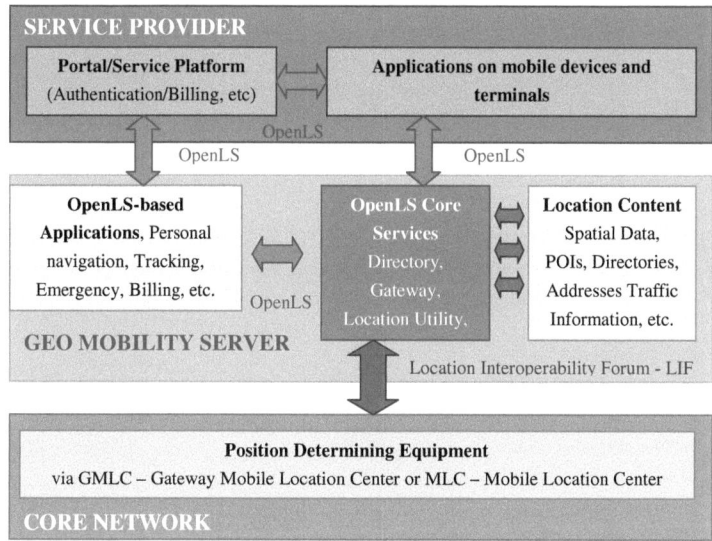

Figure 62: OGC Geo Mobility Server - modified after the OGC OpenLS 1.1

Location-aware application can be implemented either directly into the geo mobility server or by centralized and mobile applications at the service providers. Figure 62 also highlights the origin of LBS as emergency services for mobile subscribers, due to the assignment of the localization determining equipment to the core network. This does not reflect today's reality with a plethora of mobile devices, a diversified service landscape including GPS-enabled Smartphone's, WIFI positioning services and further localization techniques such as RFID or Bluetooth. Given the fact that the current specification is three years old, it also highlights the tremendous dynamics of the location-based and mobile services.

6.2. OpenLS Core Services

The OpenLS core subsumes a set of five services. The *directory service*: provides access to an online directory (e.g. Yellow Pages) in order to find the location of a *specific* or *nearest* place, product or service. The *gateway service* fetches the position of mobile terminals from a given network. The *location utility* service subsumes geo-coding or reverse geo-coding to resolve a given address to a coordinate or vice versa. The *routing service* specifies the calculation of a route from starting to an endpoint, including visit locations and means of transportation. And finally the *presentation service* allows summarizing results of other OpenLS services in map presentations.

6.2.1. General Architecture and Data Types

The general architecture to these five services is depicted in Figure X. The basic input for all location based services is the location itself. It can be gathered either via the gateway service directly from a telecommunication network operator or via an explicit user command like an address input or a pointing gesture on a map. The location itself can, in a later step, serve as input for identifying some points of interest via the directory service, as an input for visualization on the map via the presentation services or as starting- or end location for a route service request.

Abstract Data Type - ADT	Definition
Position	Point location in a well-known coordinate system
Address	Street address or intersection
Point of Interest – POI	The location where someone can find place, product, service
Area of Interest	A polygon, bounding box or circle as a search template
Location	A location (Position, Address or POI)
Map	The portrayal of maps and feature overlays (routes & POI)
Route Directions	Turn-by-turn navigation instructions for a route
Route Geometry	Geometry data for a route
Route Maneuvers	Navigation maneuvers data for a route
Route Summary	Metadata pertaining to a route

Table 10: OGC OpenLS 1.1 - Abstract Data Types

Basic information elements used by OpenLS core services are xml-encoded abstract data types. Those data types facilitate the data exchange between the different OGC compliant location-based services that are implemented either within a GMS or stand-alone. Generally all abstract data types consist of well-known structures and data types which are defined as application schemas [see Table 1]. The overall processing chain and interplay between the core location services is depicted in Figure XY. Location information gathered either from a network operator or given by the user (e.g. as an address or point) are common inputs. Dependent on the service request, this location information is used to query a directory service, compute a route or visualize the location graphically on a map. The final outcomes like route instructions, maps, or points of interest lists are generated by the presentation service.

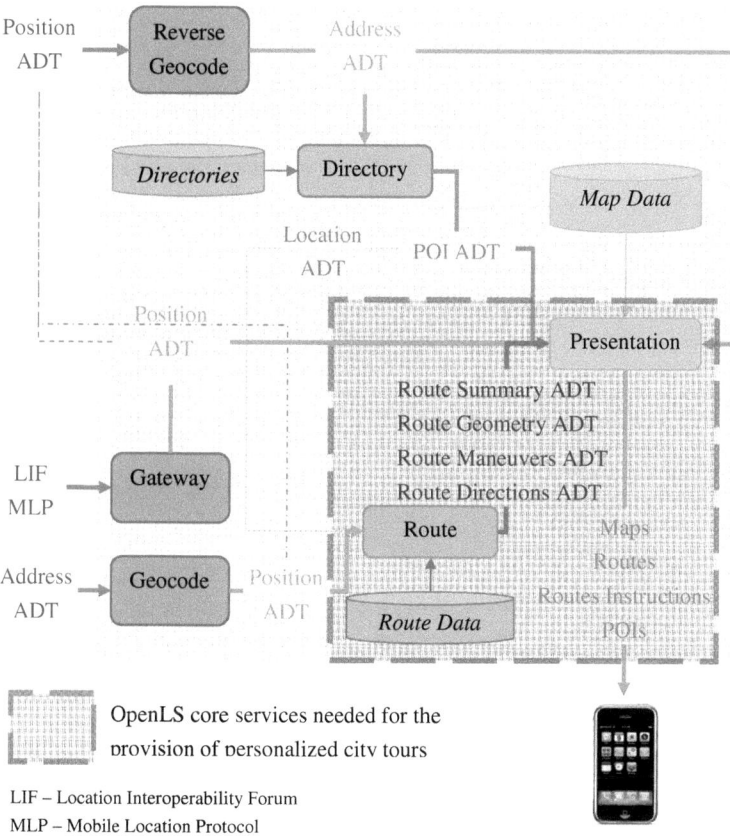

Figure 63: Abstract data types and the core services, modified after the OGC OpenLS Specification 1.1

6.2.2. Implementations and Extensions

Even today, three years after the publication of the current official specification 1.1., the absolute number of OpenLS compliant services is quite limited. This applies for scientific as well as for commercial implementations, which might be due to two reasons: First, location-based services – especially mobile and connected services – have just recently gotten momentum because of the availability of wireless high-speed connectivity and the success of the mobile internet. Second, the Open Geospatial Consortium gets more attention and awareness due to increasing national and international efforts on interoperability between spatial data and spatial service providers like the NSDI[42], INSPIRE[43] or the GDI-DE[44]. In the following, approaches which implement the core services are examined.

The OpenLS location utility service subsumes geocoding and reverse-geocoding in order to determine locations by address or geographic coordinates. This service serves the basic requirement for the provision of location-bases services, the location. Although it is implemented in various services along the initiatives aiming at spatial data infrastructures, the scientific literature on these services is quite rare. A paper by Hui-Ting [Hui-Ting, et al. (2005)] investigates the feasibility of this specification for the address scheme in Taiwan which differs from classical schemes in western countries.

OpenLS Address ADTS		Hierarchy	MOI[45] specification - 2005
freeFormAddress		Full Address	Full Address
Street Address	Building	Number	No.
	Street	Road	Alley
			Lane
			Road Sec. (Street/Place name
Place		Political unit	Neighborhood
			Village
			District Code
			City Code
PostalCode		PostalCode	Null
Point		Coordinate	N Coordinate
			E Coordinate

Table 11 Translation between the OpenLS address ADTs and the address specification of the ministry of interior / Taiwan [modified after Hui-Ting, et al. (2005)]

The OpenLS directory service provides search capacity for Points of Interests like places or services. Its implementation in a 3D Information system was described by Schilling [Schilling, et al. (2009)].

---

[42] NSDI – National Spatial Data Infrastructure - http://www.fgdc.gov/nsdi/nsdi.html
[43] INSPIRE – Infrastructure for Spatial Information in Europe - http://www.ec-gis.org/inspire/
[44] GDI-DE – Geodaten Infrastruktur Deutschland - http://www.gdi-de.org/de/f_start.html
[45] MOI – Ministry of Interior Taiwan

Chapter 6. Personalized City Tours

The Open LS route services has been topic of various research projects that aims to provide more enhanced routing functionality and routing descriptions. One of the few yet existing implementations and extension of the route service was described by Kim and Park [Kim and Park (2004)] who employ the specification on a Korean route network. An extension by Hansen, et al. [Hansen, et al. (2006a, 2006b)] focuses on route instructions and landmarks. The authors introduce cognitive route directions that make direction concepts more precise, referring to landmarks and subsuming route directions. They extend the route service with an extended direction model [Klippel, et al (2004)], the structure of intersections, and further descriptions of landmarks. Furthermore they added spatial chunking to reduce the number of instructions [Dale, et al. (2003)].

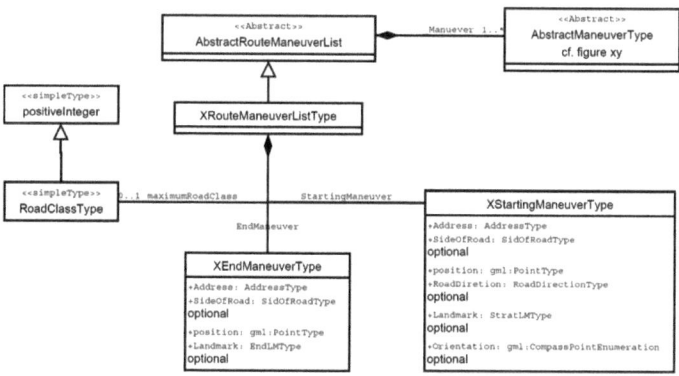

Figure 64: Route maneuver type [Hansen, et al. (2006b)]

Since starting and endpoint of a route are crucial elements to provide advanced route instructions Richter et al. extends the route maneuver service specification with dedicate route maneuvers types incorporating the potential orientation of the user [see Figure 64].

Neis and Zipf [Neis and Zipf (2007)] employ the route service to compute accessibility areas as polygons around a location (starting point, address, POI) which are accessible given further parameters like time, speed or distance. The calculations are based on a street network considering additional attributes (one-way tracks, speed limits).

Yet another extension of the route services was described by Weiser [Weiser, et al. (2006)] in the context of emergency situations. This Emergency Route Service – ERS – considers actual avoid areas (flooded or blocked roads, evacuated or poisoned areas or landslides) during route processing.

Neis additionally presented a Route Service 3D that facilitates a route service and maps its route geometry results onto a digital elevation model – DEM [Neis et al. (2007)]. All 2D points are

Personalized City Tours - An Extension of the OGC® OpenLS Specification

extended with height information and additional geometry points are added to avoid intersections in the DEM.

The OpenLS presentation service is defined as *a network-accessible service that portrays a map made up of a base map derived from any geospatial data and a set of ADT's as overlays* [OGC (2003)]. So far the amount of official implementations and research publication are very limited.

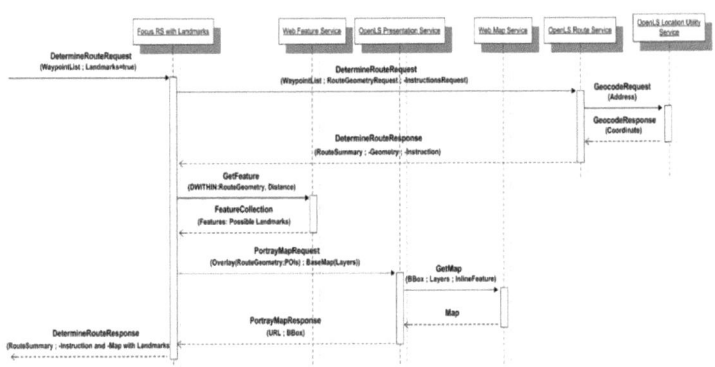

Figure 65: Orchestrated OpenLS services for the provision of focus maps [Neis and Zipf (2007)]

Neis and Zipf [Neis and Zipf (2007)] present an approach that orchestrate different OpenLS services for the provision of focus maps [Zipf and Richter (2002)], visualizing routes in urban areas on a map where – with increasing distance to the route – the level of detail on the map is decreased. Figure 65 visualized the orchestration of different OpenLS core services.

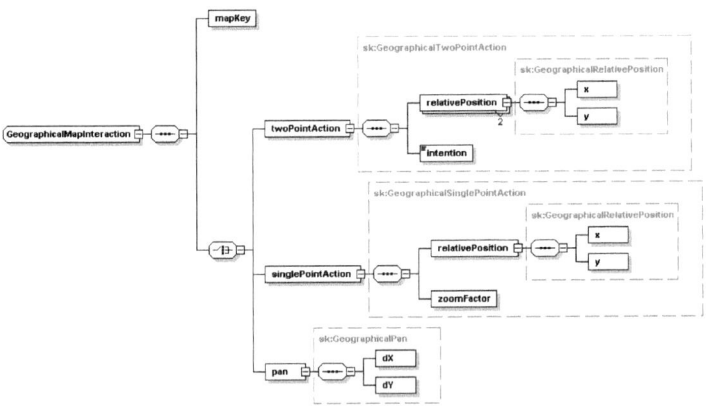

Figure 66: XML-encoded agent communication - map interaction request

Chapter 6. Personalized City Tours

Zipf and Haeussler [Haeussler and Zipf (2003)] discuss the OpenLS core services with regard to the provision of multimodal map and routing service [Zipf and Haeussler (2004)] in an agent-based application. XML-encoded messages analogous to OpenLS service requests were employed to facilitate communication between different service agents.

Figure 66 visualizes a map services request, analogous to the OpenLS PortrayMapRequest. This request is tailored to map interaction like panning, zooming and rotation in a multimodal fashion, distinguishing three interaction types:

- A simple pointing gesture associated with a speech command, like – "Zoom in there [pointing gesture]"

- A complex pointing gesture associated with a speech command, like - "Move the map from here [pointing gesture] to there [pointing gesture]"

- A speech command, like - "Zoom in".

Company	Products	Services
Audodesk	Autodesk LocationLogic XML Web Services 2	Core
Compusult Ltd.	Web Enterprise Suite 3.1	Core
deCarta	Drill Down Web Service Server	Core, DS, GS, LUS, PS, RS, NS
ESRI	ArcIMS 9.0, 9.1,	Core, DS, LUS, PS, RS
	ArcWeb Service 2006	Core, DS, LUS, RS, PS, GS
Deodan Holding BV	Movida 1.3	Core
Leica Geosystems Geospatial Imaging	RedSpider Enterprise 3.4 and 3,5	Core
MapInfo Corporation	Envinsa 4.0	Core
Novo Group	Navici	Core

Table 12: Commercial OpenLS-compliant and registered products [OGC (2008)]

Core – core services, DS – directory service, GS – gateway service, LUS – location utility service, PS – presentation service, RS – route service, NS – navigation service.

Generally implementations – scientific or commercial one – mainly focus on outdoor navigation services. In contrast Kolodziej [Kolodziej (2004)] discussed the usage of OpenLS for the provision of indoor location based services. Since October 31, 2008 indoor navigation is a part of an OGC Test Bed Initiative which aims at developing, testing and delivering proven candidate specifications into the OGC's Specification Program [OGC (2008b)].

Only 9 commercial products, offered by 8 companies, compliant with the OGC OpenLS specification do currently exist.

6.2.3. The OpenLS Route Services Specification – a Closer Look

Common routing in car navigation or pedestrian navigation usually happens usually in a four stage process. First, the user defines his general route requirements like destination, locations he intends to visit en route, his preferred route style and the like. Second, these requirements are considered while calculating the route before third, presenting the route for example on a map. Finally fourth, the route is executed. Additional external events like a traffic jam or additional requirements can trigger a re-calculation of the route. Figure 67 visualizes this general routing work flow.

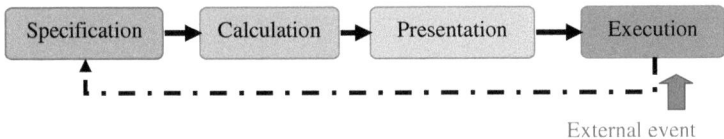

Figure 67: Typical route planning procedure

This classical route calculation procedure is also represented by the OpenLS core services. Figure 68 visualizes its most important service components. The basic request – named *DetermineRouteRequest* – serves as an envelope for the specification of the route planning procedure. Generally this request consists of the route specification, either by means of the *RoutePlan* or the *RouteHandle* request. The first one specifies a new route and the later one provides reference to an already processed route. In addition the *RouteRequest* specifies the desired service outcome be means of route presentation. It provides three different possibilities like turn-by-turn route instructions, the route geometry itself or one or more maps visualizing the route. Additional parameters are the distance unit and whether a handle to the route it is requested or not.

A *RouteHandle* request refers to a general service identifier and can hold reference to a dedicated, already computed route via a route ID.

The *RoutePlan* request as such contains the route specification. It includes, a list of waypoints, referring to the starting location, end location and possibly a set of visiting locations. An optional *AvoidList* might contain a list of spatial objects that should be avoided during the route calculation like a specific area, locations to be omitted or specific segments of the routing graph. Furthermore *RoutePreferences* can by specified as plain text.

Chapter 6. Personalized City Tours

The *RouteMapRequest* describes general map parameters, familiar with the Web Map Service specification[46]. It contains a general bounding box, the width and height of the map, the format of the map image and additional styling parameters like background color and transparency.

A set of route geometries is requested by the *RouteGeometryRequest*. This request specifies a set of bounding boxes, the maximum scale at which the route will be displayed, whether the starting point of the route should be contained and the maximum number of points.

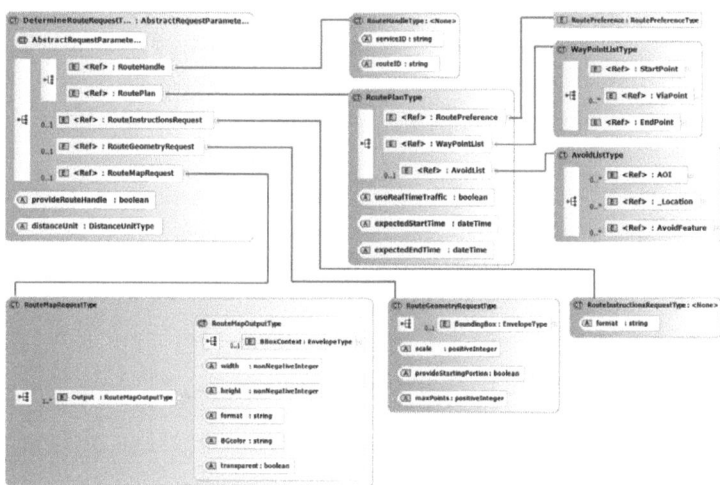

Figure 68: The OGC OpenLS 1.01. Route service request suite

Finally the *RouteInstructionRequest* asks for a set of turn by turn instructions describing the route characteristics.

The answer of an OpenLS route service is – analogous to the *DetermineRouteRequest* – a *DetermineRouteResponse*. It contains first of all a *RouteHandle* as future reference to the *DetermineRouteRequest* . Furthermore a general summary of the route is returned. This *RouteSummary* contains the overall distance of the route, its spatial extend as bounding box and a total time estimate for executing the route.

The return type *RouteGeometry* contains the basic route geometry as line string allowing for further analysis or visualization.

---

[46] OpenGeospatialConsortium – Web Map service, found under specification:
http://www.opengeospatial.org/standards/wms at 2008.07.20

Yet another possible return type within the *DetermineRouteResponse* is a list of route instructions. The instructions, as textual descriptions associated with distance measures and durations, are turn-by-turn instructions to follow the route.

The *RouteMap* response returns a reference to a computed map image. Its spatial extent is defined by a bounding box or center point. The parameter *ContentType* specifies the return format by means of a reference to the physical file as uniform resource locator – URL, the file format and its size (height and width).

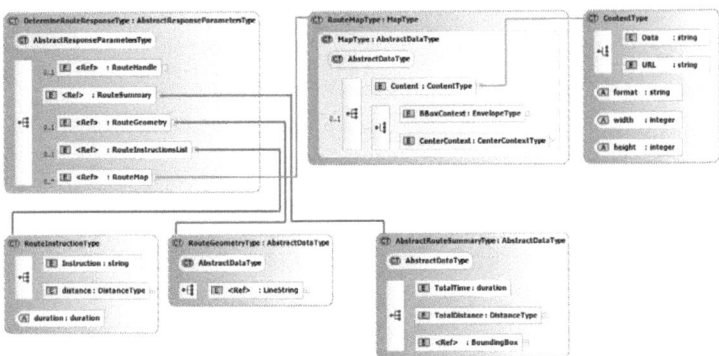

Figure 69: DetermineRouteResponse

In its current state of specification the OpenLS route service reveals several important and useful features that are not yet dealt with in depth or are missing at all. *RoutePlan* does not yet allow specifying the means of transportation for the route or even request a multimodal routing with regard to the request specification. Furthermore there is no handle to specify the routing algorithm as such (like Dijkstra or A*), which is not very important for the computation of classical shortest path problems. But for complex optimization problems (like the TSP) a wide array of potential algorithms available and should be specified in the request. Waypoints are specified as plain list with a given ordering. There are many cases imaginable in which a later optimization of the ordering done by a routing algorithm results in a more optimal route. The parameter *RoutePreference* is specified as plain text (more precisely as data format String). In the majority of cases this element indicates the kind of route that is requested e.g. the fastest, shortest or nicest route. But for the provision of individual route considering personal preferences this rather simplified element is obviously not sufficient.

The route response also displays some limitations. The *RouteInstructionType* allows for textual instructions while symbolic visualizations like direction arrows or generalized visualizations of intersections often present more suitable instructions. A concept for dealing with abstract representation of route instructions was proposed by Kray [Kray (2003)] who employs so called preverbal messages that encodes elements like target locations, referring locations, turn angles and metric information in an xml message.

6.3. Tour Proposal Service Specification

In the following a cascade of open location (OpenLS), web processing (WPS) and web feature services (WFC) is presented that orchestrates the provision of personalized city tours. It reflects and incorporates elements of human computing interaction, adaptation, personalization, advanced spatial information theory and combinatorial optimization. Major concepts and theories of these research areas have already been presented in the previous chapters.

6.3.1. Service Cascade for the Generation of Tour Proposals

On a more fine grained level of consideration one can distinguish three phases for the processing of personalized tours, 1) personalization, 2) computation of the tour itself and 3) presentation of the tour. This procedure can be mapped to a cascade of web processing and open location services. A central tour planning module or component serves as interface to a user agent and controls the different phases and its sub ordinary services. Besides a personalization service, respectively user model server provides access to user preferences and a context server serves as central aggregation point for available sources of context information like for example weather information. A visualization of this cascade can be found in Figure 70.

Any service that target at individual users, who aim to consider their preferences, needs, interests and abilities, needs to employ some kind of personalization services. This applies for the provision of personalized city tours, too. Chapter 4.1 has discussed some deductive and inductive reasoning approaches like Bayesian networks, Fuzzy logics, nearest-neighbor algorithms or neural networks, all aiming to reason to given user inputs in analogy to other inputs or similar users.

Yet another important aspect, interweaved with personalization, is the information and awareness about the current or future context a user, respectively city visitor, might be in. In contrast to the wide array of solely context-aware applications, published in scientific literature or available as commercial services, Zipf and Jöst [Zipf and Jöst (2005)] propose a model that combines both, a user model allowing for personalization and a context-model allowing for context-aware applications [see Chapter 4.2].

Coming back to city tours, one can easily identify two aspects that are characteristic for any sightseeing tour. First, a city tour consists of visiting locations, like sights, places, viewpoints or restaurants for lunch. Second, paths between the different visiting locations are of great importance

Personalized City Tours - An Extension of the OGC® OpenLS Specification

as they allow for experiencing the special atmosphere of the visited city. Because of a graph being the mathematical and computational basis for any routing service [see Chapter 5.5], personalization and contextualization aims at transferring the above mentioned characteristics into data structure.

The first step to do so is to obtain the basic spatial features from a spatial data repository and to build up the initial graph. In the following available locations are rated and weighted according to given user preferences and context information.

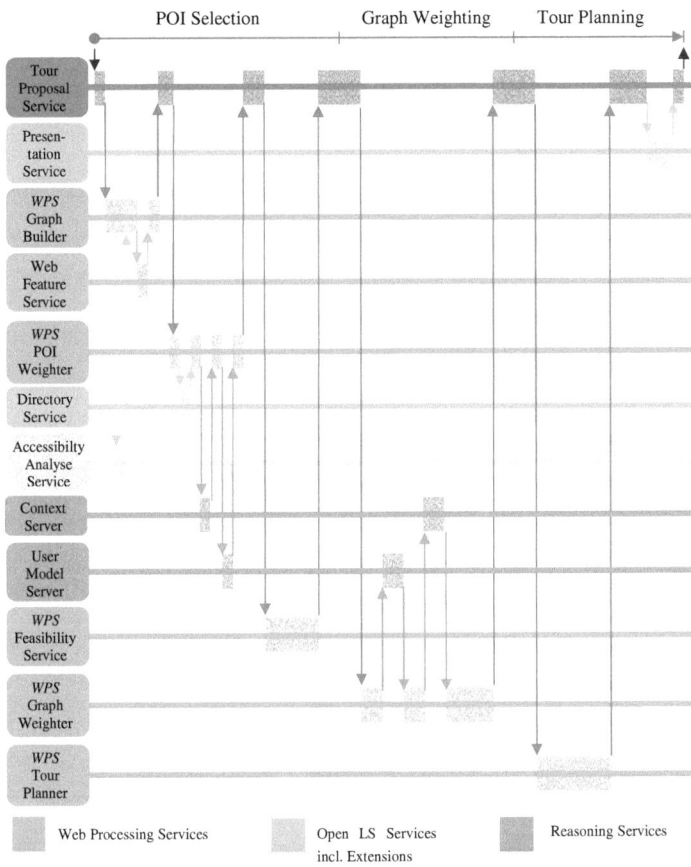

Figure 70: Service cascade for personalized tour proposal. Orchestration of OGC OpenLS, Web Processing and Feature Service.

A later step aims at verifying potential visit locations with regard to their feasibility, given spatio-temporal constraints. Additionally, this step reduces the computational complexity for the tour generation algorithm by limiting the graph size. The final preparation step weights the edges of the

Chapter 6. Personalized City Tours

graph –corresponding to the paths through the tour area – considering spatial properties as such and summing up location weights along the edges, mapping them onto the individual edges. The tour planning is the key element for the provision of personalized city tours. A heuristic approach is required because the task that has to be solved is among the NP complete traveling salesmen problems. More precisely the task itself belongs to the enhanced profitable tour problems (EPTSP) that aim at maximizing tour profits while at the same time minimizing the tour costs. Chapter 5.5.2.3 has reviewed approaches dealing with EPSTPs.

After having a tour computed its result need to be communicated to the user. A visual presentation by means of a map incorporating the tour can be processed by the OpenLS Presentation service.

6.3.2. Services, Components and Interfaces

The different services of the processing chain will be discussed in the following. Specific emphasis will be laid on the core service interfaces and the basic computational principles which the services employ.

6.3.2.1. Tour Proposal Service – *DetermineTourRequest*

In the previously sketched service cascade serves the tour proposal service as a central component. It provides external interfaces to other services like a user agent or visualization services. But it also controls the overall processing cascade of various Web Processing and OpenLS services.

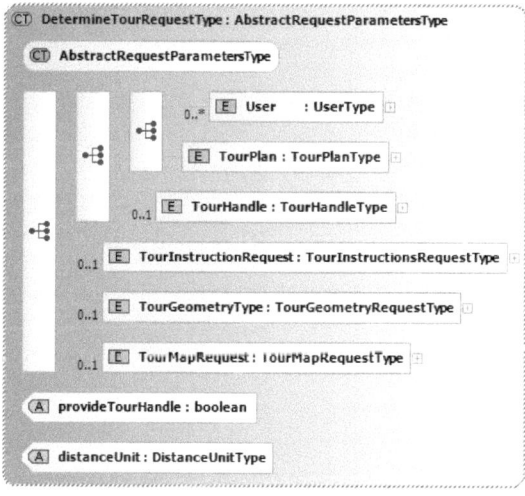

Figure 71: DetermineTourRequest

The primary request that initiates the provision of personalized tour proposals is the *DetermineTourRequest*. This request specifies the general parameters and constraints that a tour proposal inevitably has to follow. Analogous to the *DetermineRouteRequest*, as standard OpenLS service request, it also specifies the requested output format for example as list of tour instructions, as tour geometry or visualized on a tour map etc.

An important set of parameters, necessary for any personalization service, is the information about one or more users. The description about a single user can be restrained to a unique identifier or a set a name value pairs specifying individual properties like for example his interest in historic buildings or has favorite type of lunch.

The *TourPlan* request element serves as a container for the general tour parameters within the *DetermineTourRequest*. First of all it contains a list of locations to be visited, namely a mandatory starting location, and a set of optional visiting locations. In contrast to the analogous *RoutePlan* request element of the OpenLS specification the end location is not mandatory as the tour might end at the start location. A Boolean element named *preserveOrder* allows for specification whether the order of locations to be visited has to be kept or not.

Locomotion type is another element to be specified in the *TourPlan* request. This element is not available in the OpenLS *RoutePlan* element either, as this specification focuses on motorized locomotion and more precisely, locomotion by car.

For personalized city tours the elements can be more manifold like locomotion on foot, by bike, via public transportation or for handicapped people in a wheelchair. Additionally the *Locomotion* type can be précised with the speed range to be considered during computation of the tour. This is especially reasonable in order to comply with the requested tour duration.

Figure 72: General UserType Element as Abstract Data Type.

Chapter 6. Personalized City Tours

Yet another facet of the *TourPlan* request elements allows for specification of areas, locations or spatial features to be avoided during tour computation, for example highly frequented streets or dangerous areas. This element is analogous the OGC Route Service *AvoidListType*.

Finally, the *TourDuration* element specifies the overall tour duration including an expected starting and end time, an optional variance as offset and optional breaks.

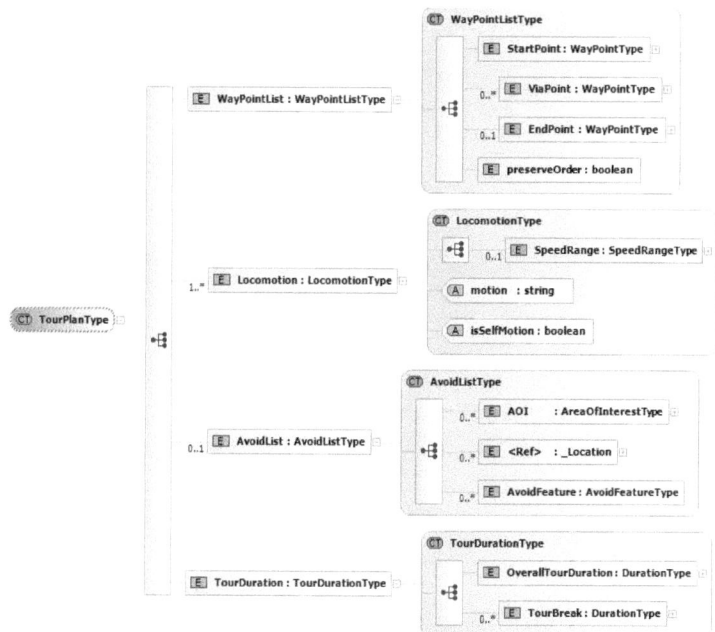

Figure 73: TourPlan Request

6.3.2.2. WPS Graph Builder

The service WPS Graph Builder aims at constructing a graph by means of querying a web feature service with given additional input constraints. As OGC web processing service, it supports three basic requests response pairs: first a *Capability request/response*, to obtain general information about the service itself, second a *DescribeProcess request/response* to obtain detailed description about an individual process offered by the service and third the *Execute request/response* – which is the central element in this context – to perform a data processing with given input data and obtaining either feedback about the actual status of the processing or the final process results [see Chapter 5.3.3.2].

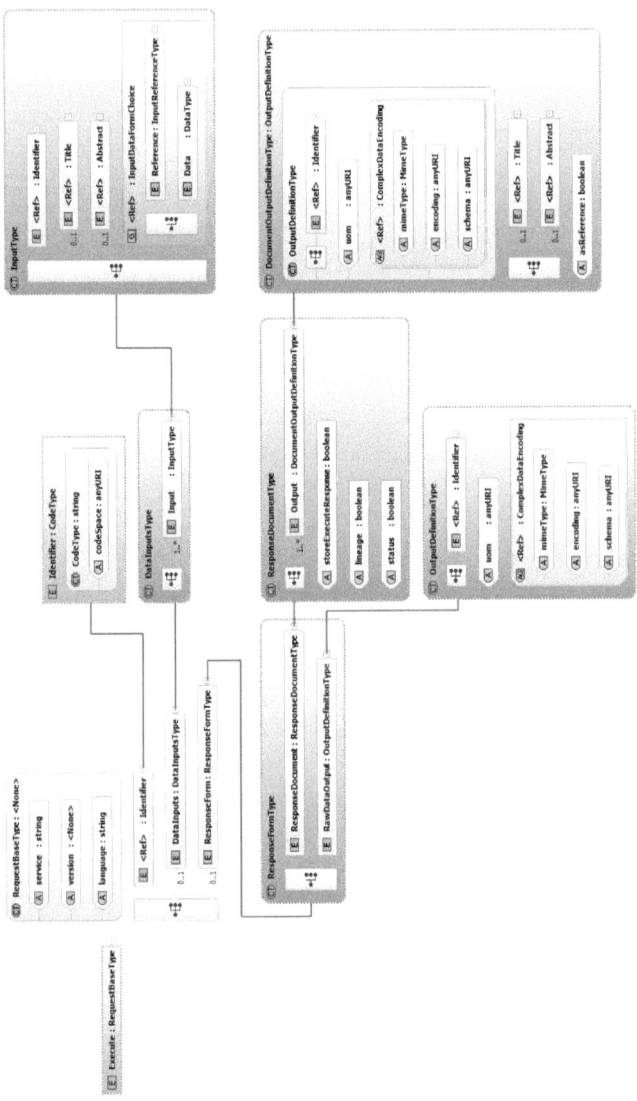

Figure 74 OGC Web Processing Request – *ExecuteRequest*

Chapter 6. Personalized City Tours

Execute request/response – which is the central element in this context – to perform a data processing with given input data and obtaining either feedback about the actual status of the processing or the final process results [see Chapter 5.3.3.2].

An *Execute requests* contains at first service information like service name, version number, language and provides reference to a service identifier. The format of the service response is specified via the *ResponseFormType* element either as raw data format or as response document. Output formats refer to an encoding which is specified as universal resource identifier (URI), a schema reference and a multipurpose internet mail extension (MIME type) format.

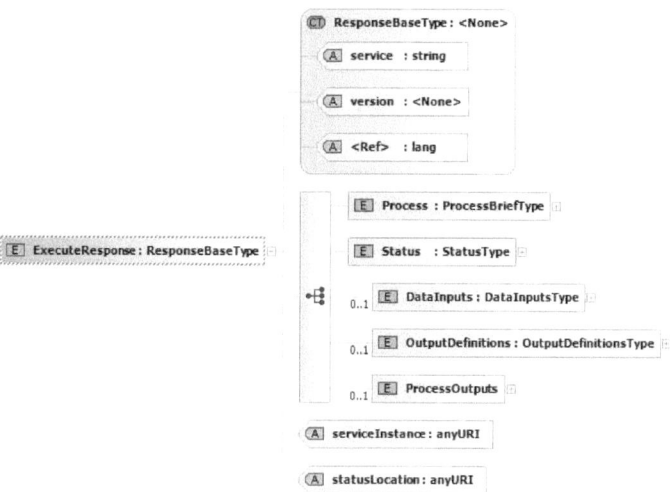

Figure 75: OGC Web Processing Request – *ExecuteResponse*

The Execute response consist of a brief process description, the current status (process accepted, started, paused, succeeded or failed), its initial inputs, the requested output format and the process output, if available [see Figure 75].

The core services request of the WPS GraphBuilder is the *GetGraphRequest* [see Figure 76]. Its basic elements are either a generic area to be covered or an accessibility definition. The generic area contains a spatial extent (like the boundaries of a city) and associated motion types, as proposed by Zipf and Röther [Zipf and Röther (2000)]. To allow for a more realistic representation of the spatial dimension which has to be considered, the spatial extent is represented not by a simple bounding box but rather by a? polygon. This allows for example to dismiss areas that should be avoided (e.g. dangerous areas). The locomotion element corresponds to the type of line features that have to be considered while building the graph. This could be for instance whether only car roads should be incorporated or also additional bicycling tracks, in case the routing is aimed for a biking tour and the like. In the proposed specification also combination of locomotion types can be defined to allow for multimodal tour generation but this is currently not covered in more detail in this thesis.

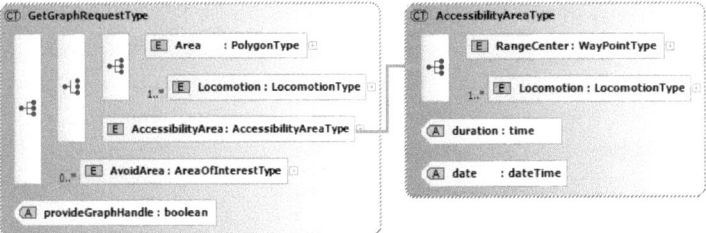

Figure 76: WPS GraphBuilder - *GetGraph* request including an AccessibilityArea ADT

An accessibility area definition follows the question "what is the most distant point to be reached on a network, given a starting location, a time budget and a locomotion type. A service that computes a service area incorporating distinct start and end locations of a tour was presented by Jöst [Jöst (2000)], Neis [Neis and Zipf (2007)] propose an extension of the OGC RouteService – called Accessibility Area Service - that allows for computation of such an area. An optional integration of this service in the overall tour service cascade is proposed.

Finally a *GetGraphRequest* can incorporate areas to be avoided, for example specified previously in the *TourPlan* request

In consequence of the service request, the response contains the graph as basic data structure. An optional reference to it serves for later retrieval. In order to construct the graph the *Graph Builder* queries a *Web Feature Service* for the requested features and builds a graph as abstract data type.

The *Graph* ADT is comprised of edges and nodes and two Boolean values indicating whether the graph is directed and is weighted. A single node is represented by related edges whereas an edge is represented by two nodes. In addition both elements can contain their originating spatial properties by means of line geometry for the edge and point geometry for the node. A general weight property serves as measure for the costs or profits to add this element to a tour. This weight property can be computed for example by a WPS Graph Weighter service (see chapter 6.3.2.5). In case the element was selected by the user it is also represented as Boolean value. For directed graphs, necessary for example to represented one ways, a direction property indicates the order of nodes.

Chapter 6. Personalized City Tours

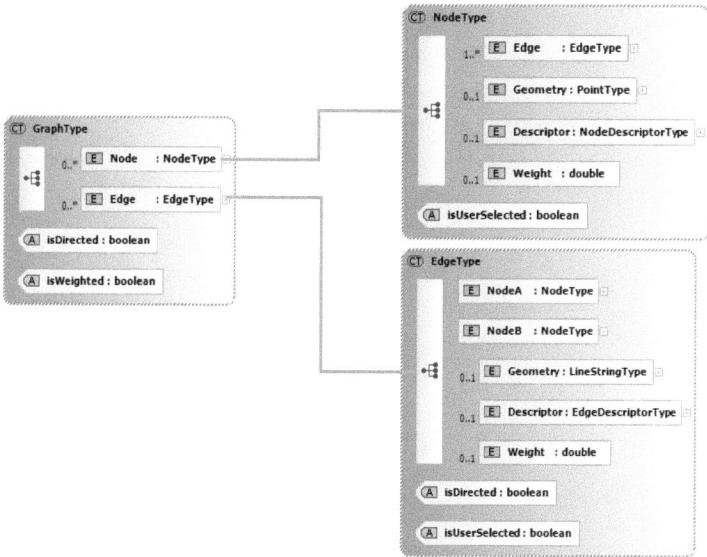

Figure 77: Graph ADT.

In order to allow for computation of weight properties based on a personalization and contextualization procedure, node and edge representation are be enhanced by optional descriptors. The descriptors on the one hand reflect spatial properties and on the other hand reflect non spatial attributes as well.

Basic primitive of a graph, the node, does not only represent intersections between line features. It can also serve as reference to places or other points of interest in close vicinity called *AssociatedDestination*. The vicinity is defined as generic spatial buffer.

A *NodeDescriptor* acts as container for those *AssociatedDestinations* and additional information describing the specific node as name value pairs. Furthermore it holds context and user weights.

An *Edge*, as element with a spatial extent and consisting of individual nodes, is specified by additional spatial attributes like distance, elevation up and down. Further attributes like means of transportation, speed range, and surface cover aspects of transportation. Analogously to the nodes, destinations in vicinity can be associated to the edge.

An *AssociatedDestinations* refers either to a waypoint that was specified previously/in the forefront of the tour by the user in the *TourPlan* request or a point of interest that was identified by a directory servic

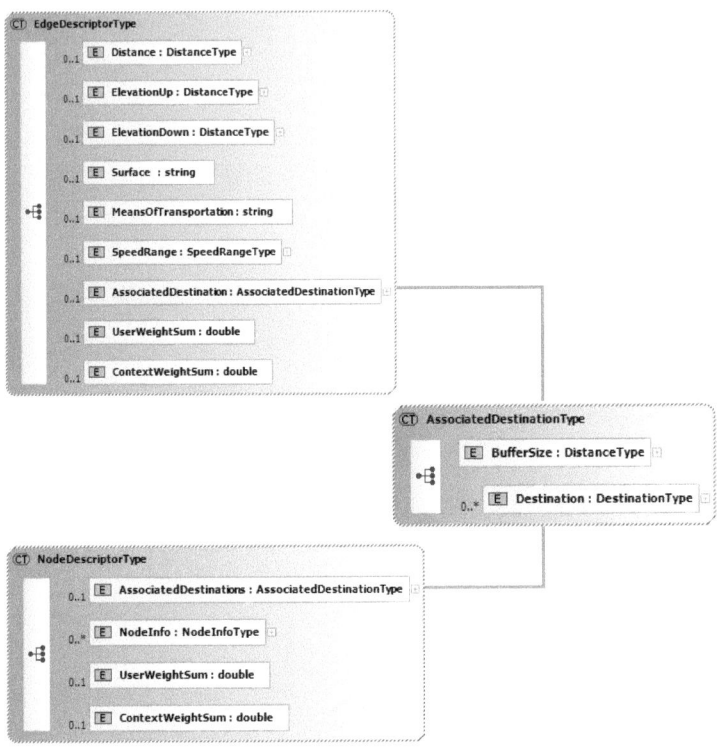

Figure 78: Edge and NodeDescriptor

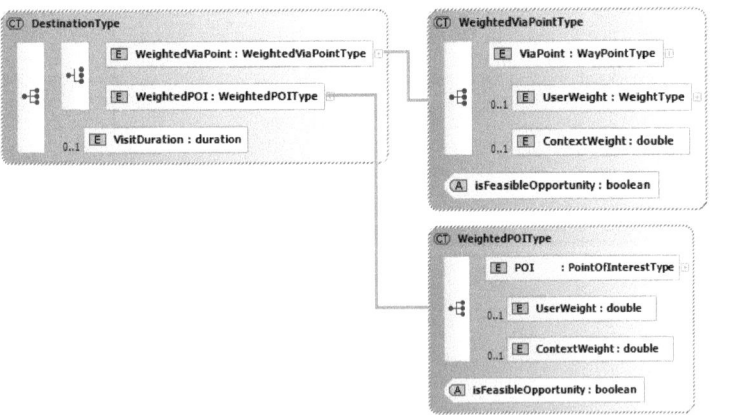

Figure 79: DestinationType

Chapter 6. Personalized City Tours

After having constructed the graph the *WPS Graph Builder* returns this data structure to the *TourProposal Service*. At this stage, edges and nodes hold their originating spatial properties and processed spatial attributes like elevation.

6.3.2.3. WPS POI Weighter - WPS LS

The Web Processing Service – *POI Weighter* performs the task to identify potential visit locations to be incorporated in the tour proposal. At first it queries an OpenLS *Directory Service* in order to obtain all POIs given the graph extent. Second a context server is queried in order to get actual contextual parameters gathered and aggregated from external sensors and services. As third step the service queries a User Model Server for stored models about the user(s). Given the context information and user model, the *POI Weighter* weights the POIs in the requested area.

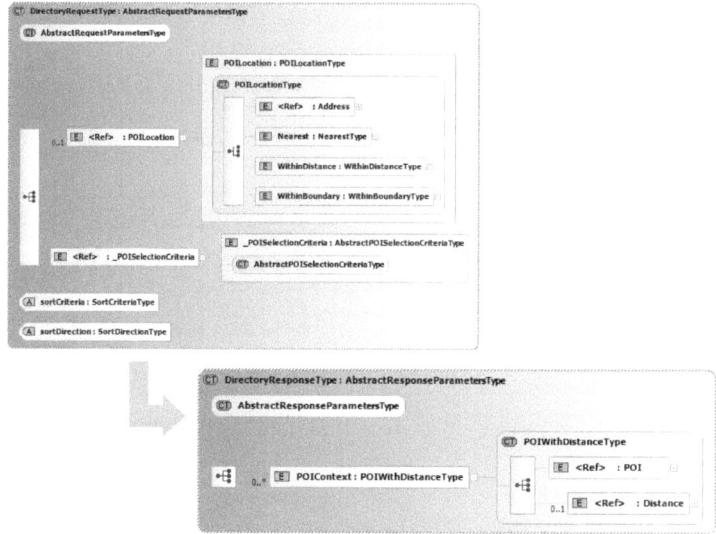

Figure 80: OpenLS Directory Request and Response

OpenLS Directory Service Request

The directory service returns a set of POIs within the specified boundaries. The *POILocation* serves as basic element of the standard OpenLS *DirectoryRequest* and holds reference either to an address, a location with a selection criterion, a location including some min and max distances or a general area of interest. Furthermore the request can include selection criteria like for example the POI type or other attributes.

The *DirectoryResponse* contains the points of interest within the given extent including optional distance measures to allow for a later refinement of the selection.

Context Server Service Request

The Context Server facilitates access to context information. Its services request also follows also the OGC web processing specification. Another OGC specification that aims at providing access to real-time environmental data is the Sensor Observation service – SOS [OGC SOS (2008)]. But this service specification is geared to raw data inputs and not to potentially aggregated context information. In Chapter 4.2 a wide array of context-aware applications and frameworks has been introduced of which some are component based and rely on middleware architectures. These approaches like for example the Deep Map system [Zipf (1998), Malaka and Zipf (2000)] or the SOCAM System [Gu, et al. (2004)] employ a central components to store, process and distribute context information.

Especially context descriptions by means of ontology have been successful with regard to context distribution within component and service-based applications because they exhibit high formal expressiveness that allows for applying reasoning techniques. In these cases – which apply also to the service-based approach for the provision of personalized city tours – formal languages are used to encode ontologies. Examples are formal languages that follow the first-order-predicate calculus (e.g. CYCL[47]) or that are based one markups. As all OGC service specifications are described by means of XML schemas, markup-based ontology descriptions are used for the context server service. The quasi standard amount the markup-based ontology languages is the web ontology language – OWL[48]. It incorporates and revises DAML[49] + OIL[50] as predecessors facilitating information exchange in agent based applications and RDF[51] as metadata description for web resources.

The central *GetContextRequest* enhances a generic *RequestBaseType* by three additional elements: first, a *Time* element to restrain the request context information to the appropriate temporal scope; second, an optional *User* element to individualize the context information to a specific person and third, an optional *Location* element to define the spatial scope of the context information. Its response form refers to an ontology specified in OWL.

---

[47] CYCL – Ontology Language based on the openCyc project – http://www.opencyc.org
[48] OWL – Web Ontology Language – http://www.w3.org/OWL
[49] DARPA – Agent Markup Language – www.daml.org
[50] OIL – Ontology interchange language
[51] RDF – Resource Description Framework - http://www.w3.org/RDF/

Chapter 6. Personalized City Tours

Figure 81: *GetContextRequest*

Prominent examples of context ontologies are the CONON [Wang, et al. (2004)], COMANTO [Roussaki, et al. (2006)], and CoBrA [Chen, et al. (2003)]. A first approach that combines context information and user models is GUMO, the general user modeling ontology [Heckmann, et. al (2005)]. It describes five kinds of context types: location, physical environment, social environment product information, and travel context.

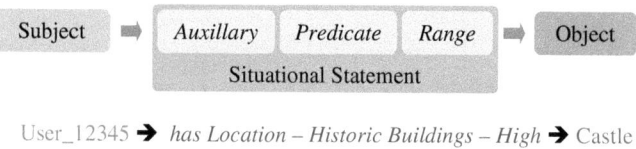

User_12345 ➔ *has Location – Historic Buildings – High* ➔ Castle

Figure 82: Situational statements in GUMO

GUMO relies on situational statements [Heckmann (2003)] which specify subject object relations via explicitly defined auxiliaries, predicates and ranges [see Figure 82]. It is encoded in the web ontology language.

The *GetContextResponse* incorporates the context information in OWL format and also includes – if available – the spatial, temporal und user constraints.

User Model Service Requests

A User Model Server – UMS manages models about individual users needed for the provision of personalized services. It facilitates the creation, update and deletion of user models. Furthermore it allows for deduction and induction across multiple users and user actions – for example by clustering individual users in groups by employing statistical algorithms. A range of approaches and methods have been introduced in Chapter 4.1.

Personalized City Tours - An Extension of the OGC® OpenLS Specification

User models generally consist of three elements: First, the profile data describing user properties; second, observations about the user and third, inferred properties like user interests and personal preferences.

In the past User Model Servers have been implemented as monolithic and embedded components, but these approaches have shown various drawbacks [Zhang, et al. (2006)]: first, the information about the user is only utilizable within the application; second, the source of information about the user is limited to one application, and third, the user has no control about his user profile as it is enclosed in the application. To face these drawbacks – while following the trend of service oriented applications – cross-system personalization has been investigated in the scientific community in recent years. In this context a wide range of approaches has been employed ranging from multi-agents systems like [Jöst and Stille (2002), Vassileva and McGalla (2005)], ontology-based approaches e.g. [Heckmann (2005), Middleton, et al. 2004)] or in a web service environments [Dolog, et al. (2004)]. Figure 83 visualizes a User Model Schema specification exposed by the multi-agent application Deep Map.

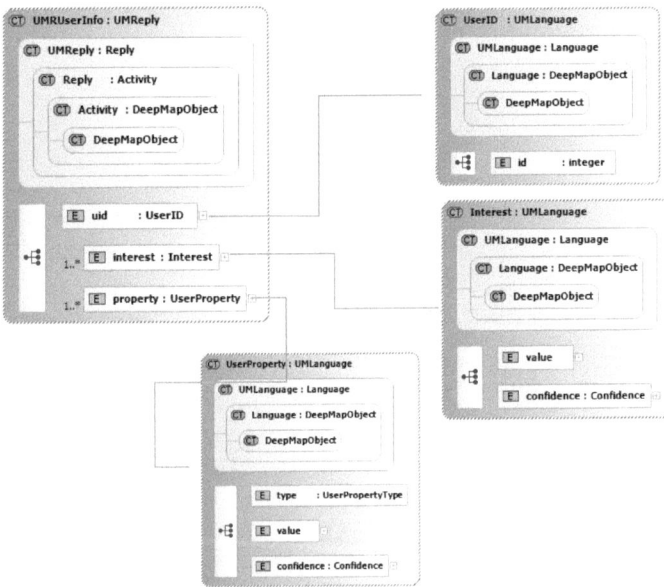

Figure 83: User Model service request exposed by the Deep Map application

Zhang proposes an ontology-based user role model employed in a web services environment, to model the user and the roles according to the service they address [Zhang, et al. (2006)]. This concept matches the ontology-driven context-modeling and the OGC web service specifications

Chapter 6. Personalized City Tours

perfectly. For that reason the *GetUserModelRequest* also follows the OGC web processing service schema. One or more *UserTypes* definitions that correspond to stored user models are the most important elements of this request.

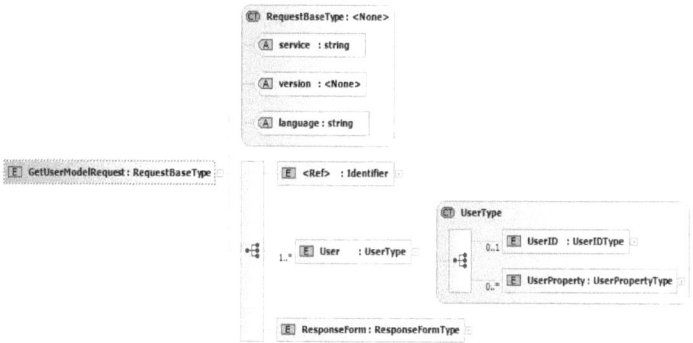

Figure 84: *GetUserModelRequest*

Its corresponding response, the *GetUserModelResponse*, returns a user model for each specified user. The user model specified as Ontology – like GUMO - is encoded according to the OGC WPS specification as *DocumentOutputDefinitionType*.

Processing user and context weight – an example

Already in 2001 Posland, et al. discusses personalization for mobile tourism service [Poslad, et al. (2002)]. Winter et al. states in his article: *"personalized LBS must allow for focalization, i.e. the adaptation to different decision situations"* [Winter, et al. (2004)]. Given all possible points of interest in the area of interest, information about the current context and the user model, the WPS POI weigther aims in weighting the Point of Interest in order to allow for a selection during route calculation. This process is dependent on the information available for the points of interest (e.g. descriptions, categorizations, Meta data and the like) as well as the context and user models. Various machine learning approaches (e.g. genetic algorithms or neural networks) can serve in computing context and user weights for a given graph element based on information contained in the user model and the current context [see Chapter 4.1.2.2].

Niaraki and Kim propose an analytical hierarchy process – AHP [Saaty and Vagas (2001)] for structuring various and heterogeneous input variables for the provision of personalized ontology-driven car routes in order to allow for comparison and computation [Niaraki and Kim (2008)]. An approach by Voelkl and Weber aiming at pedestrian route planning for impaired assigns normalized vectors to each route segments and employ a cost function based on weighted addition [Voelkl and Weber (2008)].

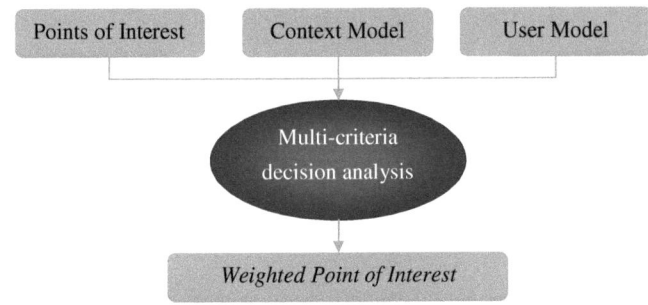

Figure 85: Example for assigning Point of Interests with context and user weights

Another approach that has been employed in GIS science since 1990 is the multi-criteria decision analysis – MCDA [Janssen and Rietveld (1990)]. Analogous to humans who use multiple, context-dependent decision criteria to determine the best solution for a given problem, MCDA tries to mimic this behavior. This methodology aggregates standardized attributes of potential decision options into an evaluation score for each alternative. Raubal and Rinner adopt MCDA to LBS in a hotel selection scenario [Raubal and Rinner (2004)] by employing an ordered weighted averaging algorithm – OWA. This type of algorithms aims at standardizing selection criteria to allow for computational comparison – for example in a numerical range from 0 to 1 or – involving a user feedback step – e.g. from good to poor. An OWA algorithm assigns these criteria with additional importance weights according to user preferences. Furthermore order weights are associated to define which criterion to choose first. Having ordered the criteria by descent values instead of summarizing them, evaluation scores are calculated as the sum of the re-ordered standardized selection criterion values with an additional weighting of the positions. Yager [Yager (1988)] proposed to calculate order weights automatically based on a general decision strategy rather than allowing for human-driven ordering. Such a decision strategy might be an *optimistic selection,* ranking a single outstanding value highest or *pessimistic selection,* ranking the least poor properties the highest.

As user and context models represents accumulated information about the user and his surrounding both models usually consist of standardized selection criteria. Also importance weight and decision strategies can be intrinsic elements of the models as such.

Given the graph extent, having queried the user model and context server and finally computed individual weights for each point of interest, the WPS POI Weighter service returns the list of weighted points of interest found in the area of interest. A weighted POI element is comprised of the general information about the point of interest, the user and context weight and a Boolean parameter which indicate that this POI represents a feasible opportunity with regard to spatio-temporal constraints. This flag is set by the following *WPS Feasibility Service.*

Chapter 6. Personalized City Tours

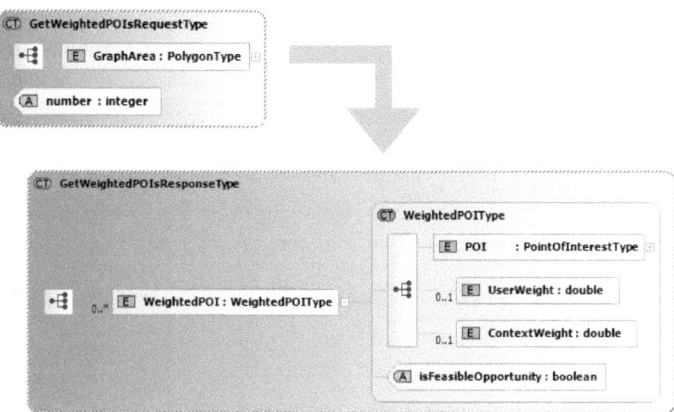

Figure 86: WPS Location service – *GetWeightedPOIs* request response pair requests

6.3.2.4. WPS Feasibility Service

This web processing service attempts to compute feasible sets of visit locations considering spatio-temporal constraints. By means of these feasible visit locations it allows for reduction of the graph size in order to minimize the computational complexity during later tour calculation.

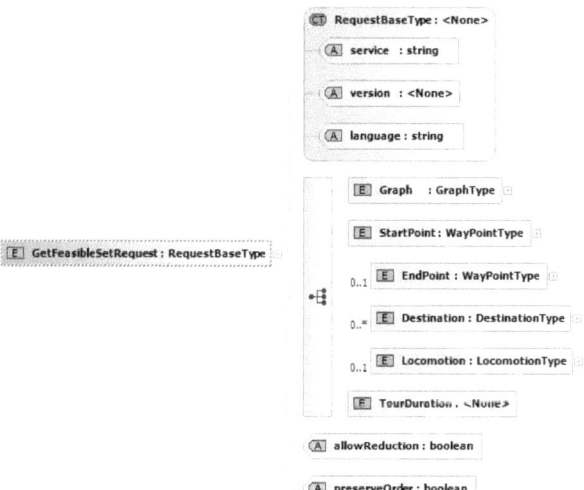

Figure 87: WPS Feasibility Service – *GetFeasibbleSet*

Personalized City Tours - An Extension of the OGC® OpenLS Specification

It considers the overall tour time and a given set of potential visit locations with regard to spatial-temporal constraints they expose. Limitations might be opening times or visit durations as well as traveling times to the destinations as such. Space time accessibility measures as part of the research field time geography are the theoretical fundaments to cope with spatio-temporal conditionality.

One of its basic concepts – the space time path – traces the movement of an individual in space and time. An extension of this concept is the space-time prism that measures the ability to reach destinations in space and time, given locations and durations of fixed activities [Lenntorp (1976)].

Frameworks allowing for computation of spatio-temporal constraints have been introduced in chapter 5.6.

Basic input elements allowing for computation of spatio-temporal constraints at the WPS Feasibility service are incorporated in the *GetFeasibileSetRequest*. This request includes spatial and temporal elements computed from predecessor processing services.

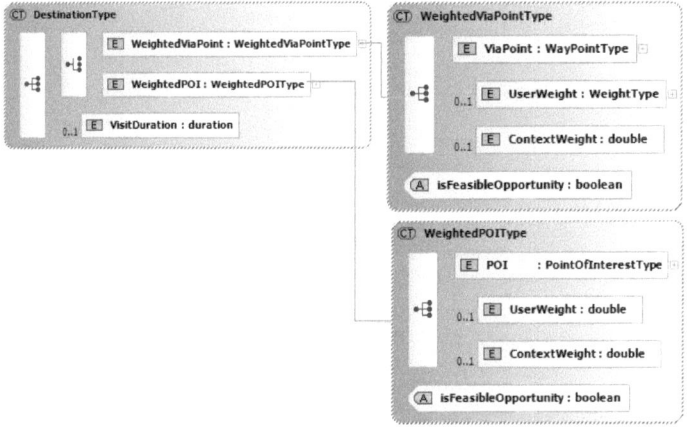

Figure 88: WPS Feasibility service– *DestinationType*

At first it contains the basic *Graph* yet only limited by the initially specified spatial extent. Furthermore it includes the *Startpoint*, (and if available the requested *Endpoint* of the tour) and the list of potential *Destinations* to be visited during the city tour. Additionally means of transportation incorporated in the element *Locomotion* and the *TourDuration* build the overall spatial and temporal frame. A Boolean parameter *allowReduction* indicates whether the WPS Feasibility service can eliminate unfeasible destinations or not. The Boolean element *PreserveOrder* is true in case the order of destinations has to be kept. This can set additional boundaries to the reachability of further destinations.

Chapter 6. Personalized City Tours

The *Destination* elements represent the basis for the identification of feasible opportunity sets. They consist of either *WeightedViaPoints* to be visited – specified by the user directly – or *WeightedPOIs* received by the WPS Location Selector. Both elements can be associated with an optional *VisitDuration* specifying an average visit time at the location. The Boolean parameter *isFeasibleOpportunity* is set during processing

Figure 89: WPS Graph Reducer – *GetFeasibileSetResponse*

This given set of spatio-temporal constraints allows for computation of space-time accessibility measures in the given graph extent with one of the approaches introduced in chapter 5.6 like for example [Kwan (1998)], [Miller (1999)], [Weber and Kwan (2002)], [Dijst and Vidakovic (2002)], [Kim and Kwan (2003)].

The *GetFeasibleSetResponse* includes a *ReducedGraph* and the set of *FeasibleOpportunities*. Feasible opportunities are indicated with a Boolean parameter. Additionally the response highlights whether the graph and the list of destinations are reduced and/or the ordering of destination is altered with Boolean properties.

6.3.2.5. WPS Graph Weighter

In order to allow for computation of a personalized city tour – as heuristic travel salesmen solution – this web processing service generates a weighted graph which is defined after Dell'Amico, et al. as:

A graph that contains edges with non-negative costs $c(e)$ for each edge $e \in (E)$ and nodes with non-negative node prizes $p(n)$ for each node $n \in (N)$.

[Dell'Amico et al. (1995)]

These edge costs and vertices prizes are computed by means of cost functions that consider and weights the spatial properties like edge distance, elevation - and in some rare cases also non-spatial attributes like context-parameters in the transportation sector. An approach by Rogers, et al. (1999) calculates the edge cost as sum of the weighted attributes. These weights for the attributes like steepness were collected iteratively via explicit user feedback [Rogers, et al.(1999)]. A quite similar approach by Balke et al. extends the concept of user defined weights by the mathematical concepts of strict partial orders to model general domain preferences (like prefer dry road over wet road) upfront [Balke, et al. (2003)]. Cziferszky and Winter compute a set of feasible tours by giving an overall tour length in a hiking scenario. A later sequential selection process tries to identify the optimal route incorporating additional parameters attached again with a weighting factor while eliminating least optimal routes [Cziferszky and Winter (2002)]. Another approach by Ten Hagen, et al. facilitates semantic matching of user preferences and constructed tour elements in a hierarchical order of vertice attributes like building type, etc., [ten Hagel, et al. (2005)].

The challenge during the computation of a weighted graph that considers spatial and non-spatial attributes is to balance both of these heterogeneous aspects. To facilitate a leveling between different attribute types and heterogeneous value ranges the individual weights need to be normalized. The proposed algorithm at first aligns all destinations within a buffer distance to edges and nodes. Second, node costs are computed and normalized over all possible nodes. Third, user preferences and context parameters are queried from external services and the edge weights are computed while incorporating edge properties and associated destination weights. Finally, the edge weights are normalized.

To calculate a singular node prize all user weights uw and context weights cw for all destinations D in the buffered area are summed up and divided by the number of destinations. An optional factor wf allows for leveling the ratio between user preferences and context parameters and the feasible weight fwf emphasizes whether a destination is indicated as feasible solution according to spatio-temporal constraints.

$$p(n)_j = Destinationweight = \frac{\sum_{i=1}^{D} \frac{((uw_i \bullet wf_n) + cw_i)}{2}}{D} \bullet fwf$$

Equation 2: Calculation of the vertex prize – p(v)

To normalize individual vertices prizes in the range lower than 1 and greater than 0, all prizes $p(n)_j$ are level regardively divided by the prize maximum $p(n)_{max}$.

$$\overline{p(n)}_j = \frac{Destinationweight_j}{Destinationweight_{max}} = \frac{p(n)_j}{p(n)_{max}}$$

Equation 3: Calculation of the normalized vertex prize

Edge cost $c(e)$ are calculated by weighting the spatial properties according to user preferences and context parameters and incorporating the individual destination weight. Approaches to compute individual weights based on multi-dimensional feature vectors like the analytical hierarchy process – AHP or multi-criteria decision analysis – MCDA have been introduced in a previous sub-chapter.

$$c(e)_j = \frac{(Destinationweight \bullet dwf) + \frac{(uw_e \bullet wf_e) + cw_e}{2}}{2}$$

Equation 4: Calculation of the edge costs - c(e)

The weighting factor *wf* allows again for leveling user and context inputs and an additional destination weight factor *dwf* balanced destination and spatial weights.

$$\overline{c(e)}_j = \frac{c(e)_j}{c(e)_{max}}$$

Equation 5: Calculation of the normalized edge costs

Similar to the vertex prize normalization are the edge costs $c(e)$ divided by the maximum cost $c(e)_{max}$ value computed during the weighting procedure.

The corresponding service request– *WeightGraphRequest* reflects the above introduced weighting factors [see Figure 90]. It incorporated the graph as such and its destinations. Optional user model and context element allow for computation of the spatial-related edge weights. In case one of these elements is missing the service can query dedicated user model or context services as show in previous steps of the OGC processing chain. The corresponding service response – *WeightGraphResponse* returns a weighted Graph as core element.

6.3.2.6. WPS Tour Planner – WPS TP

Having build a graph, queried and weighted potential points of interest; having reduced and weighted the graph, the tour planner service – as central element –aims in computing a personalized city tour. This includes the incorporation of potential visit locations, connecting street of houses while obeying additional restrictions like tour duration. Chapter 5.5 has introduced general concepts of graph based algorithms ranging from rather simple shortest path solutions to complex enhanced profitable tour problems. The computation of personalized city tours with their multidimensionality belongs to the later one.

Figure 90: WPS Graph Weighter – *WeightGraphRequest*

Heuristic solutions for the NP-complete PTP have been introduced for example by Arkin, et al. (1998), Ramesh, et al. (1992), Laporte and Martello (1990), Leifer and Rosenwein (1994), Tasgetiren (1984), Golden, et al. (1987) and many others. In the following a heuristic algorithm will be introduced that follows an iterative extension/collapse method and that was employed for the provision by personalized city tours by Jöst and Stille [Jöst and Stille (2002)]

First this algorithm reduces the graph by elimination on unnecessary nodes via computing all pairs of shortest paths between the nodes of interest employing Dijkstras shortest path algorithm [Stille (2001)].

Chapter 6. Personalized City Tours

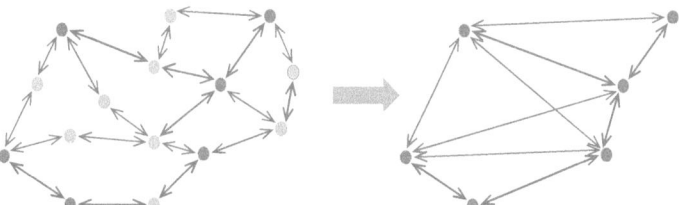

Figure 91: Graph reduction [Stille (2001)]

At second the algorithm produces an initial feasible tour on the reduced graph. An iterative extension/collapse method tries to improve this initial solution in the following.

In an extension phase the unitary and average gains for all nodes are computed and all nodes that maximize the overall profits are added to the tour. After adding nodes the unitary gains for all remaining nodes are recomputed in order to consider also nodes that have not been considered in the previous cycle. The following collapse phase focuses on the reduction of the tour in order to remain the overall feasibility. For that reason a collapse node is identified that maximizes the ratio price/time of the tour without losing feasibility. As visualized in Figure 92 both phased a computed in alternative sequence iteratively.

In comparison to an exact solution (by reduction to an asymmetric TSP with a branch- and bound algorithm) that runs in the worst case exponentially, this extend and collapse algorithm has a running time of $O(n^2\log_2 n)$ while achieving more than 90% of the exact solution objective function [Stille (2001)]. In comparison to the approximation algorithm by Goemans and Williamson – that runs with $O(n^2\log_n)$ [Goemans and Williamson (1992)] the proposed algorithm has a 5 – 15 % better solution quality.

The TourPlanRequest provides the input elements to allow for the computation personalized city tours. At first it incorporates a weighted graph. Second it holds reference to the user specified start and end location. A set of destinations specify requested visit location and points of interest that match the user's preferences and the current context. Finally the tour duration defines the temporal constraints of the tour.

Personalized City Tours - An Extension of the OGC® OpenLS Specification

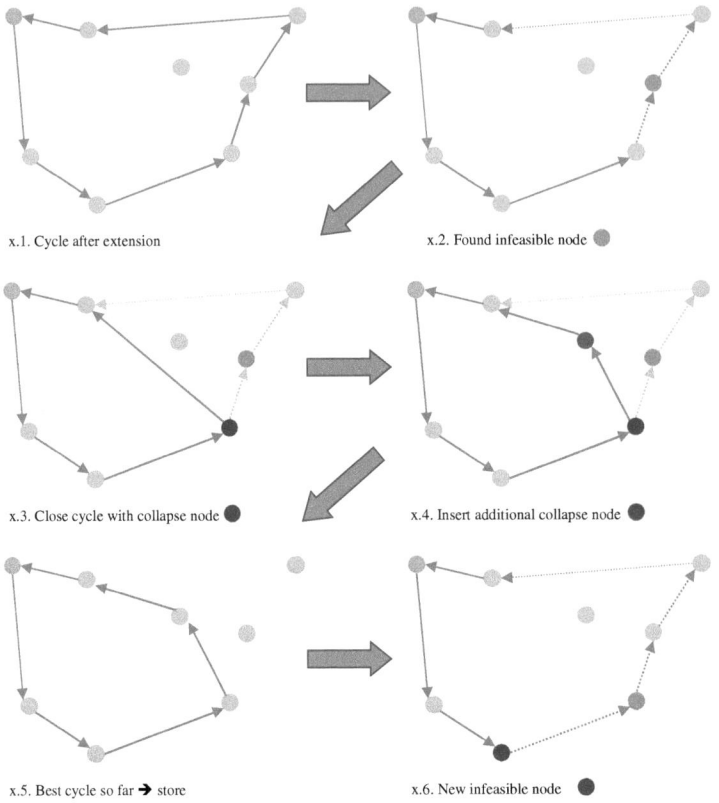

x.1. Cycle after extension

x.2. Found infeasible node

x.3. Close cycle with collapse node

x.4. Insert additional collapse node

x.5. Best cycle so far ➔ store

x.6. New infeasible node

Figure 92: Collapse and extension cycles [Stille (2001)]

The TourPlanResponse is similar to the request despite that fact that it contains a set of tour elements instead of the weighted graph. Those tour elements refer to individual edges of type *EdgeType* in the graph (see Figure 79).

Chapter 6. Personalized City Tours

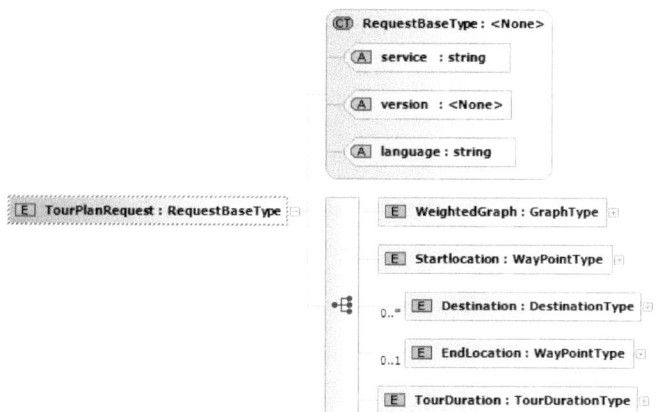

Figure 93 WPS Tour Planner – *TourPlanRequest*

6.3.2.7. Tour Proposal Service – *DetermineTourResponse*

After having revived a computed tour proposal from the *WPS Tour Planner*, the *WPS TourProrosal* prepares the final tour result be means of computing its visual or textual representation. The result is incorporated in the *DetermineTourResponse*. This response is comprised of summary of the tour, an optional handle to the tour as reference for a later usage and a list of tour destinations.

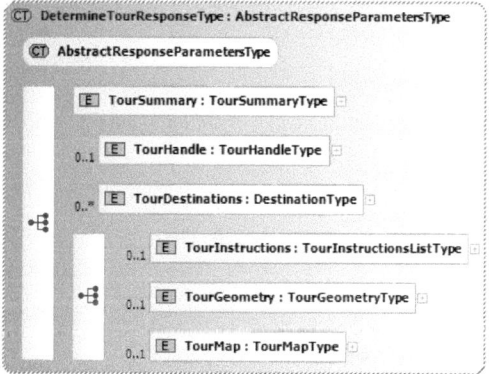

Figure 94: DetermineTourResponse

Generally there are two types of destinations, those that are defined previously by the user and those that are suggested by the tour proposal service. A more precise definition of this service element can be seen in Figure 88. With regard to the major building blocks this response is analogous to the OpenLS RouteResponse except for the tour destinations that refer to locations to be visited during the tour (see Figure 94).

The tour summary (see Figure 95) depicts the core characteristics of the tour by means of the overall duration, distance, elevation, locomotion type, its spatial extent and number of locations to be visited. Duration as such refers not only to the time needed to follow the tour given the specified locomotion type but also the time for visiting points of interest.

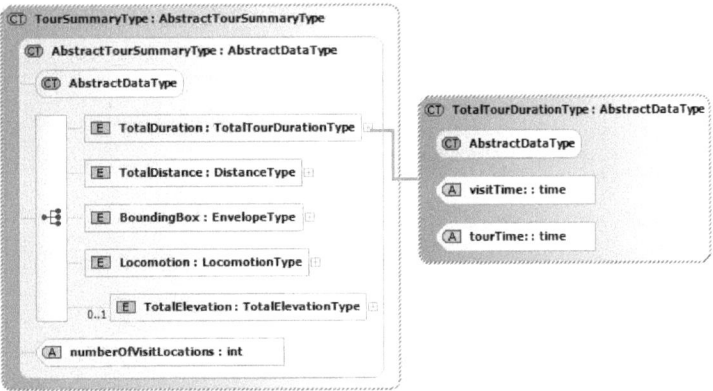

Figure 95: DetermineTourResponse – TourSummary and TourDuration

The visiting time can reflect initial inputs by the user at the service request or estimations according to the point of interest type. Distance measure, elevation (up and down) and the bounding box represent the spatial properties of tour.

Final outcome of the tour proposal service can contain three main elements: First a list of turn by turn tour instructions, second tour geometry or third a map visualizing the tour. The instruction list is comprised of individual turn by turn instructions that emphasize specifically on pedestrian way finding.

In contrast to the car navigation oriented *RouteInstructionType* that has its orientation via distance measures along the route can a tour instruction also refer to position values. Furthermore it allows for incorporation of Points of interest as landmarks.

Chapter 6. Personalized City Tours

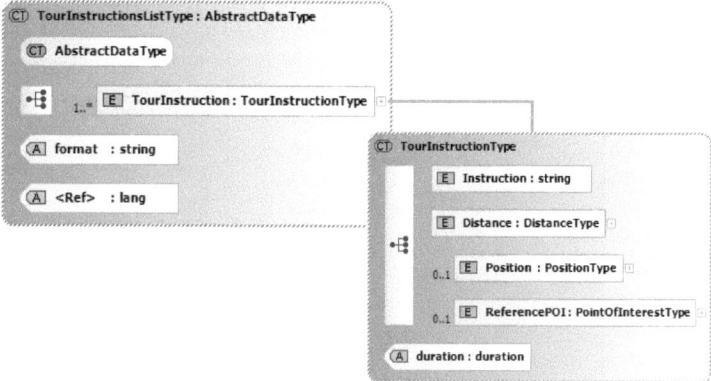

Figure 96: DetermineTourResponse – TourInstructionsList

The TourGeometry similar to the Route Geometry elements of the OpenLS Route Service holds the tour geometry as GML LineString.

Analogously the TourMap element is similar to OpenLS RouteMap element. It represents general map context definition be means of the spatial extent to be drawn on the map, the output width and size and further attributes like the background color or the file format. This interface specification facilitates facilitates a static, non-adaptive mapping.

Chapter 7. Conclusion

Tourism and especially city tourism is an important phenomenon of our times that poses huge economical, cultural, social and environmental effects. In Germany in 2005 round 1.26 day trips had cities as destinations [DTV (2006)] and in 2006 was the direct economical impact quantified with 78 billion US dollars [TSA (2007)]. Those two figures highlight the scale of today's city tourism.

Studies on the profile of current and "next generation" of travelers reveal a increasing shift towards the usage of digital information services before, during and after a journey. According to [PhocusWright (2008)], these "next generation" travelers are highly educated, affluent, and use heavily mobile devices for taking pictures, text message, access the mobile internet and play mobile video games.

Visitors of cities find themselves in a great dilemma: *What to choose in the wide range of opportunities a city offers given the usually quite limited time budget.* Personalized City tours – which consider preferences and interests of individual visitors while taking context information and spatio-temporal constraints into account - can provide an answer to this dilemma.

Following the geographic tradition this thesis took an integrative approach in order to propose a methodology, architecture and standard specification for the provision of personalized city tours. It investigates broadly facets of personalization and user modeling in information services. Furthermore it files a wide array of context-aware approaches into indoor, outdoor and generic

Chapter 7. Conclusion

frameworks. Personalization and context-awareness are combined into a generic and unify model that serves as foundation for the tour proposal services [Zipf and Jöst (2005)].

After introducing spatial data models and geographic information system this thesis focuses on today's heterogeneous and distributed software environments. It discusses interoperability for spatial data and services with specific emphasis on ontologies. As City tours can be added to the field of Location-based services, an introduction into those is given with specific emphasis on today's services, applications and devices.

Foundation for any navigation services is the graph theory, yet for examples used for computing shortest path tours from A to B. Sightseeing city tours as such pose complex constraints to any routing algorithm, e.g. the tour duration might be limited or the set of locations to be visited is undefined or even unknown. For this reason the mathematical field of Traveling Salesmen Problems is introduced. Those TSPs are NP-complete meaning not solvable in polynomial time. They demand for heuristic solutions that are provided by combinatorial optimization which aims at problem reduction and simplification. This thesis introduces Time Geography – a research field that investigates the spatial and temporal capabilities and restrictions of humans for participating in urban live – as means for reducing combinatorial complexity during a tour generation process.

To allow for an open, interoperable and flexible provision of personalized city tours an extension of the OpenLS specification is proposed. This new OpenLS Framework is founded on the OpenLS Route Service specification. It incorporates a range of new OGC Web Processing Services responsible for dedicated tasks like for example weighting of points of interests or reducing graph complexity.

An OpenLS Tour Proposal Service serves as central element of the processing cascade. During the processing cascade user preferences, context constraints and spatio-temporal constraints are transferred into the spatial by means of a weighted graph. Methods on fusioning of heterogeneous data like analytical hierarchy process [Saaty and Vagas (2001)] or multi-criteria decision analysis [Janssen and Rietveld (1990)] are discussed and a dedicated graph weighting algorithm is proposed.

For computation of the tours as such a heuristic algorithm is proposed that follows an iterative extension/collapse method. It adds and removes potential visit locations until an optimum is reached. This algorithm was proposed by [Stille (2001)] and suggested for personalize city tours by [Jöst and Stille (2002)].

Additionally to the functional aspects for the provision of personalized city tours, the herein presented service framework focuses on openness and compatibility. The services – for example the WPS POI Weighter – can also be used in other usage scenarios like a spatial search. Different implementation could also compete for the best result. A future evaluation of different service implementations of the OpenLS Tour Proposal Framework shall verify the feasibility of the approach. Those complex evaluations are addressed by the OGC by means of official Test Bed Projects that aim at a global participation of institutions and companies submitting service implementations.

The presented OpenLS Tour Proposal Framework – as extension of the OpenLS Specification – focuses on the aspect of tour generation while leaving out the subsequent tour presentation. In recent years mapping services and frameworks have been introduced that could complement the presented approach for personalized city tours with adaptive mapping into a generic framework for the personalized and context-aware provisioning of spatial information. [Zipf (2002)] introduced a framework for adaptive map generation. It follows a multistage process describing the base map generation, task and user specific overlays e.g. labels, symbols, routes and presentation constrained posed by the output devices. [Reichenbach (2001, 2004)] focuses specifically on the adaptation process of spatial information visualization as such. A wide array of research articles target at the problem of pedestrian way finding and landmark selection. Nothegger et al. introduced the concept of salience of features. Their approach tries to mimic human landmark selection while addressing different aspects of a landmark. It considers visual, semantic, structural and upfront visibility during tour execution [Nothegger, et al. (2004)]. An approach by Kolbe emphasizes on visual attractiveness of potential landmarks by means of visual attributes like form factor, color, expressiveness [Kolbe (2004)]. Data mining is employed by Elias, who used a classification algorithm on ALK data and 3D sceneries that where generated from airborne lasers can data [Elias (2006)].

In most real life scenarios, tourist discover not only as pedestrian a city but employ also public transportation to visit sights or to commute from their hotels to the city center. A future extension of the presented framework could focus also on multimodal city tours.

The presentation of the city tours is facilitated by the OGC presentation service which basically encapsulate web mapping services. Another extension of this OpenLS Tour Service could address aspects of adaptive and multimodal user interfaces and presentations, as for example proposed by Oviatt, et al 2004.

References

[Aamodt and Plaze (1994)]
Aamodt, A., and Plaza, E. (1994): Case-Based Reasoning: Foundational Issues, Methodological Variations, and System Approaches. In: *Artificial Intelligence Communications*, 7 (1), pp. 39 – 59.

[ABI Research (2008)]
Abi Research, found on 11/25/2008 at: http://www.abiresearch.com/products/market_research/Consumer_Navigation_Systems_and_Devices

[Abowd, et al. (1997)]
Abowd, G. D., Atkeson, C. G., Hong, J., Long, S., Kooper, R., and Pinkerton, M. (1997): Cyberguide: A Mobile Context-Aware Tour Guide. In: GVU Center, Georgia Institute of Technology, *Technical Report*. GITGVU-96-27.

[Abowd (2000)]
G. D. Abowd, (2000): Classroom 2000: An Experiment with the Instrumentation of a Living Educational. In: *IBM Systems Journal – Special issue on HCI / Pervasive computing*, Volume 38, Number 4, pp. 508 – 530.

[Abu-Hakima (1993)]
Abu-Hakima, S. (1993): The Use of Context in Diagnostic Systems. In: *Proceedings of the IJCAI-93 Workshop on Using Knowledge in its Context*, Research Report 93/13, Laforia University Paris 6, pp. 13 – 20.

[Alexandroff (1961)]
Alexandroff, P. (1961): *Elementary Concepts of Topology*, Dover Publications, Inc., New York, NY.

[Ahn, et al. (2008)]
Ahn, J., Brusllovsky, P., He, D., Grady, J., and Li, Q. (2008): Personalized Web Exploration with Task Models. In: *Proceeding of the 17th International Conference on World Wide Web*, Beijing, China.

[Aleksandrov, et al. (2000)]
Aleksandrov, L., Maheshwari, A., and Sack, J. (2000): Approximation Algorithms for Geometric Shortest Path Problems. In: *Proceedings of the Thirty-Second Annual ACM Symposium on Theory of Computing*, Portland, Oregon, United States.

[Allen and Perrault (1980)]
Allen, J. F. and Perrault, C. R. (1980): Analyzing Intentions in Utterances. In: *Artificial Intelligence*,15(3), pp. 143 – 178.

[Alspector, et al. (1997)]
Alspector, J., Kolcz, A., & Karunanithi, N. (1997): Feature-Based and Clique-Based User Models for Movie Selection: A Comparative Study. In: *User Modeling and User-Adapted Interaction* 7(4), pp. 279 – 304.

[Antenucci, et al. (1991)]
Antenucci, J., Brown, K. and Crosswell, P. (1991): *Geographic Information Systems - A guide to the technology*. New York.

[Appelgate, et al. (1998)]
Appelgate, D., Bixby, R. Chvatal, V. and Cook, W. (1998): On the Solution of Travelling Salesman Problems. In: *Documenta Mathematica, Extra Volume 1998, III*, pp. 645 – 656.

[Atlas (2007)]
Association for Tourism and Leisure Education, found on 11/13/2007 at http://www.atlas-euro.org/.

[Arens, et al. (1993)]
Arens, Y., Hovy, E., and van Mulken, S. (1993): Structure and Rules in Automated Multimedia Presentation Planning. In: *Proceedings of the 13 International Joint Conference on Artificial Intelligence*, Chambery, France.

[Arnborg, et al. (1993)]
Arnborg, S., Courcelle, B., Proskurowski, A., and Seese, D. (1993): An Algebraic Theory of Graph Reduction. In: *Journal of the ACM* 40, 5. pp. 1134 – 1164.

[Arkin, et al. (1998)]
Arkin, E. M., Mitchell, J. S. B., and Narasimhan, G. (1998): Resource-Constrained Geometric Network Optimization. In: *Proceedings of the 14th Annual ACM Symposium on Computing Geometry*, Minneapolis, Minnesota, USA, pp. 307 – 316.

[Arora (2003)]
Arora. S. (2003): Approximation Schemes for NP-hard Geometric Optimization Problems: A Survey. In: *Mathematical Programming*, 97, pp. 43 – 69.

[Awerbuch et al. (1998)]
Awerbuch, B., Azar, Y., Blum, A., and Vempala, S. (1998): New Approximation Guarantees for Minimum-Weight k-trees and Prize Collecting Salesmen. In: *SIAM Journal on Computing*, 28(1), pp. 254 – 262.

[Bauer (1996)]
Bauer, M. (1996): Acquisition of User Preferences for Plan Recognition. In: *Proceedings of the Fifth International Conference on User Modeling*. Boston, MA, USA.

[Bala, et al. (1995)]
Bala, J., Huang, J., Vafaie, H., DeJong, K., and Wechsler, H. (1995): Hybrid Learning Using Genetic Algorithms and Decision Tress for Pattern Classification. In: *Proceedings of the 14th International Joint Conference on Artificial Intelligence, IJCAI*, Montreal, Canada, pp. 719 – 724.

[Baldauf, et al. (2007)]
Baldauf, M., Dustdar, S., Rosenberg, F. (2007); A Survey on Context Aware Systems. In: *International Journal of Ad Hoc and Ubiquitous Computing*, Vol. 2, No. 4, pp. 263 – 277.

[Balke, et al. (2003)]
Balke, W., Kießling, W., and Unbehend, C. (2003): A Situation-Aware Mobile Traffic Information System. In: *Proceedings of the 36th Annual Hawaii international Conference on System Sciences*, Hawaii, USA.

[Baumann (1994)]
Baumann, P. (1994): Management of Multidimensional Discrete Data. In: *Very Large Databases Journal 3*, 4, pp. 401– 444.

[Bardram (2005)]
Bardram, J. E (2005): The Java Context Awareness Framework (JCAF)—A Service Infrastructure and Programming Framework for Context-Aware Applications. In: Gellersen, H., Want, R., and Schmidt, A., (Eds.): *Proceedings of the 3rd International Conference on Pervasive Computing*, Lecture Notes in Computer Science, Munich, Germany, May 2005. Springer Verlag.

References

[Battig and Montagues (1968)]
Battig, W. F., and Montague, W. E., (1968): Category Norms for Verbal Items in 56 Categories: A Replication and Extension of the Connecticut Norms. In: *Journal of Experimental Psychology*, 80, No. 3, Part 2, pp. 1 – 46.

[Bellavista, et al. (2006)]
Bellavista, P., Corradi, A., Montanari, R., and Stefanelli, C. (2006): A Mobile Computing Middleware for Location- and Context-Aware Internet Data Services. In: *ACM Transactions on Internet Technologies*, 6, 4, pp. 356 – 380.

[Bellman (2003)]
Bellman, R. E. (2003): *Dynamic Programming*. Courier Dover Publications, Mineola, New York

[Benthien (1997)]
Benthien, B. (1997): *Geographie der Erholung und des Tourismus*. Gotha: Justus Perthes.

[Bieger (2005)]
Bieger, Th. (2005): *Management von Destinationen*. München: Oldenbourg.

[Bidel, et al. (2003)]
Bidel, S., Lemoine, L., and Piat, F. (2003): Statistical Machine Learning for Tracking Hypermedia User Behavior. In: *Proceedings of the 2nd workshop on machine learning, information retrieval and user modeling*, pp. 56 – 65.

[Bishr (1998)]
Bishr, Y. (1998): Overcoming the Semantic and Other Barriers to GIS Interoperability. In: *International Journal of Geographical Information Science*, 12, pp. 299 – 314.

[Blessing, et al. (2006)]
Blessing, A., Klatt, S., Nicklas, D., Volz, S., Schütze, H. (2006): Language-Derived Information and Context Models. In: *Proceedings of 3rd IEEE PerCom Workshop on Context Modeling and Reasoning*.

[Bobick, et al. (1999)],
Bobick, A., et al. (1999):The KidsRoom: A Perceptually-Based Interactive and Immersive Story Environment. In: *Presence*, 8 (4), pp. 369 – 393.

[Bolchini, et al. (2007)]
Bolchini, C., Curino, C. A., Quintarelli, E., Schreiber, F. A., and Tanca, L. (2007): A data-oriented survey of context models. In: *SIGMOD Records*. 36 (4), pp. 19 – 26.

[Bolt (1980)]
Bolt, R. A. (1980): Put-that-there: Voice and gesture at the graphics interface. In: *Computer Graphics*, 14 (3), pp. 262 – 270.

[Bondy and Murty (1976)]
Bondy, J. A., and Murty, U. S. R. (1976): *Graph theory with applications*. Elsavier Science Publishing Co., Inc., New York.

[Boy (1991) a]
Boy, G. (1991): Intelligent Assistant Systems. In: *Knowledge-Based Systems Series*, Vol. 6, Academic Press, London.

[Boyle and Encarnacion (1994)]
Boyle, C. and Encarnacion, A. O., (1994): Metadoc: An Adaptive Hypertext Reading System. In: *User Modeling and User-Adapted Interaction*, 4(1), pp. 1 – 19.

[Boucelma, et al. (2003)]
Boucelma, O., Garinet, J. and Lacroix, Z. (2003): The VirGIS WFSBased Spatial Mediation System. In: *Proceedings of 12th ACM Conference on Information and Knowledge*. New Orleans, Lousianna, USA.

[Brachman (1979)]
Brachman, R. J. (1979): On the Epistemological Status of Semantic Networks. In: Findler, N. V. (Ed.) *Associative Networks: Representation and Use of Knowledgeby Computers*. Academic Press: 3-50.

[Brézillion (2002)]
Brézillion, P. (2002): Context in Problem Solving: A Survey. In: *Knowledge Engineering Review*. 14, 1, pp. 47 – 80.

[Brimicombe (2002)]
Brimicombe, A. J., (2002): GIS - Where are the Frontiers now? In: *Proceedings GIS 2000*, Bahrain, pp. 33 – 45.

[Brown, et al. (1990)]
Browne, D., M. Norman, M., Riches, D., (1990): Why Build Adaptive Systems? In: Browne, D., Totterdell, P., Norman, M., (Eds.): *Adaptive User Interfaces*. Academic Press, London, 1990, pp. 15 – 57.

[Brox, et al. (2002)]
C. Brox,, Y. Bishr, W. Kuhn, K. Senkler & K. Zens (2002): Toward a Geospatial Data Infrastructure for Northrhine-Westphalia. In: *Computer, Environment and Urban Systems* 26: pp. 19 – 37.

[Brusilovsky (1996)]
Brusilovsky, P. (1996): Methods and Techniques of Adaptive Hypermedia. In: *User Modeling and User-Adapted Interaction* 6 (2-3), pp. 87 – 129.

[Buehler and Farley (1994)]
Buehler, K. and Farley, J. A. (1994): Interoperability of Geographic Data and Processes: The OGIS Approach. In: *StandardView* 2, 3, pp. 163 – 168.

[Buliung and Kanaroglou (2006)]
Buliung, R. N., and Kanaroglou, P.S., (2006): A GIS Toolkit for Exploring Geographies of Household Activity/Travel Behaviour. In: *Journal of Transport Geography* 14, pp. 35 – 51.

[Burckhardt, et al. (1983)]
Burckhardt, J. J., Euler, L., and Jenni, M., (1983): Leonhard Euler, 1707-1783: Beiträge zu Leben und Werk - Gedenkband des Kantons Basel Stadt, found on 01/14/2008 at http://books.google.de/books?id=vi7me3h-KCkC

[Burns (1979)]
Burns, L. D. (1979): *Transportation, Temporal, and Spatial Components of Accessibility*. Lexington Books, Lexington

[Byun and Cheverst (2001)]
Byun H.E. and K. Cheverst (2001): Exploiting User Models and Context-Awareness to Support Personal Daily Activities. In: *Proceedings of International Workshop on User Modeling for Context-Aware Applications*. Sonthofen, Germany.

[Cahour and Karsenty (1993)]
Chaour, B. and Karsenty, L. (1993): Context of Dialogue: A Cognitive Point of View. In: *Proceedings of the IJCAI, Workshop on Using Knowledge in its Context*. Technical Report, 93/13, Laforia University Paris 6, pp. 20 – 29.

[Carberry (1990)]
Carberry, S. (1990): Incorporating Default Inferences into Plan Recognition. In: *Proceedings of the Eighth National Conference on Artificial Intelligence*, Boston, MA, USA, pp. 471 – 478.

[Carrol and Rosson (1987)]
Carroll, J.M. and Rosson, M.B. (1987): Paradox of the Active User. In: Carroll, J. M., (Ed.), *Interfacing Thought: Cognitive Aspects of Human-Computer Interaction*. Bradford Books/MIT Press, 1987

[Carver (1991)]
Carver, S.J. (1991): Integrating Multi-criteria Evaluation with Geographical Information Systems. In: *International Journal of Geographical Information Systems* 5(3). pp. 321 – 339.

[Chan (2007)]
Chan, T. M. (2007): More Algorithms for All-pairs Shortest Paths in Weighted Graphs. In: *Proceedings of the Thirty-Ninth Annual ACM Symposium on theory of Computing*. San Diego, California, USA.

[Chao, et al. (1996)]
Chao I-M., Golden B.L., and Wasil E. A., (1996): A Fast and Effective Heuristic for the Orienteering Problem. In: *European Journal of Operational Research*. Vol. 88, pp. 475-489.

[Chen (1995)]
Chen, D. Z. (1995): On the all-pairs Euclidean short path problem. In: *Proceedings of the Sixth Annual ACM-SIAM Symposium on Discrete Algorithms*. San Francisco, California, USA.

[Chen, et al. (2003)]
Chen, H., Finin, T., and Joshi, A. (2003): Using OWL in a Pervasive Computing Broker. In: *Proceedings of Workshop on Ontology's in Open Agent Systems*. Melbourne, Australia.

References

[Chen, et al. (2004)]
Chen, G., Li, M. and Kotz, D. (2004): Design and Implementation of a Large Scale Context Fusion Network. In: *Proceedings of the First Annual International Conference on Mobile and Ubiquitous Systems: Networking and Services*. Boston, MA, USA.

[Chen and Har-Peled (2006)]
Chen, K. and Har-Peled, S. (2006): The Orienteering Problem in the Plane Revisited. In: *Proceedings of the Twenty-Second Annual Symposium on Computational Geometry*. Sedona, Arizona, USA.

[Cheverest, et. al (1998)]
Cheverest, K., Davies, N., and Mitchel, K., (1998): Design of an Object Model for a Context sensitive tour GUIDE, Distributed Multimedia Research Group, Department of Computing, University of Lancaster, UK.

[Cheverest, et. al (2000)]
Cheverest, K., Davies, N., Mitchell, K., Friday, A., Efstratiou, C. (2000): Developing a Context-aware Electronic Tourist Guide: Some Issues and Experiences, Distributed Multimedia Research Group, Department of Computing, University of Lancaster, UK.

[Chin (1993)]
Chin, D. N., (1993): Acquiring User Models. In: *Artificial Intelligence Review*, 7, pp. 185 – 197.

[Churchil, et al. (2004)]
Churchill, E. F., Nelson, L., Denoue, L., Helfman, J. and Murphy, P., (2004): Sharing Multimedia Content with Interactive Public Displays: A Case Study. In: *Proceedings of the 2004 conference on Designing interactive systems: processes, practices, methods, and techniques*. Cambridge, MA, USA.

[Cocchiarella (1991)]
Cocchiarella, N. B. (1991): Formal Ontology. In: Burkhardt, H., and Smith, B., (Eds.): *Handbook of Metaphysics and Ontology*. Philosophia Verlag, Munich.

[Connor (2001)]
Connor, D. O. R. (2001): *Shortest Path Algorithms*. Lecture Notes.

[Comert (2004)]
Comert, C. (2004): Web Services and National Spatial Data Infrastructure (NSDI). *In: Proceedings of Geo-Imagery Bridging Continents, XXth ISPRS Congress*. Istanbul, Turkey.

[Cooper (1981)]
Cooper, C. P. (1981): Spatial and Temporal Patterns of Tourist Behaviour. In: *Regional Studies* 15 (H. 5).

[Cormen, et al. (2007)]
Cormen, T. H., Leiserson, C. E., Rivest, R. L., and Stein, C. (2007): *Introduction to Algorithms*. McGraw-Hill, 2nd Edition.

[Couclelis (1992)]
Couclelis, H. (1992): People Manipulate Objects (but Cultivate Fields): Beyond the Raster-Vector Debate in GIS. In: Frank, A. U., Campari, I., and Formentini, U. (Eds.): *Proceedings of the international Conference GIS - From Space to Territory: Theories and Methods of Spatio-Temporal Reasoning in Geographic Space*. Lecture Notes in Computer Science, vol. 639. Springer-Verlag, London, pp 65 – 77.

[Cost and Salzberg (1993)]
Cost, S., and Salzberg, S. (1993): A Weighted Nearest Neighbor Algorithm for Learning with Symbolic Features. In: *Machine Learning*. 10, pp. 57 – 78.

[Cziferszky and Winter (2002)]
Cziferszky, A and Winter, S., (2002): Automatisches Generieren von Wanderrouten. In: Strobl, J.; Blaschke, T.; Griesebner, G. (Eds.): *Angewandte Geographische Informationsverarbeitung XIV*. Wichmann, Heidelberg, pp. 77-86.

[Dale, et al. (2003)]
Dale, R., Geldof, S., and Prost, J.-P. (2003): CORAL: Using Natural Language Generation for Navigational Assistance. In: Oudshoorn, M. (Ed.), *Proceedings of the 26th Australasian Computer Science Conference (ACSC2003)*. Adelaide, Australia.

[Davidyuk, et al. (2004)]
Davidyuk, O., Riekki, J., Rautio, V., and Sun, J. (2004): Context-aware Middleware for mobile multimedia applications. In: *Proceedings of the 3rd international Conference on Mobile and Ubiquitous Multimedia.* College Park, Maryland, USA.

[Davies, at al. (2005)]
Davies, N., Cheverst, K., Dix, A. and Hesse, A., (2005): Understanding the Role of Image Recognition in Mobile Tour Guides. In: *Proceedings of MobileHCI'2005.* Salzburg, Austria, pp. 191 – 198.

[Deitch and Ladny (2000)]
Deitch, R. and Ladany, S. P. (2000): The One-Period Bus Routing Problem: Solved by an Effective Heuristic for the Orienteering Tour Problem and Improvement Algorithm. In: *European Journal of Operations Research* 127, pp. 69 – 77.

[Dell'Amico et al. (1995)]
Dell'Amico, M., Maffioli, F., and V¨arbrand, P. (1995): On Prize-Collecting Tours and the Asymmetric Travelling Salesman Problem. In: *International Transactions in Operational Research,* 2(3), pp. 297 – 308.

[Dettmer (2000)]
Dettmer, H. et al. (2000): *Tourismustypen.* München, Wien, Oldenbourg.

[Desvinges (1991)]
Desvinges, M., Revenu, M., Porquet, C. (1991): The Use of Context in Image Sequences Interpretation. In: *Proceedings of the 3rd IEE International Conference on Image Processing and Applications.* Barcelona, Spain. pp. 467 – 472.

[Dey, et al. (1998)]
Dey, A., Abowd, G., Pinkerton, M., Wood, A., (1998): CyberDesk: A Framework for Providing Self-Integrating Ubiquitous Software Services. In: *Proceedings of the International Conference on Intelligent User Interfaces.* San Francisco, California, USA.

[Dey and Abowd (1999)]
Dey, A. K. and Abowd, G. D. (1999): Towards a Better Understanding of context and context-awareness, Technical Report GIT-GVU-99-22, Georgia Institute of Technology, College of Computing.

[Dey, et al. (1999)]
Dey, A.K., et al. (1999): The Conference Assistant: Combining Context – Awareness with Wearable Computing. In: *Proceedings of the 3rd International Symposium on Wearable Computers.* San Francisco, California, USA.

[Diaby and Ramesh (1995)]
Diaby, M. and Ramesh, R. (1995): The Distribution Problem with Carrier Service: A Dual Based Penalty Approach. In: *ORSA Journal on Computing 7(1),* pp. 24 – 35.

[Dietvorst (1995)]
Dietvorst, A., (1995): Tourist Behaviour and the Importance of Time-Space Analysis. In: Ashworth, G. J., and Dietvorst, A., (Eds.): *Tourism and spatial transformations. Implications for policy and planning.* Wallingford, pp. 163–182.

[Dijst and Vidakovice (1997)]
Dijst, M. and Vidakovic, V. (1997): Individual Action-Space in the City. In: Ettema D.F. and Timmermans, H.J.P. (Eds.): *Activity-Based Approach to Travel Analysis.* Elsevier Science Ltd., pp. 117 – 134.

[Dijst and Vidakovic (2000)]
Dijst, M. and Vidakovic, V. (2000): Travel Time Ratio: The Key Factor of Spatial Reach. In: *Transportation* 27, pp. 179 – 199.

[Dobosiewics (1990)]
Dobosiewicz. W. (1990): A more Efficient Algorithm for the Min-Plus Multiplication. In: *International Journal on Computer Mathematics, 32,* pp. 49–60.

[Dolog, et al. (2004)]
Dolog, P., Henze, N., Nejdl, W., and Sintek, M. (2004): Personalization in Distributed E-Learning Environments. In: *Proceedings of the 13th international World Wide Web Conference on Alternate Track Paper, Posters,* New York, NY, USA.

References

[Dragunov, et al. (2005)]
Dragunov, A. N., Dietterich, T. G., Johnsrude, K., McLaughlin, M., Li, L., and Herlocker, J. L. (2005): TaskTracer: A Desktop Environment to Support Multi-Tasking Knowledge Workers. In: *Proceedings of the 10th International Conference on Intelligent User Interfaces,* San Diego, California, USA.

[Edmonds and Karp (1972)]
Edmonds, J. and Karp, R. M. (1972): Theoretical Improvements in Algorithmic Efficiency for Network Flow Problems. In: *Journal of the ACM* 19, pp. 248 – 264.

[Egenhofer (2002)]
Egenhofer, M. J. (2002): Toward the Semantic Geospatial Web. In: *Proceedings of the 10th ACM International Symposium on Advances in Geographic information Systems.* McLean, Virginia, USA.

[Egenhofer and Herring (1991)]
Egenhofer, M., and Herring, J. (1991): Categorizing Binary Topological Relationships between Regions, Lines, and Points in Geographic Databases. In: *Technical Report.* Department of Surveying Engineering, University of Maine, Orono, ME.

[Elias (2006)]
Elias, B (2006): *Extraction von Landmarken für die Navigation,* Dissertation, Universität von Hannover. Dissertation.

[Encyclopedia Britannica (2007)]
Encyclopedia Britannica (2007): The Graph Theory, found on 01/14/2008 at http://www.britannica.com/eb/article-9037754/graph-theory

[Essid, et al. (2004)]
Essid, M., Boucelma, O., Colonna, F., and Lassoued, Y. (2004): Query Processing in a Geographic Mediation System. In: *Proceedings of the 12th Annual ACM international Workshop on Geographic information Systems,* Washington DC, USA, pp. 101 - 108.

[Fan, et al. (2000)]
Fan, W., Gordon, M. D., and Pathak, P., (2000): Personalization of Search Engine Services for Effective Retrieval and Knowledge Management. In: *Proceedings of the 21st International Conference on Information Systems.* Brisbane, Queensland, Australia.

[Feillet, et al. (2005)]
Feillet, D., Dejax, P., & Gendreau, M. (2005): Traveling Salesman Problems with Profits. In: *Transportation Science.* 39 (2), pp. 188 – 205.

[Fegeas, et al. (1992)]
Fegeas, R. G., Cascio, J. L., and Lazar, R. A., (1992): An Overview of FIPS 173, the Spatial Data Transfer Standard. In: *Cartography and Geographic Information Systems* 19 (5), pp. 278 – 293.

[Finin, et al.(1994)]
Finin, T., Fritzson, R., McKay, D., and McEntire, R., (1994): KQML as an Agent Communication Language. In: *Proceedings of the Third International Conference on Information and Knowledge Management.* Gaithersburg, Maryland, USA.

[Fink, et al. (1998)]
Fink, J., Kobsa, A., and Nill, A., (1998): Adaptable and adaptive information provision for all users, including disabled and elderly people. In: *The New Review of Hypermedia and Multimedia 4,* pp. 163 – 188.

[Fink and Kobsa (2002)]
Fink, J. and Kobsa, A. (2002): User Modeling in Personalized City Tours. In: *Artificial Intelligence Review* 18(1), pp. 33 – 74.

[Flippo, et al. (2003)]
Flippo, F., Krebs, A. and I. Marsic, I., (2003): A Framework for Rapid Development of Multimodal Interfaces. In: *Proceedings of the 5th International Conference on Multimodal Interfaces,* New York, USA.

[Frank (1992)]
Frank, A. U. (1992): Spatial Concepts, Geometric Data Models, and Geometric Data Structures. In: *Computational Geoscience.* 18, 4.

[Frias-Martinez, et al. (2005)]
Frias-Martinez E., Magoulas G., Chen S. and Macredie R., (2005): Modeling Human Behavior. In: *User-Adaptive Systems: Recent Advances Using Soft Computing Techniques, Expert Systems with Applications*, vol. 29(2), pp. 320 – 329.

[Foline, et al. (2007)]
Folino, G., Forestiero, A., Papuzzo, G., and Spezzano, G., (2007): Content-based Mining for Solving Geoprocessing Problems on Grids. In: *Proceedings of the Second Workshop on Use of P2p, GRID and Agents for the Development of Content Networks*. Monterey, California, USA.

[Fonlupt and Nachef (1993)]
Fonlupt, J. and Nachef, A. (1993): Dynamic Programming and the Graphical Traveling Salesman Problem. In: *Journal of the ACM* 40, 5.

[Fonseca, et al. (2000)]
Fonseca, F., Egenhofer, M., Davis, C., and Borges, K., (2000): Ontologies and Knowledge Sharing in Urban GIS. In: *Computer, Environment and Urban Systems* 24(3): pp. 232 – 251.

[Fonseca, et al (2003)]
Fonseca, F., Davis, C. and Camara, G., (2003): Bridging Ontologies and Conceptual Schemas in Geographic Applications Development. In: *Geoinformatica*: 7(4): pp. 355 – 378.

[Foster and Kesselman (1999)]
Foster, I., Kesselman, C. (1999): Computational Grids. In: Kesselman, F., (Eds.): *The Grid: Blueprint for a New Computing Infrastructure*. Morgan-Kaufman.

[Fox, et al. (2000)]
Fox, A., Johanson, B., Hanrahan, P., and Winograd, T., (2000): Integrating Information Appliances into an Interactive Space. In: *IEEE Computer Graphics and Applications*, 20 (3), pp. 54 – 65.

[Francica and Schutzberg (2007)]
Francica, J. and Schutzberg, A. (2007): Podcast: Beyond Local Search, found on 2007/08/18 at: http://www.directionsmag.com/article.php?article_id=2526

[Frank (1997)]
Frank, A. (1997): Spatial Ontology: A Geographical Point of View. In: *Spatial and Temporal Reasoning*. (Stock, O., ed.), Dordrecht, The Netherlands, Kluwer Academic Publishers, pp. 135 – 153.

[Frank and Mark (1991)]
Frank, A., and Mark, D.M. (1991): Language Issues for GIS. In: Maguire, D.J., Goodchild, M.F., & Rhind, D.W., (Eds.): *Geographical Information Systems: Principles and Applications*. Vol. 1, London, Longman Scientific and Technical, pp. 147 – 163.

[Frederickson (1987)]
Frederickson, G. N. (1987): Fast Algorithms for Shortest Paths in Planar Graphs, with Applications. In: *SIAM Journal on Computing*, 16 (6). pp. 1004 - 1022.

[Freytag (2003)]
Freytag, T. (2003): Aktuelle Entwicklungen des Tourismus in Heidelberg - Ergebnisbericht zur Gästebefragung 2001/2002. Geographisches Institut der Universität, Heidelberg.

[Fritsch, et al. (2000)]
Fritsch, D., Klinec, D., and Volz, S., (2000): NEXUS Positioning and Data Management Concepts for Location Aware Applications. In: *Proceedings of the 2nd International Symposium on Telegeoprocessing*, Nice-Sophia-Antipolis, France.

[Gabow (1985)]
Gabow, H. N. (1985): Scaling Algorithms for Network Problems. In: *Journal of Computer and System Sciences*, 31(2). pp. 148 – 168.

[Gal, et al. (2000)]
Gal, C. Le, Martin, J., Lux, A., and Crowley, J. L. (2000): Smart Office: Design of an Intelligent Environment. In: *IEEE Intelligent Systems*, 16 (4).

References

[Garlan and Sousa (2002)]
Garlan, D. and Sousa, J. P., (2002): Aura: an Architectural Framework for User Mobility in Ubiquitous Computing Environments, School of Computer Science, Carnegie Mellon University, Pittsburg

[Gauch, et al. (2006)]
Gauch, S., Speretta, M., and Pretschner, A., (2006): Ontology-Based User Profiles for Personalized Search. In: Kishore, R., Ramesh, R., and Sharman, R. (Eds.): *Ontologies in the Context of Information Systems*, Springer Verlag.

[Gajos and Weld (2005)]
Gajos, K. and Weld, D. S. (2005): Preference Elicitation for Interface Optimization. In: *Proceedings of the 18th Annual ACM Symposium on User interface Software and Technology*, Seattle, WA, USA.

[Gass (1984)]
Gass S. (Ed.) (1984): *Linear Programming: Methods and Applications*, McGraw-Hill, Inc., New York, 5th Edition.

[Gensch (1978)]
Gensch, D. H. (1978): An Industrial Application of the Traveling Salesman Subtour problem. In: *AIIE Trans.* 10(4) pp. 362 – 370.

[Geertman and Van Eck (1995)]
Geertman, S. C. M. and Van Eck, J. R. R. (1995): GIS and Models of Accessibility Potential: An Application in Planning. In: *International Journal of Geographical Information Systems*, 9, pp. 67 – 80.

[Gibson (1977)]
Gibson, J. (1977): The Theory of Affordances. In: Shaw, R. and Bransford, J. (Eds.): *Perceiving, Acting, and Knowing - Toward an Ecological Psychology*. pp. 67-82, Lawrence Erlbaum Ass., Hillsdale, New Jersey.

[GNTB (2007)]
GNTB/Anholt-GMI, Nation Brands Index 2006, USA 2007

[GNTB/WTM (2005)]
GNTB/IPK-International, World Travel, Monitor/In-Flight-Survey 2005, Malta 2007, USA 200

[Goemans and Williamson (1992)]
Goemans, M. and Williamson, D., (1992): A General Approximation Technique for Constrained Forest Problems. In: *Proceedings of the 3rd ACM-SIAM – Symposium on Discrete Algorithms*, pp. 307 – 315.

[Golden, et al. (1984)]
Golden B.L., Assad A., and Dahl R., (1984): Analysis of a Large Scale Vehicle Routing Problem with an Inventory Component. In: *Large Scale Systems*, 7, pp. 181 – 190.

[Golden, et al. (1987)]
Golden B.L., Levy L., and Vohra R., (1987): The Orienteering Problem. In: *Naval Research Logistics*, 34, pp. 307 – 318.

[Goldenberg (1993)]
Goldberg, A. V. (1993): Scaling Algorithms for the Shortest Paths Problem. In: *Proceedings of the Fourth Annual ACM-SIAM Symposium on Discrete Algorithms*, Austin, Texas, USA.

[Gotz and Mayer-Patel (2004)]
Gotz, D., and Mayer-Patel, K., (2004): A General Framework for Multidimensional Adaptation. In: *Proceedings of the 12th annual ACM international conference on Multimedia*, New York, USA.

[Gu, et al. (2004)]
Gu, T., Pung, H.K. and Zhang, D.Q., (2004): A Middleware for Building Context-Aware Mobile Services. In: *Proceedings of IEEE Vehicular Technology Conference*, Milan, Italy.

[Guarino (1995)]
Guarino, N., (1995): Formal Ontology, Conceptual Analysis and Knowledge Representation. In: *International Journal of Human and Computer Studies*, 43(5/6), pp. 625 – 640.

[Guarino (1997)]
Guarino, N., (1997): Semantic Matching: Formal Ontological Distinctions for Information organization, Extraction, and Integration. In: M. Pazienza, (Ed.), *Information Extraction: A Multidisciplinary Approach to an Emerging Information Technology, International Summer School, SCIE-97*, Frascati, Italy, pp. 139 – 170.

[Guoyong, et al. (2007)]
Guoyong S., Weiwei, C., and Shi, C. J., (2007): A Graph Reduction Approach to Symbolic Circuit Analysis. In: *Proceedings of the 2007 Conference on Asia South Pacific Design Automation with EDA Technofair Design Automation Conference Asia and South Pacific*. IEEE Computer Society, Washington, DC, pp. 197 – 202.

[Graham, et al. (1995)]
Graham, R. L., Grötschel, M., and Lovász, L., (1995): *Handbook of Combinatorics, Volume I*, Elsevier, The MIT Press, Cambridge, Massachusetts.

[Grötschel and Lóvasz (1993)]
Grötschel, M., and Lóvasz, L., (1993): Combinatorial Optimization – A Survey. In: *DIMACS, Technical Report*.

[Groot and McLaughlin (2000)]
Groot, R., and McLaughlin, J., (2000) (Eds.): *Geospatial Data Infrastructure - Concepts, Cases, and Good Practice*. Oxford University Press, Oxford.

[Gruber (1995)]
Gruber, T., (1995): Toward Principles for the Design of Ontology's used for Knowledge Sharing. In: *International Journal Human-Computer Studies*, 43, I(5-6), pp. 907 – 928.

[Haegerstrand (1970)]
Haegerstrand, T., (1970): What about People in Regional Science? In: *Papers of the Regional Science Association* 24, pp. 7 – 21.

[Haeussler and Zipf (2003)]
Haeussler, J., and Zipf, A., (2003): Multimodale Kateninteraktion und inkrementelle Zielführung zur integrierten Navigationsunterstützung für Fußgänger und Autofahrer. In: *Symposium für Angewandte Geographische Informationstechnologie. AGIT 2003*. Salzburg.

[Hakimpour and Timpf (2002)]
Hakimpour, F., and Timpf, S., (2002): A Step towards Geodata Integration using Formal Ontologies. In: *Proceedings of the 5th AGILE Conference on Geographic Information Science*. Palma, Balearic Islands, Spain.

[Hansen, et al. (2006)a]
Hansen, S., Klippel, A., and Richter, K.-F., (2006): Cognitive OpenLS Specification. SFB/TR 8 Spatial Cognition. Technical report No. 012-10/2006.

[Hansen, et al. (2006b)]
Hansen, S., Richter, K-F., and Klippel, A., (2006): Landmarks in OpenLS - A Data Structure for Cognitive Ergonomic Route Directions. In: M. Raubal, H. Miller, A. U. Frank, M. F. Goodchild (Eds.): *Geographic Information Science - Fourth International Conference, GIScience* 2006. pp. 128–144, Lecture Notes in Computer Science 4197. Springer, Berlin.

[Harter and Hopper (1993)]
Harter, A., Hopper, A., (1993): A Distributed Location System for the Active Office, Olivetti Research Ltd (ORL), Cambridge, UK.

[Heckmann (2003)]
Heckmann, D., (2003): Introducing Situational Statements as an Integrating Data Structure for User Modeling, Context-Awareness and Resource-Adaptive Computing. In: ABIS2003, Karlsruhe, Germany.

[Heckmann, et. al (2005)]
Heckmann, D., Schwartz, T., Brandherm, B., Schmitz, M., and von Wilamowitz-Moellendorff, M., (2005): GUMO - the General User Model Ontology. In: *Proceedings of the 10th International Conference on User Modeling*, Edinburgh, UK.

[Heckmann (2005)]
Heckmann, D., (2005): Distributed User Modeling for Situated Interaction. In: *Proceedings of the 35. GI Jahrestagung, Informatik 2005 - Workshop Situierung, Individualisierung und Personalisierung*, ISBN 3-88579-396-2, Bonn, Germany, pp. 266 – 270.

[Heider, T. and Kirste, T. (2002)].
Heider, T., and Kirste, T., (2002): Supporting Goal-Based Interaction with Dynamic Intelligent Environments. In: *Proceedings of the 15th Eureopean Conference on Artificial Intelligence, ECAI'2002*, Lyon, France, pp. 596 – 600.

References

[Hellal, et al. (2005)]
Helal, S., Mann, W., El-Zabadani, H., King, J., Kaddoura, Y., and Jansen, E., (2005): The Gator Tech Smart House: A Programmable Pervasive Space. In: *IEEE Computer*, 38(3), pp. 50 – 60.

[Hirst (1991)]
Hirst, G., (1991): Existence Assumptions in Knowledge Representation. In: *Artificial Intelligence*, 49, pp. 199 – 242.

[Hobbs (1985a)]
Hobbs, J. R., (1985): Granularity. In: *Proceedings of International Joing Conference on Artificial Intelligence*, Los Angeles, California, USA, pp. 432 – 435.

[Hobbs (1985b)]
Hobbs, J. R., (1985): Ontological Promiscuity. In: *Proceedings of the Association of Computer Linguistics 85*, pp. 61 – 69.

[Hopper, et al. (1994)]
Hopper, A., Falcao, V., Gibbons, J., and Roy, W. (1993): The Active Badge Location System, Olivetti Resarch Ltd (ORL), Cambridge, UK.

[Horvitz, et al. (1998)]
Horvitz, E., Breese, J., Heckerman, D., Hovel, D., and Rommelse, K., (1998): The Lumiere Project: Bayesian User Modeling for Inferring the Goals and Needs of Software Users. In: *Proceedings of the Fourteenth Conference on Uncertainty in Artificial Intelligence*, Madison, WI, USA.

[Hsieh (2004)]
Hsieh, N., (2004): An Integrated Data Mining and Behavioral Scoring Model for Analyzing Bank Customers. In: *Expert Systems with Applications*, 27, pp. 623–633.

[Hui-Ting, et al. (2005)]
Hui-Ting, H., Jung-Hong, H., Chia-Yang, S., (2005): Preliminary Analysis for Constructing Geocoder Service in China Taipei. In: *Proceedings of 26th Conference of the Asian Association on Remote Sensing*, Hanoi, Vietnam.

[InternetWorldStats (2007)].
Internet World Statistics, found on (16.11.07) at http://www.internetworldstats.com/emarketing.htm

[Iwanska (1995)]
Iwanska, I., (1995): Summary of the IJCAI'95 Workshop on Context in Natural Language Processing, found on 04/15/05 at: http://www.cs.wayne.edu/summary

[Jameson (1996)]
Jameson, A., (1996): Numerical Uncertainty Management in User and Student Modeling: An Overview of Systems and Issues. In: *User Modeling and User-Adapted Interaction*, 5, pp. 193–251.

[Jaimes and Sebe (2007)]
Jaimes, A. and Sebe, N., (2007): Multimodal Human Computer Interaction: A Survey. In: *Computer Vision and Image Understanding - Special Issue on Vision for Human-Computer Interaction*. Volume 108, pp. 1 – 2.

[Janssen and Rietveld (1990)]
Janssen, R., and Rietveld, P., (1990): Multicriteria Analysis and Geographical Information Systems: An application to Agricultural Land Use in the Netherlands. In: Scholten, H. J. and Stillwell, J. C. H., (Eds.): *Geographical Information Systems for Urban and Regional Planning*. Kluwer Academic Publishers, Dordrecht, pp. 129 – 139.

[Jennings and Wooldridge (1999)]
Jennings, N., Wooldridge, M., (1999): Intelligents Agents: Theory and Practice. In: *The Knowledge Engineering Review*, 10(2).

[Jennings (2001)]
Jenning, N., (2001): An Agent-based Approach for Building Complex Software Systems. In: *Communications of the ACM*, Vol. 44, 4.

[Johnson, et al. (2000)]
Johnson, D. S., Minko, M., and Phillips, S., (2000): The Prize Collecting Steiner Tree Problem: Theory and Practice. In: *Proceedings of the 11th Symposium on Discrete Algorithms*. San Francisco, CA, USA, pp. 760-769.

[Jöst (2000)]
Jöst, M (2000): *Deep Map – Touristeninformationssystem für die Stadt Heidelberg. Systemarchitektur und kommunikation am Beispiel eines Tourenplanungsmoduls.* Zulassungsarbeit, Ruprecht-Karls Universität Heidelberg, Germany

[Jöst and Stille (2002)]
Jöst, M. and Stille, W., (2002): A User-Aware Tour Proposal Framework using a Hybrid Optimization Approach. In: *Proceedings of the 10th ACM International Symposium on Advances in Geographic information Systems.* McLean, Virginia, USA.

[Jöst and Merdes (2004)]
Jöst M, and Merdes, M., (2004): Listening to Agents - Transparent Representation and Presentation of Agent Communication in Mobile Systems. In: Proceedings of the Net.ObjectDays 2004. Leipzig, Germany, pp. 55 – 68.

[Jöst, et. al (2005)]
Jöst, M., Haeussler, J., Merdes, M., and Malaka, R., (2005): Multimodal Interaction for Pedestrians: An Evaluation Study. In: *Proceedings of the International Conference on Intelligent User Interfaces – IUI 2005.* San Diego, CA, USA.

[Joerding (1999)]
Joerding, T., (1999): Temporary User Modeling for Adaptive Product Presentations in the Web. In: *Proceedings of the 7th International Conference on User Modeling.* Banff, Canada.

[Judd and Steenkiste (2003)]
Judd, G., and Steenkiste, P., (2003): Providing Contextual Information to Pervasive Computing Applications. In: *Proceedings of the First IEEE International Conference on Pervasive Computing and Communications.* Fort Worth, Texas, USA.

[Kasper (1996)]
Kaspar, C., (1996): *Die Tourismuslehre im Grundriss.* Bern, Stuttgart, Wien: Haupt.

[Kaspar (1998)]
Kaspar, C., (1998): Das System Tourismus im Überblick. In: Haedrich, G., Kaspar, C., Klemm, K., und Kreilkamp, E. (Hrsg.): *Tourismus-Management.* Berlin, New York: Walter de Gruyter.

[Kaul (1999)]
Kaul, E. (1999): *Sozioökonomische Kategorisierung von Heidelberg Touristen.* Diplomarbeit. Geographisches Institut. Universität Heidelberg.

[Khuller and Raghavachari (1996)]
Khuller, S., and Raghavachari, B., (1996): Graph and Network Algorithms. In: *ACM Computing Survey,* 28, 1, pp. 43 – 45.

[Kemp, at al. (2007)]
Kemp, Z., Tan, L., and Whalley, J., (2007): Interoperability for Geospatial Analysis: A Semantics and Ontology-based Approach. In: *Proceedings of the Eighteenth Conference on Australasian Database.* Ballarat, Victoria, Australia.

[Kidd, et al. (1999)]
Kidd, C., Orr, J. R., Abowd, G. D., Atkeson, C. G., Essa, I. A., MacIntyre, B., Mynatt, E., Starner, T. E., and Newstetter, W., (1990): The Aware Home: A Living Laboratory for Ubiquitous Computing. In: *Proceeding of the 2nd International Workshop on Cooperative Buildings.* Pittsburg, USA.

[Kim and Kwan (2003)]
Kim, H.-M., and Kwan, M.-P., (2003): Space-time Accessibility Measures: A Geocomputational Algorithm with a Focus on the Feasible Opportunity Set and Possible Activity Duration. In: *Journal of Geographical Systems,* 5(1), pp. 71 – 91.

[Kim and Park (2004)]
Kim, S.-S., and Park, J.-H., (2004): Efficient Routing Service for Open LBS Services. In: *Proceedings of the 12th International Conference on Geoinformatics – Geospatial Information Research: Bridging the Pacific and Atlantic.* Gävle, Sweden.

[Kindberg and Barton (2001)]
Kindberg, T., and Barton, J., (2001): A Web-Based Nomadic Computing System. In: *Computer Networks,* 35 (4), pp. 443 – 456.

References

[Kindberg, et al. (2002)]
Kindberg, T., Barton, J., Morgan, J., Becker, G., Caswell, D., Debaty, P., Gopal, G., Frid, M., Krishnan, V., Morris, H., Schettino, J., Serra, B., and Spasojevic, M., (2002): People, Places, Things: Web Presence for the Real World. In: *Mobile Network Applications,* 7, 5.

[Klippel, et al. (2004)]
Klippel, A., Dewey, C., Knauf, M., Richter, K.-F., Montello, D. R., Freksa, C., and Loeliger, E.-A., (2004): Direction Concepts in Wayfinding Assistance Systems. In: Baus, J., Kray, C., Porzel, R. (Eds.): *Workshop on Artificial Intelligence in Mobile Systems 2004 (AIMS'04).* SFB 378, Memo 84, Saarbruecken, Germany, pp. 1 – 8.

[Knights and Lanza (2001)]
Knights, D., and Lanza, J., (2001): Localization and Identification of Visual Landmarks. In: *Proceedings of the Sixth Annual CCSC Northeastern Conference on the Journal of Computing in Small Colleges.* Middlebury, Vermont, United States, pp. 312 - 313.

[Kobsa and Fink (2000)]
Kobsa, A., and Fink, J., (2000): A Review and Analysis of Commercial User Modeling Servers for Personalization on the World Wide Web. In: *User Modeling and User-Adapted Interaction* 10, pp. 209 – 249.

[Kobsa, et al. (2001)]
Kobsa, A., Koenemann, J., Pohl, W., (2001): Personalized Hypermedia Presentation Techniques for Improving Online Customer Relationships. In: *The Knowledge Engineering Review* 16(2), pp. 111 – 155.

[Kölmel and Wirsing (2002)]
Kölmel, B. and Wirsing, M., (2002): Nutzererwartungen an Location-based Services – Ergebnisse einer empirischen Analyse. In: Zipf, A. und Strobl, J. (Hrsg.): *Geoinformation mobil.* Herbert Wichmann Verlag. Heidelberg.

[Kolbe (2004)]
Kolbe, T., (2004): Augmented Videos and Panaorams for Pedestrian Navigation. In: Gartner, G. (Eds.): *Proceedings of the Symposium on Location-based Services and TeleCartography.* Vienna, Austria.

[Kolodziej (2004)]
Kolodziej, K. W., (2004): *OpenLS for Indoor Positioning: Strategies for Standardizing Location-based Services for Indoor Use.* PhD Thesis, MIT.

[Konstan, et al. (1997)]
Konstan, J. A., Miller, B. N., Maltz, D., Herlocker, J. L., Gordon, L. R., and Riedl, J., (1997): GroupLens: Applying Collaborative Filtering to Usenet News. In: *Communications of the ACM,* 40(3), pp. 77 – 87.

[Korpipää and Mäntyjärvi (2003)]
Korpipää, P., and Mäntyjärvi, J., (2003): An Ontology for Mobile Device Sensor-Based Context Awareness. In: Blackburg, P., Ghidinim, C., Turner, R. M., and Giunchiglia, F. (Eds.): *Modeling and Using Context, 4th International and Interdisciplinary Conference, CONTEXT 2003.* Stanford, CA, USA, pp. 451-458

[Kray (2003)]
Kray. C. (2003): *Situated Interaction on Spatial Topics.* PhD Thesis, Akademische Verlags-Gesellschaft AKA, Berlin.

[Kramer (2005)]
Kramer, C. (2005): Zeit für Mobilität. Räumliche Disparitäten der individuellen Zeitverwendung für Mobilität in Deutschland. In: *Erdkundliches Wissen 138,* Stuttgart.

[Krulwich (1995)]
Krulwich, B., (1995): Learning User Interests Across Heterogeneous Document Databases. In: *Proceedings of AAAI Spring Symposium On Information Gathering from Heterogeneus, Distributed Environments.* Stanford, CA, USA.

[Kruskal (1956)]
Kruskal, J. B., (1956): On the Shortest Spanning Subtree of a Graph and the Traveling Salesman Problem. In: *Proceedings of the American Mathematical Society.* Volume 7, No. 1, pp. 48 – 50.

[Kwan and Hong (1998)]
Kwan M.-P. and Hong, X. D., (1998) Network-based Constraints-oriented Choice Set Formation using GIS. In: *Geographical Systems* 5, pp. 139 – 162.

[Kwan (1998)]
Kwan, M.-P., (1998): Space-Time and Integral Measures of Individual Accessibility: A Comparative Analysis Using a Point-Based Framework. In: *Geographical Analysis* 30:3, pp. 191 – 216.

[Landau, et al. (1981)]
Landau, U., Prashker, J. N., and Hirsh, M., (1981): The Effect of Temporal Constrains on Household Travel Behavior. In: *Environment and Planning* A 13, pp. 435 – 448.

[Landau, et al. (1982)]
Landau, U., Prashker, J. N., and Alpern, B., (1982): Evaluation of Activity Constrained Choice Sets to Shopping Destination Choice Modeling. In: *Transportation Research A* 16A, pp. 199 – 207.

[Langheinrich (2007)]
Langheinrich, M., (2007): Gibt es in einer total informatisierten Welt noch eine Privatsphäre? In: Friedemann Mattern (Ed.): *Die Informatisierung des Alltags – Leben in smarten Umgebungen*. Springer, pp. 233 – 264.

[Laporte and Martello (1990)]
Laporte, G. and Martello, S., (1990): The Selective Traveling Salesmen Problem. In: *Discrete Applied Mathematics* 26, pp. 193 – 207.

[Leifer and Rosenwein (1994)]
Leifer, A. C., and Rosenwein, M.B., (1994): Strong Linear Programming Relaxations for the Orienteering Problem. In: *European Journal of Operations Research 73*, pp. 517 – 523.

[Lenntorp (1976)]
Lenntorp, B., (1976): Path in Space-Time Environments: A Time-geographic Study of the Movement Possibilities of Individual. In: *Lund Studies in Geography*. Series B, Number 44.

[Lesh and Etzioni (1995)]
Lesh, N., and Etzioni, O., (1995): A Sound and Fast Goal Recognizer. In: *Proceedings of the Fourteenth International Joint Conference on Artificial Intelligence*. Montreal, Canada. Palo Alto, CA: Morgan Kaufmann, pp. 1704 – 1710.

[Leureiro, et al (2006)]
Loureiro, E., Bublitz, F., Barbosa, N., Perkusich, A., Almeida, H., and Ferreira, G., (2006): A Flexible Middleware for Service Provision over Heterogeneous Pervasive Networks. In: *Proceedings of the 2006 International Symposium on on World of Wireless, Mobile and Multimedia Networks, International Workshop on Wireless Mobile Multimedia*. IEEE Computer Society, Washington, DC, pp. 609 – 614.

[Le Sommer, et al. (2006)]
Le Sommer, N., Guidec, F., and Roussain, H. (2006): A Context-aware Middleware Platform for Autonomous Application Services in Dynamic Wireless Networks. In: *Proceedings of the First international Conference on integrated internet Ad Hoc and Sensor Networks*. Nice, France.

[Lloyd, et al (1996)]
Lloyd, R., Patton, D., and Cammack, R., (1996): Basic-level Geographic Categories. In: *Professional Geographer*. 48: pp. 181 – 194.

[Lohann (1989)]
Lohmann, M., (1989): Städtereisende und Städtereisen - Marktforschung im Städtetourismus. In: *Deutsches Seminar für Fremdenverkehr (Hrsg.): Im Städtetourismus erfolgreich inszenieren!* Berlin.

[Ludwig, et al. (2006)]
Ludwig, B., Mandl, S., and von Mammen, S., (2006): What's on Tonight: User-centered and Situation-aware Proposals for TV Programmes. In: *Proceedings of the 11th International Conference on Intelligent User interfaces*. Sydney, Australia.

[Lutz (2005)]
Lutz, M., (2005): Ontology-based Service Discovery in Spatial Data Infrastructures. In: *Proceedings of the 2005 Workshop on Geographic information Retrieval*. Bremen, Germany.

[Mahalanobis (1940)]
Mahalanobis, P.C., (1940): A Sample Survey of the Acreage Under Jute in Bengal. In: *Sankhyu* 4 (1940), pp. 511 – 530.

[Makin, et al. 1997]
Makin, J., Healey, R.G., Dowers, S., (1997): Simulation Modelling with Object-oriented GIS: A Prototype Application to the Time Geography of Shopping Behavior. In: *Geographical Systems* 4 (4), pp. 397 – 429.

References

[Malaka, et al. (2000)]
Malaka, R., Porzel, R., Zipf, A., and Chandrasekhara, V., (2000): Integration of Smart Components for Building your Personal Mobile Guide. In: *Proceedings of AIMS 2000. Workshop on Artificial Intelligence in mobile Systems*. Berlin, Germany

[Malaka and Zipf (2000)]
Malaka, R., and Zipf, A., (2000): DEEP MAP - Challenging IT Research in the Framework of a Tourist Information System. In: Fesenmaier, D. Klein, S. and Buhalis, D. (Eds.): *Information and Communication Technologies in Tourism 2000. Proceedings of ENTER 2000*. Barcelona, Spain.

[Markupoulos (1997)]
Markupoulos, P., (1997): *A Compositional Model for the Formal Specification of User Interface Software*. PhD thesis, Department of Computer Science, Queen Mary and Westfield College, University of London.

[Markupoulus and Marijnissen (2000)]
Markopoulos, P., Marijnissen, P. (2000): UML as a Representation for Interaction Design. In: *Proceedings of OZCHI 2000*. Sydney, Australia.

[Marmasse and Schmandt (2000)]
Marmasse, N. and Schmandt, C., (2000): Location-aware Information Delivery with comMotion. In: *Proceedings of the HUC 2000*. Bristol, UK, pp. 157 – 171.

[Maskery and Meads (1992)]
Maskery, H., and Meads, J., (1992): Context: In the Eyes of Users and in Computer Systems. In: *SIGCHI Bulletin* 24(2), pp. 12 – 21.

[Maskery et al. (1992)]
Maskery, H., Hopkins, G., and Dudly, T. (1992): Context: What does it mean to Application Design. In: *SIGCHI Bulletin* 24(2), pp. 22 – 30.

[Mayhew (1997)]
Mayhew, S., (1997): *A Dictionary of Geography*. Oxford, New York: Oxford University Press.

[Middleton, et al. 2004)]
Middleton, S. E., Shadbolt, N. R., and De Roure, D. C. (2004): Ontological User Profiling in Recommender Systems. In: *ACM Transactions on Information Systrmd* 22, 1, pp. 54 – 88.

[Miller (2005)]
Miller, H. J., (2005): Place-based versus People-based Accessibility. In: Levinson D. and Krizek, K. J., (Eds.): *Access to Destinations*. London, Elsevier, pp. 63 - 89.

[Miller (1991)]
Miller, H. J., (1991): Modelling Accessibility Using Space-time Prism Concepts within Geographical Information Systems. In: *International Journal of Geographical Information Systems* 5, pp. 287 – 301.

[Miller (1999)]
Miller, H. J., (1999): Measuring Space-time Accessibility Benefits within Transportation Networks: Basic Theory and Computational Methods. In: *Geographical Analysis* 31, pp. 187 – 212.

[Miller and Johnson-Laird (1976)]
Miller, G. A., and Johnson-Laird, P. N., (1976): *Language and Perception*. Cambridge, MA: Harvard University Press.

[Mittal and Paris (1995)]
Mittal, V. O. and Paris, C. L., (1995): Use of Context in Explanations Systems. In: *International Journal of Expert Systems with Applications*, 8(4), pp. 491 – 504.

[Min, et al. (2001)]
Min, H., Smolinski, T., and Boratyn, G., (2001): A GA-based Data Mining Approach to Profiling the Adopters of E-Purchasing. In: *Proceedings of the 2001 IEEE International Conference on Information Reuse and Integration*. LasVegas, Nevada, USA.

[Moore (1978)]
Moore, W. G., (1978): *A Dictionary of Geography: Definitions and Explanations of Terms Used in Physical Geography*. Barnes and Noble Books, New York, 2nd Edition.

[Musser and Osman (2003)]
Musser, D. R. and Osman, B., (2003): Algorithm Concepts, found on 11/15/2008 at: http://www.cs.rpi.edu/~musser/gp/algorithm-concepts/

[Naguib, et al. (2001)]
Naguib, H., Coulouris, G. and Mitchell, S., (2001): Middleware Support for Context-Aware Multimedia Applications. In: *Proceedings of the IFIP TC6 / WG6.1 Third International Working Conference on New Developments in Distributed Applications and Interoperable Systems*. Berlin, Germany, pp .9-22.

[Nasraoui and Petenes (2003)]
Nasraoui O., and Petenes C., (2003): Combining Web Usage Mining and Fuzzy Inference for Website Personalization. In: *Proceedings of WebKDD 2003 – KDD Workshop on Web mining as a Premise to Effective and Intelligent Web Applications*. Washington DC, USA.

[Neis and Zipf (2007)]
Neis, P., and Zipf, A. (2007): Realizing Focus Maps with Landmarks using OpenLS Services. In: *4th International Symposium on LBS and Telecartography*. 2007. Hongkong, China.

[Neis, et al. (2007)]
Neis, P., Schilling, and Zipf, A., (2007): 3D Emergency Route Service (3D-ERS) based on OpenLS Specifications. In: *3rd International Symposium on Geoinformation for Disaster Management, GI4DM07*. Toronto, Canada.

[Neis and Zipf (2007)]
Neis, P., and Zipf, A., (2007): A Web Accessibility Analysis Service based on the OpenLS Route Service. In: *International Conference on Geographic Information Science of the Association of Geograpic Information Laboratories for Europe (AGILE)*. Aalborg, Denmark.

[Newell (1982)]
Newell, A., (1982): The Knowledge Level. In: *Artificial Intelligence*, 18, pp. 87-127.

[Niaraki and Kim (2008)]
Niaraki, A. S., and Kim, K., (2008): Ontology-based Personalized Route Planning System using a Multi-criteria Decision Making Approach. In: *Expert Systems with Applications* (2008) – In Press.

[Nielson Media (2007)]
Nielson Media: found on 11/24/07 at http://www.telephia.com/html/NielsenMobileRebrand.html

[Norman (1988)]
Norman, D., A., (1988): Psychology of Everyday Action. In: *The Design of Everyday Things*. New York: Basic Book, 1988. pp. 45 – 46.

[Norvig and Russel (2003)]
Norvig, P., and Russel, S. J., (2003): *Artificial Intelligence: A Modern Approach*. Prentice Hall, 2nd Edition.

[Nothergger, et al. (2004)]
Nothegger, C., Winter, S., and Raubal, M., (2004): Computation of the Salience of Features. In: *Spatial Cognition and Computation*, 4(2), pp. 113 – 136.

[Nunes (1991)]
Nunes, J., (1991): Geographic Space as a Set of Concrete Geographical Entities. In: Mark, D., and Frank, A., (Eds.): *Cognitive and Linguistic Aspects of Geographic Space*. Kluwer Academic, pp. 9 – 33.

[Nutter (1987)]
Nutter, J. T. (1987): Epistemology. In: S. Shapiro (Ed.) *Encyclopedia of Artificial Intelligence*. John Wyley.

[Odgen and Richards (1946)]
Odgen, C. K., and Richards, I. A., (1946): *The Meaning of Meaning*. Routledge & Kegan Paul LTD, London, 8th Edition.

[OGC OpenLS (2004)]
The OpenLocation Specification, found on 2004/07/11 at: http://www.opengeospatial.org/standards/olscore

[OGC WPS (2005)]
Web Processing Service, found on 2005/04/19, at: http://www.opengeospatial.org/standards/requests/28

[OGC History (2007)]
The OGC History, found on 2007/10/23 at: http://www.opengeospatial.org/ogc/history

References

[OGC GML (2007)]
Geographic Markup Language, found on 2007/10/23, at: http://www.opengeospatial.org/standards/gml

[OGC CAT (2007)]
Catalog Service, found on 2007/10/25, at: http://www.opengeospatial.org/standards/cat

[OGC FIL (2007)]
Filter Encoding, found on 2007/10/24, at: http://www.opengeospatial.org/standards/filter

[OGC SLD (2007)]
Styled Layer Descriptor, found on 2007/10/20, at: http://www.opengeospatial.org/standards/sld

[OGC WMS (2007)]
Web Mapping Service, found on 2007/10/20, at: http://www.opengeospatial.org/standards/wms

[OGC (2008)]
OpenGeospatialConsortium – Registered Products, found on 06.02.2008 at:
http://www.opengeospatial.org/resource/products/byspec

[OGC (2008b)]
OpenGeospatialConsortium – OGC WebServices, Phase 6, found on 07.02.2009 at:
http://www.opengeospatial.org/standards/requests/50

[OGC SOS (2008)]
Sensor Observation Service, found on 2009/01/13, at: http://www.opengeospatial.org/standards/sos

[Olson, et al. (1990)]
Olson, J.R., Olson, G.M., (1990): The Growth of Cognitive Modeling in Human-Computer Interaction since GOMS. In: *Human-Computer Interaction*. Vol. 5, pp. 221 – 265.

[Oppermann, et al. (1999)]
Oppermann, R., Specht, M. Jaceniak, I., (1999): Hippie: A Nomadic Information System, GMD, Institute for Applied Information Technology

[Oppermann and Specht (2000)]
Opperman, R. and Specht, M., (1999): User Modeling and Adaptivity in Nomadic Information Systems, GMD, Institute for Applied Information Technology

[Oviatt, et al. (2004)]
Oviatt, S., Coulston, R., and Lunsford, R., (2004): When Do We Interact Multimodally? Cognitive Load and Multimodal Communication Patterns. In: *Proceedings of the Sixth International Conference on Multimodal Interfaces (ICMI 2004)*. Pennsylvania, USA.

[Papakonstantinou, et al. (1995)]
Papakonstantinou, Y., Garcia-Molina, H., and Widom, J., (1995): Object Exchange Across Heterogeneous Information Sources. In: *Proceedings of ICDE Conference*. Taipei, Taiwan, pp. 251 – 260.

[Pascoe (1996)]
Pascoe, J., (1996): The Stick-e Note Architecture: Extending the Interface Beyond the User, Computer Laboratory, University of Kent

[Paul and Ghosh (2006)]
Paul, M., and Ghosh, S. K., (2006): An Approach for Service Oriented Discovery and Retrieval of Spatial Data. In: *Proceedings of the 2006 International Workshop on Service-Oriented Software Engineering*. Shanghai, China.

[Pekny and Miller (1990)]
Pekny, J. F., and Miller, D.L., (1990): An Exact Parallel Algorithm for the Resource Constrained Travelling Salesman Problem with Application to Scheduling with an Aggregate Deadline. In: *ACM 18th Annual Computing Scientific Conference*. pp. 208 – 214.

[Petrusin and Sinitsa (1993)]
Petrushin, V. A., and Sinitsa, K. M., (1993): Using Probabilistic Reasoning Techniques for Learner Modeling. In: P. Brna, S. Ohlsson, & H. Pain (Eds.): *Artificial Intelligence in Education: Proceedings of AIED 93*, Charlottesville, VA, USA, pp. 418 – 425.

[Perkowitz and Etzioni (1998)]
Perkowitz, M., and O. Etzioni, O., (1998): Adaptive Web sites: Automatically Synthesizing Web Pages. In: *Proceedings of Fifteenth National Conference on Artificial Intelligence.* Madison, WI, USA.

[Peuquet (1984)]
Peuquet, D. J., (1984): A Conceptual Framework and Comparison of Spatial Data Models. In: *Cartographica.* pp. 66 – 113.

[Pfaltz, et al. (2003)]
Pfaltz, J. L., Nagl, M., and Böhlen, B., (Eds.): (2003): *Applications of Graph Transformations with Industrial Relevance.* Second Edition, Springer. Heidelberg.

[PhocusWright (2008)]
PhocusWright (2008): The Next Generation Travelers, found on 22.10.2008 at: http://www.phocuswright.com/library/pressrelease/526

[Poslad, et al. (2001)]
Poslad, S., Laamanen, H., Malaka, R., Nick, A., Buckle, P. and Zipf, A., (2001): CRUMPET: Creation of User-Friendly Mobile Services Personalised for Tourism. In: *Proceedings of: 3G 2001 - Second Int. Conf. on 3G Mobile Communication Technologies.* London. UK.

[Pohl, et al. (1995)]
Pohl, W., Kobsa, A., and Kutter, O., (1995): User Model Acquisition Heuristics Based on Dialogue Acts. In: *International Workshop on the Design of Cooperative Systems.* Antibes-Juan-les-Pins, France. pp. 471 – 486.

[Pohl (1998)]
Pohl, W., (1998): Logic-Based Representation and Reasoning for User Modeling Shell Systems. In: *User Modeling and User-Adapted Interaction*, 9 (3).

[Popp and Lödel (1996)]
Popp, H., and Lödel, D., (1996): Fuzzy Techniques and User Modeling in Sales Assistants. In: *User Modeling and User-Adapted Interaction* 5(3-4), pp. 349 – 370.

[Porzel, et al. (2006)]
Porzel, P., Gurevych, I. and Malaka, R., (2006): In Context: Integrating Domain- and Situation-specific Knowledge. In: Wahlster, W. (Ed.) *SmartKom - Foundations of Multimodal Dialogue Systems.* pp. 269 – 284.

[Price, at al (2006)]
Price, B., Greiner, R., Häubl, G., and Flatt, A., (2006): Automatic Construction of Personalized Customer Interfaces. In: *Proceedings of the 11th International Conference on Intelligent User Interfaces.* Sydney, Australia.

[Pretschner (1999)]
Pretschner, A., (1999): *Ontology Based Personalized Search.* Master's thesis, University of Kansas, Lawrence.

[Quack (2004)]
Anton-Quack, C. und Quack, H.-D., (2004): Städtetourismus – eine Einführung. In: Becker, Ch., Hopfinger, H., und Steinecke, A., (Hrsg.): *Geographie der Freizeit und des Tourismus.* München, Wien: Oldenburg. S. 193 – 203.

[Ramesh, et al. (1992)]
Ramesh, R., Yoon, Y.-S., and Karwan, M.H., (1992): An Optimal Algorithm for the Orienteering Tour Problem. In: *Computers and Operations Research* 18. pp. 151 – 165.

[Raptis, et al. (2005)]
Raptis, D., Tselios, N., and Avouris, N., (2005): Context-based design of mobile applications for museums: a survey of existing practices. In: *Proceedings of the 7th international Conference on Human Computer interaction with Mobile Devices and Services.* Salzburg, Austria.

[Rasmussen and Pejtersen (1995)]
Rasmussen, J., and Pejtersen, A., (1995) Virtual Ecology of Work. in: Flack, J., Hancock, P., Caird, J., and Vicente, K., (Eds.): *Global Perspectives on the Ecology of Human-Machine Systems*.1, pp. 121 – 156, Lawrence Erlbaum Associates, Hillsdale, New Jersey.

[Raubal, et al. (2004)]
Raubal, M., Miller, M., and Bridwell, S., (2004): User Centered Time Geography for Location-Based Services. In: *Geografiska Annaler B* 86(4), pp. 245 – 265.

References

[Raubal and Rinner (2004)]
Raubal, M., and Rinner, C., (2004): Multi-Criteria Decision Analysis for Location Based Services. In: Brandt, S. A., (Ed.) *Proceedings of the 12th International Conference on Geoinformatics.* Gävle, Sweden, pp. 47 – 53.

[Reichenbacher (2001)]
Reichenbacher, T., (2001): Adaptive Concepts for a Mobile Cartography. In: *Supplement Journal of Geographical Sciences*, 11, pp. 43 – 53.

[Reichenbacher (2004)]
Reichernbacher, T., (2004): *Mobile Cartography – Adaptive Visualiuation of Spatial Information on Mobile Devices.* Phd thesis, University of Munich, Germany.

[Rich (1979)]
Rich, E., (1979): User Modeling via Stereotypes. In: *Cognitive Science 3*, pp. 329 - 354.

[Rogers, et al. (1999)]
Rogers, S., Fiechter, C.-N., and Langley, P., (1999): An Adaptive Interactive Agent for Route Advice. In: *Proceedings of the third International Conference on Autonomous Agents.* Seattle, WA, May 1999, pp. 198 – 205.

[Rueger (2006)]
Rueger, B., (2006): *Das WLAN-Stadtinformationsportal Heidelberg Mobil im Kontext des Städtetourismus: Stationsvorschläge für Touristentouren und benutzerorientierte Informationsaufbereitung.* Diplomarbeit. Geographisches Institut der Universität Heidelberg.

[Rugg and Schmidth (1986)]
Rugg, R., and Schmidt, W., (1986): Testing the Interim Proposed Standard for Cartographic Features. In: H. Moellering, (Ed.) *Issues in Digital Cartographic Data Standards: Report #7, Digital Cartographic Data Standards: A Report on Evaluation and Empirical Testing.* Columbus, Ohio: National Committee for Digital Cartographic Data Standards.

[Roh, et al. (2003)]
Roh, T. H., Oh, K. J., and Han, I., (2003): The Collaborative Filtering Recommendation Based on SOM Cluster-indexing CBR. In: *Expert Systems with Applications*, 25, pp. 413 – 423.

[Roussaki, et al. (2006)]
Roussaki, I., Strimpakou, M., Kalatzis, N., Anagnostou, M., and Pils, C., (2006): Hybrid Context Modeling: A Location-based Scheme using Ontologies. In: *4th IEEE Conference on Pervasive Computing and Communications Workshops.* Pisa, Italy, pp. 2 – 7.

[Rossi, et al. (1995)]
Rossi, G., Schwabe, D., Lucena, C.J. P., and Cowan, D. D., (1995): An Object-Oriented Model for Designing the Human-Computer Interface Of Hypermedia Applications. In: *Proceedings of the International Workshop on Hypermedia Design (IWHD'95).* Montpellier, France.

[Saaty and Vargas (2001)]
Saaty, T.L., and Vargas, L.G., (2001): *Models, Methods, Concepts & Applications of the Analytic Hierarchy Process.* Kluwer Academic Publishers, Dordrecht, MA, 2001, pp. 45 – 51.

[Salber, et al. (1999)]
Salber D., Dey A. K. and Abowd, G. D., (1999): The Context Toolkit: Aiding the Development of Context-enabled Applications. In: *Proceedings of CHI'99.* Pittsburgh, Pennsylvania, USA, pp. 434 – 441.

[Saimotion (2001)]
Eisenhauer, M., and Femke, R., (2001): Contextualization in Nomadic Computing, found on 14.12.2006 at http://www.ercim.org/publication/Ercim_News/enw47/eisenhauer.html

[Sas, et al (2003)]
Sas, C., Reilly, R., and O'Hare, G., (2003): A Connectionist Model of Spatial Knowledge Acquisition in a Virtual Environment. In: *Proceedings 2nd Workshop on Machine Learning, Information Retrieval and User Modeling, 9th International Conference on User Modeling.* Johnstown, Pennsylvania, USA, pp. 40 – 48.

[Schiex, et al. (1995)]
Schiex, T., Fargier, H., and Verfaillie, G., (1995): Valued Constraint Satisfaction Problems: Hard and Easy Problems. In: *Proceedings of the 14th International Joint Conference on Artificial Intelligence.* Montreal, Canada, pp. 631 – 637.

[Schilit, et al. (1994)]
Schilit, B. N., Adams, N. and Want R., (1994): Context-aware Computing Applications. In: *Proceedings Workshop on Mobile Computing Systems and Applications*. Santa Cruz, CA, USA, pp. 85 – 90.

[Schilit (1995)]
Schilit, W. N., (1995): *System Architecture for Context-aware Mobile Computing*. PhD thesis, Columbia University, USA.

[Schilling, et al. (2009)]
Schilling A., Over M., Neubauer S., Neis, P., Walenciak and Zipf, A., (2009): Interoperable Location-based Services for 3D cities on the Web using User Generated Content from OpenStreetMap. In: *Proceedings of the 27th Urban Data Management Symposium – UDMS*. Ljubljana , Slovenia.

[Smith (1996)]
Smith, B., (1996): Mereotopology: A Theory of Parts and Boundaries. In: *Data and Knowledge Engineering*, 20, pp.287 – 303.

[Schmidt-Belz, et al. (2003)]
Schmidt-Belz, B., Zipf, A., Poslad, S., Laamen, H., (2003): Location-based Mobile Tourist Services – First User Experiences. In: *Proceedings of the International Congress on Tourism and Communications Technologies – ENTER*. Helsinki. Finland.

[Schmidt and Zafft (1975)]
Schmidt, A. H., and Zafft, W. A., (1975): Programs of the Harvard University Laboratory for Computer Graphics and Spatial Analysis. In: Davis, J. C., and McCullagh, M. J., (Eds.): *Display and Analysis of Spatial Data*. John Wiley and Sons, London, pp. 231 – 243.

[Seidel (1992)]
Seidel, R., (1992): On the All-Pairs-Shortest-Path Problem. In: *Proceedings of the Twenty-Fourth Annual ACM Symposium on Theory of Computing*. Victoria, British Columbia, Canada, pp. 745 - 749.

[Shani, et al. (2005)]
Shani, G., Heckerman, D., and Brafman, R. I., (2005): An MDPBased Recommender System. In: *Journal of Machine Learning Research*, 6, 2005, pp. 1265 - 1295.

[Shekhar, et al (1997)]
Shekhar, S., Coyle, M., Goyal, B., Liu, D., and Sarkar, S., (1997): Data Models in Geographic Information Systems. In: *Commununications of the ACM* 40, 4, pp.103 - 111.

[Sheth and Larson (1990)]
Sheth, A., and Larson, J., (1990): Federated Database Systems for Managing Distributed, Heterogeneous, and Autonomous Databases. In: *ACM Computing Surveys*, 22 (3).

[Shin and Lee (2002)]
Shin, K., and Lee, Y., (2002): A Genetic Algorithm Application in Bankruptcy Prediction Modeling. In: *Expert Systems with Applications*, 23, pp. 321 – 328.

[Sleeman (1985)]
Sleeman, D., (1985): A User Modelling Front-End Subsystem. *International Journal of Man-Machine Studies 23*, pp. 71 – 88.

[Schmidt-Belz, et al. (2002)]
Schmidt-Belz, B., Stefan P., Nick, A. and Zipf, A., (2002): Personalized and Location-based Mobile Tourism Services. In: *Workshop on Mobile Tourism Support Systems. In Conjunction with on the Fourth International Symposium on Human Computer Interaction with Mobil Device*. PISA, Italy.

[Smith and Mark (1998)]
Mark, D. M., Smith, B., and Tversky, B., (1999): Ontology and Geographic Objects: An Empirical Study of Cognitive Categorization. In: Freksa, C., and Mark, D. M., (Eds.): *Spatial Information Theory: A Theoretical Basis for GIS*. Berlin: Springer-Verlag, Lecture Notes in Computer Science No. 1661, pp. 283 - 298.

[Smith and Mark (1999)]
Smith B., and Mark, D. M., (1998): Ontology and Geographic Kinds. In: Poiker, T. K., and Chrisman, N., (Eds.): *Proceedings. 8th International Symposium on Spatial Data Handling* (SDH'98). Vancouver: International Geographical Union, pp. 308 - 320.

References

[Sonntag, et al. (2007)]
Sonntag, D., Engel, R., Herzog, G., Pfalzgraf, A., Pfleger, N., Romanelli, M., and Reithinger N., (2007): SmartWeb Handheld – Multimodal Interaction with Ontological Knowledge Bases and Semantic Web Services. In: *Proceedings of International Workshop on AI for Human Computing*. Hyderabad, India.

[Spira (1973)]
Spira, P. M., (1973): A New Algorithm for Finding all Shortest Paths in a Graph of Positive Arcs in Average Time $0(n^2 \log^2 n)$. In: *Journal on Computing*, 2(1), pp. 28 – 32.

[Specht (2002)]
Specht, D., (2002): Interoperable Coordinate Transformation and Identification of Coordinate Systems. In: Goodchild, M., and Kimerling, A. J., (Eds.): *Discrete Global Grids*. Santa Barbara, CA, USA.

[Springer, et al. (2006)]
Springer, T., Kadner, K., Steuer, F., and Yin, M., (2006): Middleware Support for Context-Awareness in 4G Environments. In: *Proceedings of the 2006 international Symposium on on World of Wireless, Mobile and Multimedia Networks. International Workshop on Wireless Mobile Multimedia*, pp. 203 – 211.

[Shriram and Sugumaran (2007)]
Shriram, R., and Sugumaran, V., (2007): Adaptive Middleware Architecture for Information Sharing on Mobile Phones. In: *Proceedings of the 2007 ACM Symposium on Applied Computing*. Seoul, Korea, pp. 800 – 804.

[Srivastava, et al. (2001)]
Srivastava, M. B., Muntz, R., and Potkonjak, M., (2001): Smart Kindergarten: Sensor-Based Wireless Networks for Smart Problem-Solving Environments. In: *Proceedings of Conference on Mobile Computing and Networking*. Rome, Italy.

[Stollberg and Zipf (2007)]
Stollberg, B., and Zipf, A., (2007): OGC Web Processing Service Interface for Web Service Orchestration - Aggregating Geo-processing Services in a Bomb Threat Scenario. In: *Proceedings of the Web&Wireless GIS Conference 2007*. Cardiff, UK.

[Strang and Linnhoff-Popien (2004)]
Strang, T., and Linnhoff-Popien, C., (2004): A Context Modeling Survey. In: *Proceedings of the First International Workshop on Advanced Context Modeling, Reasoning and Management at UbiComp*. Nottingham, UK.

[Tacken (1997)]
Tacken, M., (1997): Changing Travel Behavior and Time Policy. In: Ettema, D.F., and Timmermans, H.J.P., (Eds.): *Activity-Based Approach to Travel Analysis*. Elsevier Science Ltd., pp. 313 – 328.

[Tasgetiren (1984)]
Tasgren, M. F., (1984): A Genetic Algorithm with an Adaptive Penalty Function for the Orienteering Problem. In: *Journal of Economic and Social Research* 4 (2), pp. 1 – 26.

[ten Hagen, et al. (2005)]
ten Hagen, K., Modsching, M, and Kramer, R. ,(2005): A Location Aware Mobile Tourist Guide Selection and Interpreting Sights and Services by Context Matching. In: *Proceedings of the Second Annual International Conference on Mobile and Ubiquitous Systems: Networking and Services*. San Diego, California.

[Thornton, et al. (1997)]
Thornton, P. R., Williams, A. M., and Shaw, G., (1997): Revisiting Time-space Diaries: An Exploratory Case Study of Tourist Behaviour in Cornwall, England. *In: Environment and Planning* A 29. 1997, pp. 1847 – 1867.

[Thorup (1999)]
Thorup, M., (1999): Undirected Single-source Shortest Paths with Positive Integer Weights in Linear Time. In: *Journal of the ACM* 46, 3, pp. 362 – 394.

[Timpf (2002)]
Timpf, S., (2002): Ontologies of Way-finding: A Traveler's Perspective. In *Networks & Spatial Econ 2002*, 2(1), pp. 9 – 33.

[Tokuda and Fukuda (1993)]
Tokuda, N., and Fukuda, A., (1993): A Probabilistic Inference Scheme for Hierarchical Buggy Models. In: *International Journal of Man Machine Studies*, *38*, pp. 857 – 872.

[Toth and Vigo (2002)]
Toth, P., and Vigo, D., (2002): The Vehicle Routing Problem. In: *SIAM Monographs on Discrete Mathematics and Applications*.

[TourMIS (2006)]
found on 11/03/2007 at http://tourmis.wu-wien.ac.at

[TravelMole (2006)]
TravelMole found on 11/18/2007 at http://www.travelmole.com.

[TSA (2007)]
TSA/ WTTC World Travel and Tourism Council (2007): The 2006 Travel and Tourism Economic Research Country League Tables, UK.

[Tsiligirides (1984)]
Tsiligirides, T., (1984): Heuristic methods applied to orienteering. In: *Journal of the Operational Research Society*, 35(9), pp. 797 – 809.

[Turner (1993)]
Turner, H. M., (1993): Context-sensitive Reasoning for Autonomous Agents and Cooperative Distributed Problem Solving. In: *Proceedings of the IJCAI-93 Workshop on Using Knowledge in its Context*. Research Report 93/13, Paris, France

[Tversky (1990)]
Tversky, B., (1990): Where Partonomies and Taxonomies Meet. In: S. L. Tsohatzidis (Ed.), *Meanings and prototypes: Studies on Linguistic Categorization*. London: Routledge, pp. 334 – 344 .

[Tversky and Hemenway (1983)]
Tversky, B., and Hemenway, K., (1983): Categories of Environmental Scenes. In: *Cognitive Psychology*, 15, pp. 121 – 149.

[VanDeMeer (2002)]
VanDeMeer, J., (2002): Hype vs.Reality of Location-Based Services - LBS at the end of 2001, DirectionsMagazine, found on 2007/12/11 at http://www.directionsmag.com/article.php?article_id=144&trv=1

[Vassileva and McGalla (2003)]
Vassileva, J., and McCalla, G., (2003): Multi-Agent Multi- User Modelling. In: *User Modelling and User-Adapted Interaction*. 13(1), pp. 179 – 210.

[Voelkel and Weber (2008)]
Voelkel, T., and Weber, G., (2008): RouteCheckr: Personalized Multicriteria Routing for Mobility Impaired Pedestrians. In: *Proceedings of the 10th international ACM SIGACCESS Conference on Computers and Accessibility*. Halifax, Nova Scotia, Canada, pp. 185 – 192.

[Voelker and Bershad (1995)
Voelker, G.M., and Bershad, B.N., (1995): Mobisaic – An Information System for a Mobile Wireless Computing Environment, Department of Computer Science and Engineering, University of Washington, Seattle, TR 95-04-01.

[Volz and Sester (2000)]
Volz, S., and Sester, M., (2000): Nexus - Distributed Data Management Concepts for Location Aware Applications. In: *Proceedings of the international workshop on emerging technologies for geo-based applications*. Ascona, Switzerland.

[Wache, et al. (2001)]
Wache, H., Vogele, T., Visser, U., Stuckenschmidt, H., Schuster, G., Neumann, H. and Hubner, S., (2001): Ontology-based Integration of Information - A Survey of Existing Approaches. In: Stuckenschmidt, H., (Ed.), *Workshop: Ontologies and Information Sharing, in conjunction with IJCAI-01*. pp.108 – 117.

[Wahlster, eds. (2000)]
Wahlster, W., (Ed.)(2000): *Verbmobil: Foundations of Speech-to-Speech Translation*. Springer, Berlin.

[Wahlster, eds. (2006)]
Wahlster, W., (Ed.)(2000): *Verbmobil: SmartKom - Foundations of Multimodal Dialogue Systems*. Springer, Heidelberg.

[Wallerath (2000)]
Wallerath, W., (2000): *Tourismusmarketing mittels GIS-gestützte Informationssysteme für das Internet*, Diplomarbeit. Geographisches Institut. Universität Heidelberg.

References

[Wang, et al. (2004)]
Wang, X. H., .Gu, T., Zhang, D. Q and Pung, H. P., (2004): Ontology Based Context Modeling and Reasoning using OWL. In: *IEEE International Conference on Pervasive Computing and Communication - PerCom'04*. Orlando, Florida, USA.

[Weber and Kwan (2002)]
Weber, J., and Kwan, M.-P., (2002): Bringing Time Back - A Study on the Influence of Travel Time Variations and Facility Opening Hours on Individual Accessibility. In: *The Professional Geographer* 54, pp. 226 – 240.

[Weber and Kwan (2003)]
Weber, J. and Kwan, M.-P., (2003): Evaluating the Effects of Geographic Contexts on Individual Accessibility: A Multilevel Approach. In: *Urban Geography*, 24(8), pp. 647 – 671.

[Weibull (1980)]
Weibull, J. W., (1980): On the Numerical Measurement of Accessibility. In: *Environment and Planning* A, 12, pp. 53 – 67.

[Weiner, et al. (1973)]
Weiner, P., Savage, S. L., and Bagchi, A., (1973): Neighborhood Search Algorithms for Finding Optimal Traveling Salesman Tours must be Inefficient. In: *Proceedings of the Fifth Annual ACM Symposium on theory of Computing*, Austin, Texas, USA, pp. 207 – 213.

[Weiser (1991)]
Weiser, M., (1991): The computer of the 21st century. In: *Scientific America*, 9, 1991

[Weiser, et al. (2006)]
Weiser, A., Neis, P., and Zipf, A., (2006): Orchestrierung von OGC Web Diensten im Katastrophenmanagement - am Beispiel eines Emergency Route Service auf Basis der OpenLS Spezifikation. In: *GIS - Zeitschrift für Geoinformatik*. 09/2006. pp. 35 – 41.

[Winter (1998)]
Winter, S., (1998): Bridging Vector and Raster Representation in GIS. In: *Proceedings of the 6th ACM international Symposium on Advances in Geographic information Systems*. Washington, D.C., USA.

[Winter, et al. (2004)]
Winter, S., Raubal, M., and Nothegger, C., (2004): Focalizing Measures of Salience for Route Directions. In: Zipf, A., Meng, L., and Reichenbacher, T., (Eds.): *Map-based mobile services - Theories, Methods and Implementations*. Springer, Berlin

[Wood (1998)]
Wood, A., (1998): CAMEO: Supporting Agent-Application Interaction, *PhD Thesis*, University of Birmingham, UK, 1998.

[Wu and Miller (2002)]
Wu, Y. H., and Miller, H. J., (2002): Computational Tools for Measuring Space-Time Accessibility with Transportation Networks with Dynamic Flow. In: *Journal of Transportation and Statistics, (special issue on accessibility)*, 4 (2/3), pp. 1 – 14.

[Xue, et al. 2008)]
Xue, W., Pung, H., Palmes, P. P., and Gu, T., (2008): Schema Matching for Context-aware Computing. In: *Proceedings of the 10th international Conference on Ubiquitous Computing*. Seoul, Korea.

[Yager (1988)]
Yager, R. R., (1988): On Ordered Weighted Averaging Aggregation Operators in Multi-criteria Decision Making. In: *IEEE Transactions on Systems, Man and Cybernetics* 18(1), pp. 183 – 190.

[Yannakakis (1988)]
Yannakakis, M., (1988): Expressing Combinatorial Optimization Problems by Linear Programs. In: *Proceedings of the Twentieth Annual ACM Symposium on theory of Computing*. Chicago, Illinois, USA, pp. 223 – 228.

[Yan, et al. (1996)]
Yan, T., Jacobsen, M., Garcia-Molina, H., and Dayal, U., (1996): From User Access Patterns to Dynamic Hypertext Linking. In: *Proceedings of the 5th International World Wide Web Conference*. Paris, France.

[Zadeh (1965)]
Zadeh, L., (1965): Fuzzy Sets. In: *Information and Control* 8, pp. 338 – 353.

[Zeimpekis, et al, (2002)]
Zeimpekis, V., Giaglis, G. M., and Lekakos, G., (2002): A Taxonomy of Indoor and Outdoor Positioning Techniques for Mobile Location Services. In: *SIGecom Exch.* 3, 4, pp. 19 – 27.

[Zhang, et al. (2006)]
Zhang, F., Song, Z., and Zhang, H., (2006): Web Service Based Architecture and Ontology Based User Model for Cross-System Personalization. In: *Proceedings of the 2006 IEEE/WIC/ACM international Conference on Web Intelligence.* Hongkong, China, pp. 849 – 852.

[Zipf (1998)]
Zipf, A., *(1998): DEEP MAP* - A Prototype Context Sensitive Tourism Information System for the City of Heidelberg. In: *Procedings of the GIS-Planet Conference.* Lisbon, Portugal.

[Zipf and Malaka (2001)]
Zipf, A., and Malaka, R., (2001): Developing "Location Based Services" (LBS) for tourism - The service provider's view. In: Sheldon, P. J., Wöber, K. W., and Fesenmaier, D. R., (Eds.): *Proceedings of the 8th International Conference on Information and Communication Technologies in Tourism, ENTER 2001.* Montreal, Canada.

[Zipf (2002)]
Zipf, A., (2002): User-Adaptive Maps for Location-Based Services (LBS) for Tourism. In: *Proceedings of the 9th International Conference on Information and Communication Technologies in Tourism, ENTER 2002.* Insbruck, Austria.

[Zipf and Aras (2002)]
Zipf, A., and Aras, H., (2002): Proactive Exploitation of the Spatial Context in LBS - through Interoperable Integration of GIS-Services with a Multi Agent System (MAS). In: *Proceedings of the International Conference on Geographic Information Science of the Association of Geographic Information Laboratories in Europe (AGILE).* Palma, Spain.

[Zipf and Jöst (2005)]
Zipf, A., and Jöst, M., (2005): Implementing Adaptive Mobile GI Services Based on Ontologies - Examples for Pedestrian Navigation Support. In: *CEUS - Computers, Environment and Urban Systems - An International Journal. Special Issue on LBS and UbiGIS.* Pergamon Press, Elsevier.

[Zipf and Richter (2002)]
Zipf, A., and Richter, K.F., (2002): Using Focus Maps to Ease Map Reading. Developing Smart Applications for Mobile Devices. In: *Künstliche Intelligenz, Special Issue: Spatial Cognition.* pp. 35 – 37.

[Zipf and Haeussler (2004)]
Zipf, A., and Haeussler, J., (2004): An Evaluation of the OpenLS Specifications for Multi-Modal Mobile Applications. In: *The Journal of Geographic Information Sciences. Special Issue on LBS and UbiGIS.* CPGIS. 10, 2, pp. 117 – 127.

[Zipf and Röther (2000)]
Zipf, A und Röther, S., (2000): Tourenvorschläge für Stadttouristen mit dem ArcView Network Analyst. In: Liebig (Hrsg.)(2000): *ArcView Arbeitsbuch.* Hüthig Verlag. Heidelberg.

I want morebooks!

Buy your books fast and straightforward online - at one of the world's fastest growing online book stores! Environmentally sound due to Print-on-Demand technologies.

Buy your books online at
www.get-morebooks.com

Kaufen Sie Ihre Bücher schnell und unkompliziert online – auf einer der am schnellsten wachsenden Buchhandelsplattformen weltweit!
Dank Print-On-Demand umwelt- und ressourcenschonend produziert.

Bücher schneller online kaufen
www.morebooks.de

OmniScriptum Marketing DEU GmbH
Heinrich-Böcking-Str. 6-8
D - 66121 Saarbrücken
Telefax: +49 681 93 81 567-9

info@omniscriptum.com
www.omniscriptum.com

Printed by Books on Demand GmbH, Norderstedt / Germany